November 2013

Dear Angela,
    I thank God for crossing our paths on this earth. You are just a little angel and Greg and I think the world of you!

God's Blessings to you and your precious family!

Love, Deborah

Nourishments

FOOD FOR THE SOUL

DEBORAH BUCKINGHAM

Published by Gregory and Deborah Buckingham;
they can be reached at soulnourishments@gmail.com.

1st Printing, 2013.
ISBN:978-0-9893230-0-0
Printed in the United States of America

14 13 12 11 10 / 10 9 8 7 6 5 4 3 2 1

Table of Contents

Acknowledgments

Avery special thank you to Brenda Noel and Dawn Sherill-Porter of ECHO Creative Media. Brenda's input was truly invaluable. The depth of knowledge she and Dawn provided, both in God's Word and how to communicate it effectively, made all the difference in the editing process. Brenda and I experienced an amazing ebb and flow through the entire, tedious, editing process that was nothing but a gift from Abba Father Himself!

I would also like to send a grateful "thank you" to Brecca Theele for the beautiful cover and interior design of *Nourishments*. Brecca's creative skills and easy-going attitude made working with her a pleasure. Her abilities helped greatly in the process of *Nourishments* evolving into an actual book.

I must also thank my mentor Terry Zwick for speaking courage into me for so many years, especially when I was scared to death to teach. Your support, encouragement and godly wisdom have made a real difference in my life.

Last, but in no way least, I would like to thank my family.

First, my two loves, Greyson and Julia, for giving me so many wonderful experiences in this life and so many opportunities to trust Abba Father and pray to Him. I love you both with all my heart.

And most of all, a huge "THANK YOU!" to my husband, Greg Buckingham, for his patient support through the countless hours poured into *Nourishments*. Without his support *Nourishments* would never have been realized. He is the best husband ever!

Letter from the Author

The two most important days of your life are the day you were born and the day you figure out why. You were born to know your Creator and to do life with Him; when you realize this, things will begin to make sense and your life will resonate with real meaning and purpose. But before you can truly enter into a life-changing relationship with Abba God, you must realize how incredibly deep His Love is for you.

Regardless how long you have been a Christian or how many years you have attended church or even Bible study, it can be difficult to believe you are loved and adored by your heavenly Father—your Abba God. Do you beat yourself up in frustration over your lack of ability to surrender all to Him because you just can't get to that confident place of trusting Him? Do you desire an intimate relationship with your Creator, but feel alone and empty deep within? If you are struggling to feel loved and adored by your Lord, to trust Him and walk with Him in that inner, sacred place of intimacy, then *Nourishments* is for you!

As a women's Bible study teacher for the past 15 years, it is heartbreaking when I witness women, men, and young adults attending church and Bible study year after year, yet never feeling an intimate closeness to their Abba God and never grasping the depth of His Love for them. How can anyone ever come to a point of trust in God if they don't believe in His Love?

Do you want a deeper relationship with Abba? Do you long to know the joy promised you as His child? He created you to know

Him; to really know Him. The more you know Him (this is very different than simply knowing *about* Him) the more secure and content you will be and the more loved you will feel. As your Abba, God adores you! When you really believe He does, you can move into a secure place of trusting Him.

The wisest man to ever live, King Solomon, said there is nothing "new" under the sun. Most likely, you will not be reading anything new in this devotional; my prayer is that the words found within will nourish your soul in such a way that you will thirst and hunger for more, more of Him. He is an amazing God and He wants you to know Him, to really know Him. He loves you so very much and desires that you trust Him with your life. You matter to Him and He wants to help you with the details of this life. He has wonderful plans for you—plans to live a transformed and abundant life!

The seeds for this devotional were actually planted years ago. When my kids were in school I used to write them little "nourishments" on note cards and pop them in their lunch bags. The notes included a Bible verse with a short encouragement. To their surprise, their friends often wanted to hear the "nourishment" for the day. The Lord says to taste and see that He is indeed Good; His words bring peace, hope, and joy to our souls. My little "nourishments" were my way of bringing Scripture to life for my kids. It is my prayer that *Nourishments* will impact your life with God's Truth and feed your soul with the knowledge of His Love as my little note cards did for my children.

Nourishments includes 260 devotionals meant to be read Monday through Friday, leaving Saturday and Sunday to dig deeper on your own, catch up on any devotionals you missed through the week, and attend church. In the beginning of this devotional, you will find an article that presents the Names of God and the meanings; the nature and character of our God are revealed so clearly by the names He has given Himself in Scripture. *Nourishments* also provides a glossary to help you grasp any unfamiliar words or concepts. Each of the words contained in the glossary appears in bold type throughout the text. I encourage you to make use of both these tools in your journey toward truly knowing Abba and His incredible, limitless Love for you.

Come to the refreshing Living Water and quench your thirst. Eat the manna of heaven and nourish your soul as you grow in intimacy with Him.

Please join me and sit at the feasting table of our Abba Father.

Love,
Deborah Buckingham

Names of God

T hough the Scripture verses listed after each name of God may not actually contain the name of God about which they speak, each reveals the specific aspect of God's nature.

Daniel 2:20; NKJV
Blessed be the name of God forever and ever.

Proverbs 18:10; NKJV
The name of the Lord is a fortified tower; the righteous run to it and are safe.

Jehovah –"I AM WHO I AM"
Jehovah is derived from the Hebrew word "Yahweh" and believed to come from the verb "to be." The pronunciation and spelling of Yahweh has been debated for over a thousand years. This personal name of God was believed by the Hebrew people to be too holy to be spoken aloud; so they substituted the name Adoni. The ancient Hebrew text used only consonants, so this personal name of God was written as YHWH, which is known as the tetragrammaton.

Eventually, scholars took the vowels from Adoni and added them between the consonants of the tetragrammaton. Therefore, Jehovah is a constructed name using the Latinized consonants from the Hebrew personal name for God, JHVH, and the vowels from Adoni.

Genesis 2:4; Exodus 3:13–15; Psalm 105:1–7; Jeremiah 16:19–21; John 8:58

Jehovah Raah – The LORD My Shepherd

Raah can be translated as "shepherd," and also as "friend" or "companion." God is our Shepherd and our Friend. He cares for us personally and takes care of us.

Psalm 23; Isaiah 40:11; John 10:11, 27, 28; Matt.18:12, 13; Revelation 7:17

Jehovah Sabaoth – The LORD of Hosts

Jehovah Sabaoth means "The Lord of Armies." He is the Supreme Commander and the King of all heaven and earth. Who better to protect us and fight for us?

1 Samuel 17:45; 2 Kings 3:14; 1 Chronicles 11:9; Psalm 24:10; 46:7; 80:19; Isaiah 3:15; 14:22; Jeremiah 48:1; Hosea 12:5; Micah 4:4; Zechariah 1:3

Jehovah Shalom – The LORD is Peace

Jehovah is the God of calm and tranquility; the opposite of anxiety and stress. No matter what storms we face in life, our Jehovah Shalom can bring us divine peace.

Psalm 23; Judges 6:24; Isaiah 9:6; 26:3, 4; Ephesians 2:14–18; Colossians 1:19-20

Jehovah Rapha – The LORD Who Heals

Rapha means "to restore" or "to heal." Our God has ultimate healing and restorative powers. No physical illness or desperate situation is beyond His power to restore.

Exodus 15:26; Psalm 103:1–4; 147:3; Isaiah 30:26; 53:4, 5; Jeremiah 3:22; 30:17; Matt. 8:16, 17

Jehovah Tsidkenu – The LORD Our Righteousness

Tsidkenu has at its base the Hebrew word "Tsedek," which means "straight" or "righteous." Our God is our righteousness—we cannot be righteous (see Glossary entry "righteousness") apart from Him.

Jeremiah 23:5, 6; 33:16; Romans 3:21, 22; 2 Corinthians 5:21

Jehovah Shammah – The LORD is There

This name is used only once in the Old Testament as a symbol for Jerusalem (Ezekiel 48:35). Though God's people questioned His faithfulness, God had not abandoned Jerusalem—He was there! And He will not abandon us, His people. He is there!

Ezekiel 48:35; Deuteronomy 31:6; Matthew 18:20; Matthew 28:20; Revelation 21:1–3

Jehovah Jireh – The LORD Will Provide

This name is used once in the Old Testament. It is the name given by Abraham at Mount Moriah, where God provided a sacrifice in place of Abraham's son, Isaac (Genesis 22:14).

Genesis 22:8, 13, 14; Acts 14:17; Romans 8:32; Philippians 4:19; 1 Timothy 6:17

Jehovah Nissi – The LORD My Banner

"Nissi" comes from the Hebrew word *nes,* which means "banner." In a battle, the banner was carried before the army, identifying the king or nation for which they fought. Its presence offered them encouragement and hope; for if it fell, the battle was lost. In Exodus 17:15, Moses built an altar and named it "Jehovah Nissi" because the Lord had led His people to victory in a battle against their enemies.

Exodus 17:15,16a; Psalm 20:5–8; 60:4; Isaiah 11:10

Jehovah Mekoddishkem – The Lord Who Sanctifies You

Mekoddishkem comes from the Hebrew *qâdash,* which means "sanctified" or "holy." When something or someone is sanctified, it/she/he is set apart as holy. As the people of God, we are set apart by God and for God. He gave His Son for us and, by His blood, we can be made holy in the eyes of God.

Exodus 31:13; Leviticus 20:8

El Roi – The God Who Sees

Our Lord sees everything. Whenever we feel alone or invisible or as if no one cares, we know our God sees, and He Loves us. Nothing in our lives misses His notice or concern.

Genesis 16:7–13; Psalm 33:13–15; Proverbs 15:3

Adonai – Lord and Master

God is our Master—we belong to Him and we serve Him because we love Him. He is our Loving and Holy Lord. Adonai was spoken in the place of Yahweh (or Jehovah) out of reverence for the holiness of God (See Jehovah). Adonai occurs over 400 times in the Old Testament.

Genesis 18:27; Exodus 34:9; Judges 6:15; Nehemiah 1:11; Psalm 2:4; Psalm 39:7; Isaiah 21:6; Daniel 9:9

Elohim-Powerful God

Elohim is the most general name for God. It may be the plural form of *el,* which comes from a root word meaning "strength" or "power." Elohim is used over 2,500 times in the Old Testament.

Genesis 1:1, 28; 45:9; Exodus 23:25; Deuteronomy 4:10; Joshua 9:24; 1 Kings 1:48; Psalm 36:7; Zephaniah 3:17

El Elyon – The Most High God

Elyon comes from the verb *alah* which means to go up. God is Exalted and Majestic and Preeminent; He is elevated above all things. There is no person and no thing higher or more holy than our God.

Genesis 14:18, 19, 20, 22; Numbers 24:16; Deuteronomy 32:8; Psalm 57:2; 78:35; Daniel 5:18, 21

El Shaddai – God Almighty

Our God is the strongest and the most powerful. Nothing that exists is mightier than He. There is nothing too hard for God Almighty to supply, provide, or control.

Genesis 17:1; 28:3; 35:11; 43:14; 48:3; Exodus 6:3; Numbers 24:4, 16; Ruth 1:20, 21; Psalm 68:14; Isaiah 13:6; Joel 1:15

Preface

Psalm 119:18, 35, 103 (NLT)

Open my eyes to see the wonderful truths in your instructions . . .
Make me walk along the path of your commands, for that is where
my happiness is found . . . How sweet your words taste to me; they
are sweeter than honey.

Nourishments is presented as 260 devotionals designed to be
read Monday through Friday throughout the year, leaving
Saturday and Sunday to catch up on any missed, review or dig more
deeply into the week's messages, and to attend church. All words in
bold print are defined in the Glossary for deeper understanding.

God's Word is so amazing and good for you! As a believer in
Jesus Christ, please ask the Holy Spirit within you to illuminate His
words and give you the desire to follow Him. He will open your
eyes to His wonderful truths and reveal things you've never before
seen! If you are not a believer in Jesus Christ, why wait another
second to enter into an eternal relationship with your Maker and
Savior? The Lord says in Acts 16:31 to "Believe in the Lord Jesus
and you will be saved" (NLT). Ephesians 2:8, 9 says that salvation
is a gift of grace from God Himself and all we must do is believe
God and choose to receive His free gift. John 3:16 says that God
loved you so much He gave His only Son; if you simply believe in
Him, you will be saved and will not perish. Abba God is offering
you salvation as a gift. Jesus Christ is that salvation; will you invite
Him into your heart as Lord and Savior of your life?

Get ready to be nourished with Abba's transforming soul food!

The Water of Life

Are you thirsty? Is there a thirst deep within you left unquenched? The Lord's Spirit is inviting you to come and drink deeply from His well of Truth and **Grace**. Will you fill your thirsty soul with His Love, Joy, and Hope?

He longs for your willingness to participate with Him, the Lover of your soul. He is your Creator and the Great "**I AM**." This is an open invitation to receive His gift, but you must be willing to receive it. Your willingness is all that is required of you.

Go to Him, seek Him and He will give you the desire to drink more and more from His water well of life. He will take care of everything in your life if you will go to Him.

Will you thank Him for His gift of the water of life? Will you drink of it liberally? Will you allow Him to wipe every tear from your eyes? The Lamb of God, the Lion of Judah, is asking to be your Good Shepherd. Will you say "yes" to Him?

Teshuva

Psalm 25:6–8, 11 (NLT)

Remember, O LORD, your compassion and unfailing love, which you have shown from long ages past. Do not remember the rebellious sins of my youth. Remember me in the light of your unfailing love, for you are merciful, O Lord. The Lord is good and does what is right; he shows the proper path to those who go astray . . . For the honor of your name, O Lord, forgive my many, many sins.

I t is true; the Lord's eyes miss nothing. His eyes have seen and His ears have heard everything you have ever done.

He understands His absolute knowledge can be unsettling for you because He is Holy and Pure and you have done and said many things that have caused Him sadness. His Love remains the same, because His Love is not based on your behavior. His Love is based on Who He is; He is Love. And He desires to help you and strengthen you. He knows you are not living up to your potential. He made you to live connected to Him—your Loving, Caring Creator.

He invites you to Teshuva (**repent**—turn toward Him and away from your sins). He is Merciful and Trustworthy; and He is waiting for you. He will guide you to the right path for the sake of His Name—the Name by which you were adopted into His everlasting family.

Teshuva. Don't you want to go home to Him where you belong?

Do You Know Him?

John 17:3 (NLT)
And this is the way to have eternal life—to know you, the only true God, and Jesus Christ, the one you sent to earth.

Do you know the only true God and Jesus Christ, the One God sent to earth? In this passage, John says this is the way to eternal life. Are you on your way to eternal life?

"To know," as used in John 17:3, is the Greek word *ginosko*, which means to learn about, to gain knowledge of, to understand, and to become intimately acquainted with. **Abba** God has given you all the resources you need in order to know Him. Do you have a daily Bible? Do you have a study Bible? Two incredible websites to enrich your time in the Word are biblgateway.com and blueletterbible.org.

You will never fully trust someone you do not know. Your **Abba** God stands with open and loving arms inviting you to sit and converse with Him. You cannot really know Him through second-hand theology. In other words, do not rely on a teacher or pastor for an intimate connection with **Abba**. Yes, we are told to study God's Word and good teachers help us grow in the Word. However, Jesus wants to spend time with you. He has a word just for you. Will you sit with Him?

Satisfying and Living Water

> **Isaiah 44:3, 4 (NLT)**
> For I will pour out water to quench your thirst and to irrigate your parched fields. And I will pour out my Spirit on your descendants, and my blessing on your children. They will thrive like watered grass, like willows on a riverbank.
>
> **Ezekiel 37:4 (NLT)**
> Then he said to me, "Speak a prophetic message to these bones and say, '**Dry bones**, listen to the word of the LORD!'"

Dry bones, come to Jesus and be satisfied. Stop drinking from the wells of this world filled with mud, parasites, and filth. Be nourished by His clean, sparkling, pure, satisfying, and **living water**. He does not desire to give you just enough to survive; He desires you to be whole, nourished, complete, irrigated through and through. He desires you to be saturated with His presence, full of the Spirit which He deposited in you when you believed in the Name above all names.

Soak up His Word; sit with it and absorb it in the ways He chooses to nourish you and grow you.

Is your spirit quenched? Are you thriving despite living in a **fallen world**? Your loving **Abba** is inviting you to drink from His living Word and to commune with Him. Will you drink deeply today?

Do You Love Him?

Luke 10:26-28 (NLT)

Jesus replied, "What does the law of Moses say? How do you read it?"

The man answered, "You must love the LORD your God with all your heart, all your soul, all your strength, and all your mind.' And 'Love your neighbor as yourself.'" "Right!" Jesus told him. "Do this and you will live!"

Jesus was speaking when a religious teacher stood and asked Him, "What should I do to inherit eternal life?" (Matthew 18:18, 19). Jesus led him to the answer: you must first love the Lord your God with all your heart.

Half-hearted love for the Lord is not enough. You have been **saved** from the world, from yourself, and from **the enemy**; therefore, show some passion for your Savior! Ask the Holy Spirit to increase your heart's desire to spend time with Him in order to grow your affection for Him. Ask the Holy Spirit to open your eyes to His amazing Truth and **Grace**, which will increase your appetite for more of Him. Do you love Him with all your heart? You can be sure you do if you have a heart that is hungry for more and more of Him and filled with gratitude. He is blessing you every day. Do the eyes of your heart see His **Grace**? Do you have a thankful heart?

Do you love Him with all your soul? Your soul is the essence of you—the part of you that lives on into eternity. It is the life-force within you. You are a living soul. Do you live for Jesus? Do you eat, sleep, work, play, and rest in Jesus? Do you breathe His breath of life?

Do you love with all your strength? To the best of your abilities, do you love Him? With all the power you can muster, do you seek

Him? Give Him your all; you will receive immeasurably more than you can even imagine (Ephesians 3:20).

Do you love Him with your entire mind? Do you seek to understand Him? The fear of the Lord is the beginning of wisdom (Proverbs 9:10). You are transformed by the renewing of your mind (Romans 12:2). Do you think His thoughts? You will when you plant His Word in your mind.

And, of course, as a reflection of Him, you cannot help but love others. Jesus is Love (John 10:30; 1 John 4:8). When you plant His seeds of truth in your mind and ask Him how to apply them to your life, He will show you opportunities for acts of love toward others. Love is not a gushy emotion; it is making choices to be kind, considerate, patient, forgiving of offenses, giving, and caring toward others.

Do you want to really live? Will you love the Lord your God with everything you have and love others as yourself?

Love is not a gushy emotion;

it is making choices to be

kind, considerate, patient,

forgiving of offenses, giving,

and caring toward others.

The Perfect Sacrifice

Hebrews 10:12-14 (NLT)
But our **High Priest** offered himself to God as a single **sacrifice** for sins, good for all time. Then he sat down in the place of honor at God's right hand. There he waits until his enemies are **humbled** and made a footstool under his feet. For by that one offering he forever made perfect those who are being made holy.

Why did Jesus have to die for you? Romans 3:23 says we all sin and fall short of God's glorious standard; and Romans 6:23 says, "the wages of sin is death." Since we all sin and the consequence of sin is death, what is our hope? God cannot overlook sin because He is Holy and Perfect; therefore, He gave us the solution: God requires a **sacrifice** of blood to cleanse us of sin. The Old Testament believers **sacrifice**d animals as a foreshadowing of the single **sacrifice** for sin made by the perfect Lamb of God—Jesus.

Why was blood required for the cleansing of sin? Sin is serious; it separates you from your Holy God. Your efforts always fall short of your Holy God's standard. Before Jesus' **sacrifice**, God instructed His followers to **sacrifice** animals because blood given in exchange for a life makes **atonement** (or purification) possible. A **sacrifice** of life is required for new life to be received. Because life is in the blood (Leviticus 17:11), those who are purified by the blood **sacrifice** are set free from the consequence of sin—death.

When perfect, sinless, and Holy Jesus Christ offered His life on the cross, His blood provided a way for you to be cleansed of all your sins, once and for all. Accepting His **sacrifice** means you are accepted as God's righteous, clean child. You have been set free from the bondage of sin forever. You have Christ's new life running through your veins.

Are you living your new life?

One Savior; One Way

Hebrews 10:26, 27 (NLT)
Dear friends, if we deliberately continue sinning after we have received knowledge of the truth, there is no longer any **sacrifice** that will cover these sins. There is only the terrible expectation of God's judgment and the raging fire that will consume his enemies.

Yes, God is Good. He is Good all the time; He is Good! He is Good to give His gifts of Truth and **Grace**. He is so Good that He will not force His Goodness on you. You can reject Good and choose bad. You can reject His gift of freedom and continue in bondage.

The sin referred to in this verse is not sin committed by one who has put his or her trust in Jesus. The sin here is committed by the one who hears the Truth and deliberately rejects Jesus. What is left for this person? There is no **sacrifice** or solution left to save them. There is only one Savior—one bridge to God—Jesus Christ. Jesus means "Savior" and Christ means "the **Anointed** One," Jesus Christ is a translation of the Hebrew word "**Messiah**." Jesus is the only **Anointed** Savior for mankind.

There are two possible eternal expectations for every soul—either eternal bliss with Jesus or the raging fire that will consume His enemies (Matthew 25:41). God created you; He has the right to judge you. It is no light matter to find yourself in the hands of an All-Powerful and Just God. Nobody is going to slip by Him on **Judgment Day**.

This is not a light matter, by any means. It is a reality that should cause us to share this truth with others in our lives and pray for their understanding.

For whom should you pray today? With whom should you share Jesus today?

The Land of Milk and Honey

Joshua 5:6 (NLT)

The Israelites had traveled in the wilderness for forty years until all the men who were old enough to fight in battle when they left Egypt had died. For they had disobeyed the LORD, and the LORD vowed he would not let them enter the land he had sworn to give us—a land flowing with milk and honey.

Ezekiel 11:18-20 (NLT)

When the people return to their homeland, they will remove every trace of their vile images and detestable **idols**. And I will give them singleness of heart and put a new spirit within them. I will take away their stony, stubborn heart and give them a tender, responsive heart, so they will obey my decrees and regulations. Then they will truly be my people, and I will be their God.

O h, beloved child of God, will you return to your home—to the land of milk and honey? You know you are roaming immoral streets and worshiping worthless gods. The place where you linger has left you with a heavy, unfeeling heart of stone. You should feel sadness and empathy for the plight of others, yet you are left unmoved. You are better than this. You were made to experience life and experience it to the fullest; yet it all seems so bland and boring. Do not aimlessly wander another second! Turn toward home; go to your Loving **Abba** Father. If you are in Christ, you are a new creature (2 Corinthians 5:17). In Christ, you will not be **dry bones** walking about! He promises to give you a tender, soft heart and place a new spirit in you (Ezekiel 36:26). All these things are gifts from Him.

God's Spirit deposited in you gives you understanding and wisdom. With the Holy Spirit, your heart begins to feel again at a deeper level than you thought possible. Your intentions shift; your life is no longer all about you. Rather, you desire to follow God and live for Him. In this way, you can know you are truly His and He is yours! Your life will begin to have meaning and depth. There will be peace in your heart and a sense of well-being in your soul. Return, dear one, and be welcomed home!

God's Spirit deposited in you

gives you understanding

and wisdom.

Are You Right With God?

> **Romans 3:20-22 (NLT)**
>
> For no one can ever be made right with God by doing what the law commands. The law simply shows us how sinful we are. But now God has shown us a way to be made right with him without keeping the requirements of the law, as was promised in the writings of Moses and the prophets long ago. We are made right with God by placing our faith in Jesus Christ. And this is true for everyone who believes, no matter who we are.
>
> **Galatians 2:16 (NLT)**
>
> Yet we know that a person is made right with God by faith in Jesus Christ, not by obeying the law. And we have believed in Christ Jesus, so that we might be made right with God because of our faith in Christ, not because we have obeyed the law. For no one will ever be made right with God by obeying the law.

God made you to be in relationship with Him; He desires that not one be lost; no, not one (2 Peter 3:9). He invites you right now to trust Him as Lord of your life, Lord over every detail, because He cares about every little thing in your life. He is asking you to trust Him as your Savior from sin, from bad choices, and from hell. Do you trust Him? Do you *want* to trust Him? All you have to do is say, "YES!"

People define a "good" person as one who does good works: gives to the poor, attends church and Bible study, cares for their family, and volunteers when needed. However, it is possible to do many "good" things and not be right with God. **Abba** God says it is credited to you as **righteousness** when you have faith in Him (Romans 4:5). You are living in God's approval when you trust His promises to care and provide for you. You are credited as righteous when you believe He has your back and is moving for good on your behalf.

You are right with God when the object of your faith is Jesus and not how well you are performing. Your right standing with God is all about your heart. Is your heart willing to trust Jesus? You cannot please God with your good works or self-improvement. It is your trust in Jesus that sets you right before God, not trying to be good or following a certain set of rules and traditions. Your goodness just isn't good enough. Jesus, the perfect, sinless Son of God and **Son of man**, is your solution to living "right." Will you receive His **Grace**, His gift of life? Will you claim Him as your **Messiah**, your Savior and Lord, and your Way to connection with God? Will you say, "Yes! I believe Jesus was born of a virgin, lived on earth, was crucified for me, rose from the dead, and now sits at the right hand of the Father, interceding on my behalf?" (See Romans 8:34.) You are made right with God by placing your faith in Jesus Christ. Are you right with God?

Your right standing with

God is all about your heart.

Amazing Grace

Romans 3:23, 24 (NLT)

For everyone has sinned; we all fall short of God's glorious standard. Yet God, with undeserved kindness, declares that we are righteous. He did this through Christ Jesus when he freed us from the penalty for our sins.

What is the one word that makes Christianity different from all other religions? It is **Grace**—the unearned, unmerited favor of God! Jesus freed you from the penalty for every sin you ever committed. What a pure gift! You did nothing to deserve His Kindness. As a follower of Christ, when you stand before Him, you stand clean. He looks at you now as a saint, not as a sinner. You now have the Power of God's Holy Spirit within you to live in freedom.

Are you living in your Jesus freedom? He is your Great **Advocate** who longs to help you live a life with meaning and purpose. Will you take all your inclinations to sin before Him? He will help you see how destructive sin is to your abundant life. He will help you recognize sin obstacles in your path of **righteousness**.

Your name is written in God's Book of Life (Philippians 4:3; Revelation 17:8) because you chose to receive God's gift of **Grace**— Jesus Christ. At the **Great White Throne of Judgment**, the dead will stand before God; those whose names are not in the Lamb's Book of Life will be thrown into the **lake of fire** (Revelation 20:15). However, because you have believed in Jesus and are one of "His people," He will wipe every tear from your eyes (Revelation 21:3, 4). There will be no more. This is the future for every child of God.

Isn't God's **Grace** amazing?!

He Sees You; He Hears You

Psalm 4:3, 5, 8 (NLT)

You can be sure of this: The LORD set apart the godly for himself. The LORD will answer when I call to him . . . Offer **sacrifice**s in the right spirit, and trust the LORD . . . In peace I will lie down and sleep, for you alone, O LORD, will keep me safe.

His eye is fixed on you—your every move, your coming and going. His ear is attentive to any conversation you seek with Him.

You are His child and His attention is focused on you. He always hears your cries to Him; He never grows weary of you. He is **Immutable** and Faithful. This is not what He *does* but Who He *is*.

When you demonstrate trust and confidence in Him by seeking to **glorify** and honor Him with your life—your every word and action—He will **anoint** you with a peace and rest which surpasses your understanding.

Are you **glorify**ing Him with your time and your choices? When you are prosperous and when you have conflict, **glorify** Him. He will bless your days with a deep, sweet, care-free rest.

He is Faithful Abba God

Go to the Lord with your questions regarding your future
and any decisions you need to make. Visualize yourself
placing all your questions at the foot of His throne. Visualize yourself committing your life to His will and His ways. Sit with Him
and thank Him for His amazing **Grace** in your life and His unending Mercies.

Abba God loves you so much; He knit you together in your
mother's womb (Psalm, 139:13). He created you with His divine
imprint. You are made in His image (Genesis 1:27). You are the
twinkle in His eye. Allow His Love to soothe your inner being like
a calming **balm**.

Do you think **Abba** will not direct you if you seek His will?
Be patient and wait for His clear nudging. When the time is right,
He will guide you and you will know it is time to move forward.
Since the moments in which you were being knit together, He has
known the plans He has for you. His faithful love only waits for
you to ask.

He has never and will never abandon the work of His hands—
You! But have you abandoned Him in any area of your life?

Bid Farewell to Old Ways

Isaiah 30:19b-23a (NLT)

He will be gracious if you ask for help. He will surely respond to the sound of your cries. Though the Lord gave you adversity for food and suffering for drink, he will still be with you to teach you. You will see your teacher with your own eyes. Your own ears will hear him. Right behind you a voice will say, "This is the way you should go," . . . Then you will destroy all your silver **idol**s and your precious gold images. You will throw them out like filthy rags, saying to them, "Good riddance!" Then the Lord will bless you with rain at planting time.

Do not hesitate to take everything to your Lord. He sits on His throne with His eyes on you, waiting for you to ask Him for help. He will never push Himself on you. He is the perfect gentleman—waiting for an invitation to intervene. He never wavers from His Faithfulness in answering His children's cry for direction or deliverance.

You must understand, however, that your eyes are not open to all the behind-the-scenes work He does in order to bless you with His answers at the perfect time.

Sometimes, He must allow you to wallow in the mud of **idol**s so when you taste and see how Good He is, you will no longer desire the filthy rags you once wore. He longs to clothe you with a robe of **righteousness**; He custom made it just for you. Say "good riddance" to straying from the Lord and start planting seeds of truth and **grace** as you prepare for a divine harvest of the most delicious fruits—the God-given blessings of a life lived for Him.

Is there anything coming between you and your **Abba** Father? Get rid of it today! Today is the day! Today is the day of **salvation** and freedom.

The Lord will Help

Psalm 121 (NLT)

I look up to the mountains—does my help come from there? My help comes from the LORD, who made heaven and earth! He will not let you stumble; the one who watches over you will not slumber. Indeed, he who watches over Israel never slumbers or sleeps. The LORD himself watches over you! The LORD stands beside you as your protective shade. The sun will not harm you by day, nor the moon at night. The LORD keeps you from all harm and watches over your life. The LORD keeps watch over you as you come and go, both now and forever.

He is **Jehovah**. He is the "**I Am** Who **I Am**" (Exodus 3:14). He is the One True God. He is the One who made you and holds the days of your life in His hands. He is always near you longing for you to call to Him. He desires to hold your hand today and throughout the night.

He is **Omnipresent**; wherever you are, there He is also. He delights in you simply because you are His. He is the perfect Father who takes great pleasure in showing you His Faithfulness, His Reliability, and His Dependability.

He is **Jehovah**. He is never moody or changing. He is always Loyal. Trouble and heartache will come to you in this **fallen world**; but you will never be alone and without help if you cry, "Jesus, help me!" He is watching over your coming and going. Your help can come from the Lord.

Where is your help coming from? Will you let it come from your Maker and the Lover of your soul?

Flicker to Flame

Your God has given you all you need to know Him. Open His Word in which He will give messages specifically for you. His Words are the fountain from which **living water** springs forth to nourish and quench parched, dry souls.

Jesus does not force you to go to Him using an assertive tone. He is Gentle and **Humble** in heart and with Him you will find peaceful rest for your soul (Matthew 11:29).

He understands how weak you are; after all, it is from dust that God formed you and it is to dust your body shall return. Allow Him to comfort you and strengthen you on life's difficult journey.

Will you take your ever-so-small flicker of faith and hope to Him? Will you trust Him to gently fan your flicker of faith into a bright and glorious flame of renewed hope?

He is Your Anchor

God's **Grace** is sufficient for you. He is all you need. He never stops holding your hand and lavishing you with His Love. Despite the heartache from this **fallen world** and the collateral damage you may receive through other's **unresolved sin** or **acts of the flesh**, God will demonstrate His **Mercy** toward you because your hope is in Him. The experience of trouble and **trial** is part of your journey on this earth. Will you seek harmony above your hurt feelings? Will you run into His arms for comfort? He stands with open arms waiting and hoping you will.

Will you offer yourself as a **sacrifice** that is pleasing to Him by keeping your vision on eternal glories and your focus on obedience to Him? Anchor yourself to Him, knowing He is working everything out for your good (Romans 8:28). There is no hopeless situation when you place your troubles before your **Abba** Lord! Will you boldly place every trouble before Him today?

Trouble and trial are

part of your journey

on this earth. Will you seek

harmony above your hurt

feelings?

The Lord to the Rescue

Psalm 34:19 (NLT)
The righteous person faces many troubles, but the LORD comes to the rescue each time.

Psalm 112:7, 8 (NLT)
They do not fear bad news; they confidently trust the LORD to care for them. They are confident and fearless and can face their foes triumphantly.

2 Timothy 3:11 (NLT)
You know how much persecution and suffering I [Paul] have endured. You know all about how I was persecuted in Antioch, Iconium, and Lystra—but the Lord rescued me from all of it.

God is **Sovereign**; nothing happens in your world without His knowledge. He is with you, holding your hand. He is Mighty to save you and Faithful to quiet you with His Love. Leave your anxieties and fears at His feet; He is Trustworthy. He is looking over you and your loved ones like a Good Shepherd (John 10:14).

Fix your thoughts on His character as revealed by His names. He is **Jehovah Shammah**—He is always there, an Ever-faithful, Loyal, Loving, Compassionate and Present **Abba** Father. He is full of **Mercy** and **Grace**.

His love covers you. He will always be there to deliver and rescue; this you must not doubt. Trust Him. When you begin to fret, will you say, "Jesus, I trust You?" You can trust the Lord will always come to your rescue.

Be Nourished and Grow Strong!

Jeremiah 17:7, 8 (NLT)

But blessed are those who trust in the LORD and have made the LORD their hope and confidence. They are like trees planted along a riverbank, with roots that reach deep into the water. Such trees are not bothered by the heat or worried by long months of drought. Their leaves stay green, and they never stop producing fruit.

The Lord is your Rock; He is the stability in life that your soul craves. Life on earth is full of twists and turns, ups and downs; but your Lord remains Steady and Strong, holding your hand. He assures you everything is going to be okay when you call upon His Name—the Name above all names—the Name through which mankind has the opportunity to be **saved**!

Will you cry out to Him? Cry out to Jesus, your **Advocate** (1 John 2:1)!

Drink from His nourishing, healing Word and be satisfied, relieved, and comforted. Accept His nourishment and grow strong and fruitful, despite living in a **fallen realm**.

Will you turn your focus to Jesus and **glorify** Him? If you will focus on Him you will find rest for your weary mind. Blessed are you when your confidence is in the Lord.

The Lord Watches Over You

Psalm 33:11-13, 15, 18 (NLT)

But the LORD's plans stand firm forever; his intentions can never be shaken. What joy for the nation whose God is the LORD, whose people he has chosen as his **inheritance**. The LORD looks down from heaven and sees the whole human race . . . He made their hearts, so he understands everything they do . . . But the LORD watches over those who fear him, those who rely on his unfailing love.

Your God sees your heart. He knows you desire your family to be **salt and light** everywhere they go (Matthew 5:13, 14). He knows how your heart hurts when your loved ones dishonor Him. Continue to **stand in the gap** for them. God hears your every prayer and He never fails to move on their behalf.

God is the Great Healer and the Great Protector. He is your refuge; enter in to His presence with praise for His Omniscience and Omnipotence.

Will you give thanks to Him for His unfailing Love and Faithfulness? He will never fail you and He is ever watching over you, listening to your prayers

Do Not Fear

Why do you worry and accept fear? Has **Abba** Father not promised to work all things out for your good (Romans 8:28) when you place your concerns, mistakes, and the offenses of others at the foot of His mighty throne of **Grace** and **Mercy**? He is God Almighty, **Jehovah Shalom**—the God of Peace and abundant life. He grants you a peace and well-being that you cannot discover without His involvement in your life.

Surrender every thought, worry, fear, hurt, and concern to Him and tell **Abba** you trust Him to move on your behalf. Stop trying to figure out all the "whys" and start asking "how" you can **glorify** Him as your life moves forward.

Will you praise Him for being **Omnipotent** and expectantly wait for Him to move mountains on your behalf? He loves you and longs to demonstrate His Wise and Powerful care over you.

Transformed

Acts 10:38a, 42, 43 (NLT)

And you know that God **anointed** Jesus of Nazareth with the Holy Spirit and with power . . . And he ordered us to preach everywhere and to testify that Jesus is the one appointed by God to be the judge of all—the living and the dead. He is the one all the prophets testified about, saying that everyone who believes in him will have their sins forgiven through his name.

Romans 12:2 (NLT)

Don't copy the behavior and customs of this world, but let God transform you into a new person by changing the way you think. Then you will learn to know God's will for you, which is good and pleasing and perfect.

God made you. He knows best how you should live in order to be satisfied and happy.

When you live under the shadow of His mighty wings (Psalm 91:4) honoring Him with your words, your actions, and your body (Romans 12:1), you bring glory to Him and health to your bones (Proverbs 3:8). Be oh so careful what you allow your eyes to see and your ears to hear because you may be giving the **devil** entry into your very being.

Your heart reflects what you think and your life is the demonstration of what is happening inside you (Proverbs 4:23). Your **Abba** Father is completely Honest, Kind, Loyal, and Merciful. He requires nothing less of you if you claim to follow Him. Will you ask Him for opportunities to demonstrate these characteristics to someone in your life?

No Need to Compare

Proverbs 20:11 (NLT)
Even children are known by the way they act, whether their conduct is pure, and whether it is right.

Romans 14:12 (NLT)
Yes, each of us will give a personal account to God.

Galatians 6:4, 5 (NLT)
Pay careful attention to your own work, for then you will get the satisfaction of a job well done, and you won't need to compare yourself to anyone else. For we are each responsible for our own conduct.

Your Heavenly Father's relationship with you is very personal; it is between Him and you. He has called you out of this world to **glorify** Him, to "do life" with Him, to behave according to the guidelines He has given you in His Word.

Why are you constantly comparing yourself to your brothers and sisters? Do you not understand that someday you will stand before **Abba** Father where you will be held accountable for your own actions? You are only accountable for yourself. Will you stop trying to please people—striving for their approval? Will you take your eyes off others and focus them on Jesus?

Pay careful attention to your own work; this is the route to a glorious satisfaction deep within your soul for a job well done!

Don't Be Misled

Your **Abba** Father loves you to pieces. He looks for opportunities to bless you with His **Grace** and Love. It is His good pleasure to show you **Mercy** when you certainly do not deserve it. Do not be misinformed about your Heavenly Father; He is a Just and Fair Father.

Abba Father deposited His Holy Spirit within you the moment you **humble**d yourself and surrendered to His Lordship. He designed you to operate under His influence and guidance so you will harvest great blessings, both now and for eternity. If you ignore His Spirit's calling and directing, then you leave Him no choice but to allow the consequences of your decisions to overtake you.

Are you choosing His eternal ways over your shallow, empty and shortsighted ways? Are you reaping the blessings of "doing life" according to His will? His kingdom come, His will be done (Matthew 6:10); is this the cry of your heart? If so, press on because you will reap a harvest of blessing if you do not give up.

Harmony

> **Romans 14:17–19, 23b (NLT)**
>
> For the Kingdom of God is not a matter of what we eat or drink, but of living a life of goodness and peace and joy in the Holy Spirit. If you serve Christ with this attitude, you will please God, and others will approve of you, too. So then, let us aim for harmony in the church and try to build each other up . . . If you do anything you believe is not right, you are sinning.

Keep a godly perspective. Try to look past your feelings and beyond the moment. Your heavenly Father is honored and you are blessed when you seek harmony among your brothers and sisters. This does not mean you do not have a voice for truth; it means you should use your voice to speak truth in love. To do this, you must consider the other person's feelings and speak with concern for that person. Truth spoken in love means you stop before you speak and ask the Holy Spirit within you to give you keen insight and revelation as to how you can sharpen the other person's walk and how they may be sharpening yours.

This attitude and course of action will require a **humble** spirit, which your **Abba** Father highly esteems. Do you have such a spirit today? Ask God Almighty to help you desire this **humble**ness and to stir affection and compassion in your heart for others.

Your attitude and actions are always communicating something about you. You are known by the way you act. How are you acting?

Give Him Full Access

Psalm 25:1-5 (NLT)

O LORD, I give my life to you. I trust in you, my God! Do not let me be disgraced, or let my enemies rejoice in my defeat. No one who trusts in you will ever be disgraced, but disgrace comes to those who try to deceive others. Show me the right path, O LORD; point out the road for me to follow. Lead me by your truth and teach me, for you are the God who saves me. All day long I put my hope in you.

Who is this God whom you worship? He is Merciful and Compassionate; you can trust Him with every fiber of your being. You can trust Him in every area of your life. What areas are you holding back from Him? He already knows and so do you. Will you admit to Him the areas of your life in which you don't trust Him?

Will you allow Him access to your thoughts, your fears, your hidden sins, your doubts, your weaknesses, and your hurts? Will you choose today to really trust Him? Will you trust Him for healing and wholeness? Will you trust Him to help you? Will you trust Him for strength for the journey? Will you trust Him for restoration? Will you trust His ways? Will you trust His timing?

Open every nook and cranny of your heart to Him; open His Word and ask Him for guidance and new revelations. Then choose to wait as long as it takes for His perfect timing. He has a plan and it is always for your good (Jeremiah 29:11). Will you trust Him?

Tender Heart and Tough Hide

Psalm 26:1 (NLT)
Declare me innocent, O Lord, for I have acted with integrity; I have trusted in the Lord without wavering.

Proverbs 12:16 (NLT)
A fool is quick-tempered, but a wise person stays calm when insulted.

Proverbs 12:16 (The Message)
Fools have short fuses and explode all too quickly; the prudent quietly shrug off insults.

D o you believe Jesus is your greatest **Advocate** (1 John 2:1) and Loyal Supporter? Do you believe He is praying for you (Romans 8:34)? He desires you to connect with Him constantly. His love knows no bounds where you are concerned (Romans 8:38, 39). As you get to know Him, you will more easily reflect His character to others. **Abba** God is Just and Fair and knows best how to handle every situation. Will you trust Him with the difficult people in your life?

While you live in this **fallen world**, you will encounter rudeness from others. And God sees any mistreatment of you for you are His child. If God wants you to confront with love those who mistreat you, He will give you the words and guide the tone in which you speak them (Luke 21:15). Ask Him to guide you before you open your mouth. The Lord will instruct you to allow Him to deal with the offender. This may stretch you to pain, but God is growing iron in your soul. Let Him use everything in your life to strengthen you. You will know when you are trusting Him more because your heart will be a bit more tender and your hide a bit more tough.

Do you have a tender heart and a tough hide?

The Eyes of Your Heart

Matthew 9:27–30a (ESV)

And as Jesus passed on from there, two blind men followed him, crying aloud, "Have **mercy** on us, Son of David." When he entered the house, the blind men came to him, and Jesus said to them, "Do you believe that I am able to do this?" They said to him, "Yes, Lord." Then he touched their eyes, saying, "According to your faith be it done to you." And their eyes were opened.

Jesus is the Son of God; He is also the **Son of man**. He connects with your humanness because He was also born of a woman; He was fully human as well as fully divine. When He walked the earth as a man, He lived in a family where they laughed, worked, cried, got tired, complained, ate, played, rested, and prayed together. He understands how limited you are in your humanity—you can't see tomorrow and you have only a foggy understanding of yesterday.

You will make bad decisions. Of course, you can greatly reduce the number of poor choices you make by asking Jesus for His guidance and help. Please, tuck this truth deep inside you. Remember, Jesus is the Merciful Lover of your soul.

Ask the Lord for **Mercy** and throw your trust upon Him; He is profoundly Kind. Remember to open your eyes to His deliverance and thank Him for His mercies that abound in your life.

How Strong Are You?

Psalm 27:1 (NLT)

The LORD is my light and my **salvation**—so why should I be afraid? The LORD is my fortress, protecting me from danger, so why should I tremble?

Romans 16:25a (NLT)

Now all glory to God, who is able to make you strong, just as my **Good News** says.

1 Corinthians 1:8 (NLT)

He will keep you strong to the end so that you will be free from all blame on the day when our Lord Jesus Christ returns.

Your God is not an elusive God. His Word says to seek Him with all your heart and you will find Him (Deuteronomy 4:29). There is no secret or special formula to knowing Him. He only asks for a surrendered and willing heart that desires Him.

You grow in strength and wisdom as you learn more about Him. When you open His Word, you will begin to discern His Ways and recognize His voice directing you. The more you become acquainted with Him, the calmer and stronger your spirit will be.

Are you feeling weak, fearful, and unstable? Fear not; He is with you (Matthew 28:20). He longs to strengthen you. Will you choose today to enter His cool, refreshing fortress of loving care? He is waiting for you.

Surefooted

Psalm 18:33 (NIV)

He makes my feet like the feet of a deer;
he causes me to stand on the heights.

Habakkuk 3:17–19 (NLT)

Even though the fig trees have no blossoms, and there are no grapes on the vines; even though the olive crop fails, and the fields lie empty and barren; even though the flocks die in the fields, and the cattle barns are empty, yet I will rejoice in the LORD! I will be joyful in the God of my **salvation**! The **Sovereign** LORD is my strength! He makes me as surefooted as a deer, able to tread upon the heights.

The world is full of tragedies and bad news because this world is under the **dominion of darkness** (Colossians 1:13). This world is not your real home, nor is it your future home; this is not heaven.

Abba Father has seen your troubles and He cares about the anguish of your soul. Do not look to the right or to the left; look straight into His eyes. Take hold of His promises for you (2 Peter 1:3, 4). You are His.

Take His hand and walk with Him today asking Him, moment-by-moment, where the next step leads. He will never leave you nor forsake you (Hebrews 13:5). His name is Faithful and True (Revelation 19:11). If the road ahead is rocky and steep, His Hand will smooth the way. He laid down His life so you might find the Way to everlasting life (John 14:6). Stay on His path, for there you will find strength to go on.

Where do you seek to find strength for the journey? The **Sovereign** Lord is your strength and He will make you as surefooted as a deer climbing the hills in your life (Habakkuk 3:19).

Thank the Lord

Remember to dress yourself spiritually with **Abba**'s shield of protection (Psalm 115:11), armor of truth (Ephesians 6:10–14a), and garments of **salvation** (Isaiah 61:10). You would not walk about without material clothing; why do you expose your spirit to the arrows of **the enemy** and harsh lies of this world without **Abba**'s covering of Truth, **Righteousness**, Peace, Faith (Ephesians 6:10–16), **Mercy** and Love (Colossians 3:12–14)?

Your heavenly Father is **Jehovah Jireh**—He provides you with everything you need . . . and more. Charles Spurgeon said choosing to trust God is like planting seeds in the field of your soul that will harvest into golden sheaves of **grace**. When you intentionally acknowledge God's provisions for you with thanksgiving, you protect your spirit from roots of bitterness (Hebrews 12:15) and depression (Psalm 42:5). He has given you so much; do you have eyes to see His blessings over you? Every time you thank Him, joy is cultivated deeper within your being (Philippians 4:4–7).

Have you thanked the Lord recently for all your blessings and tried to imagine what He has planned for you? (See Jeremiah 29:11.)

Guidance

Why do you listen to the voices of so many? Why do you entertain advice from those who don't follow **Abba** Father? He is **Omniscient**—He knows everything (Psalm 147:5). Is this not enough reason for you to go to Him for guidance, protection, and provision?

He is **Jehovah Raah**, the Lord your Shepherd (Psalm 23). His eye is on you because you belong to His flock and His ear is attentive to your every need. He is God. He needs nothing from you; but He desires to give you a life worth living. He knit you together in your mother's womb with specific plans in mind just for you (Psalm 139:13). It is best for you to walk in harmony with Him; and He is eager to show you the way. But you must ask Him, seek His answers by reading His Word, and wait for His response.

He will answer you at the perfect time—He is never early and never late. Will you trust Him to lead you and watch over you?

The Solid Rock

Abba Father has given you His Word as a foundation for your life. Please understand, you are an eternal being; although your life on earth is like petals on a flower that are blown away, never to return, your life matters for all of eternity. On the outside, you may appear similar to others; but God knows the materials you have chosen for your inner foundation.

When the storms of life kick up (and they surely will), your house may be shaken to its core. If you have laid a foundation of trust in **Abba** and built your life on His promises and the Power of His Names (that reveal His very character) your house will withstand the storms of life. It is better to test your foundation now than on the great Day of Judgment (2 Corinthians 5:10).

What will **Judgment Day** reveal about your life?

Make the Most of Your Days

Are you drifting through life weak, confused, empty, and without a plan? Today is the day to rejoice! God has made this day; He has kept you on earth because He has plans to use you and prosper you (Jeremiah 29:11).

You must take great care with each day God gives you because you do not know what tomorrow might bring. Seek His will for you by asking Him to direct your every step and then give Him time to unfold His perfect plans for you.

Do not trifle with God by squandering your days partying or complaining as the world does. Don't anger Him with an ungrateful attitude. Sing praise songs to Him; you have so many reasons to praise Him! The Lord will work everything out for your good (Romans 8:28); just bring all your troubles to Him (1 Peter 5:7). Remember to thank Him continually throughout the day. Live knowing God is always by your side, always looking out for you.

The Hope of all the World

Psalm 119:114 (NLT)
You are my refuge and my shield; your word is my source of hope.

Psalm 147:11 (NLT)
No, the LORD's delight is in those who fear Him, those who put their hope in his unfailing love.

Proverbs 10:28a (NLT)
The hopes of the godly result in happiness.

Matthew 12:21 (NLT)
And his name will be the hope of all the world.

Jesus, the Name above all names, is the only One through whom you are **saved**. It is Jesus who provides abundant life, both in this life and the next. His Name evokes hope and joy for those seeking **salvation**. Even though His Name is the hope of this **fallen world** and conveys His authority and excellence, not all in this world will embrace and accept Him. They forfeit so much, including hope.

Our Lord freely offers His hope through the truth of His Word. In the sixty-six books of the Bible, He has recorded His way—the way that leads to hope for all. His Word is for soft, open hearts— hearts that are willing to allow Him access. He does not force His planting of hope in your heart; this is a choice only you can make. Will you choose today to open more of yourself to His Word and, in turn, be a planting of the Lord for the display of His Splendor and reap eternal blessings?

Fight For Those You Love

Nehemiah 4:9, 14 (NLT)

But we prayed to our God and guarded the city day and night to protect ourselves . . . Then as I looked over the situation; I called together the nobles and the rest of the people and said to them, "Don't be afraid of **the enemy**! Remember the Lord, who is great and glorious, and fight for your brothers, your sons, your daughters, your wives, and your homes!"

Lamentations 2:19 (NLT)

Rise during the night and cry out. Pour out your hearts like water to the Lord. Lift up your hands to him in prayer, pleading for your children, for in every street they are faint with hunger.

Your **Abba** Father has placed you in your family, your circle of friends, your community, and your country for a reason; to **stand in the gap** and lift those you love up to Him. You may be the only one praying for them.

When we ask God to move on anyone's behalf, the **armies of heaven** are called into action. There is more power in our prayers on behalf of others than we have the privilege to see with earthly eyes. God is the Great and Glorious One! He desires to demonstrate, for you and others, how He fights on our behalf when we invite Him to our battles (Nehemiah 4:20). Lift up your hands and cry out to Him for the sake of the weak, lost, and hungry; pray diligently for the spiritually malnourished (James 5:16).

Who are the ones and what are the needs you should take before God's mighty throne of **Grace** (Hebrews 4:16)? Don't give up praying for them and lifting their needs before **Abba** Father! The Lord is listening.

God's Love

John 17:24–26 (NLT)

"Father, I want these whom you have given me to be with me where I am. Then they can see all the glory you gave me because you loved me even before the world began! O righteous Father, the world doesn't know you, but I do; and these disciples know you sent me. I have revealed you to them, and I will continue to do so. Then your love for me will be in them, and I will be in them."

Jesus came to earth as the visible image of your invisible God (John 14:9). Even though Jesus, the Son of God, is Supreme and **Sovereign** over all creation, He chose to be flesh and blood and visibly demonstrate God's Love for you.

Although He is Love, Pure, and Good, when He walked the earth, many hated Him, rejected Him, and ridiculed Him. Many lied about Him, threatened Him, and even plotted to kill Him. He persevered because He thought of you: He desired you to experience the reservoir of Love He and the Father have for you. Because He remembered you, He chose to endure the torments of hell for you rather than live eternally in heaven without you. Consider this.

You Need Him

Psalm 74:12 (NLT)
You, O God, are my king from ages past, bringing **salvation** to the earth.

Matthew 5:3 (NLT)
God blesses those who are poor and realize their need for him, for the Kingdom of Heaven is theirs.

John 3:16 (NIV)
For God so loved the world that he gave his one and only Son, that whoever believes in him shall not perish but have eternal life.

John 20:30, 31 (NLT)
The disciples saw Jesus do many other miraculous signs in addition to the ones recorded in this book. But these are written so that you may continue to believe that Jesus is the **Messiah**, the Son of God, and that by believing in him you will have life by the power of his name.

Romans 10:9 (NLT)
If you **confess** with your mouth that Jesus is Lord and believe in your heart that God raised him from the dead, you will be **saved**.

Do you recognize your need for God? Have you taken an honest inventory of your abilities to control anything in life? The idea that you can control your life is an illusion **the enemy** presents as a possibility; but He is the father of all lies and there is no truth found in him (John 8:44).

You are helpless and powerless on your own to accomplish anything of eternal value; following the Lord is the only way of living life to its fullest. He loves you so much! He has a reminder of you engraved on His hand (Isaiah 49:16). His Love for you is so great that He was willing to give you something of the greatest value—His very life. Now, that is Love!

True belief in God demonstrates a living faith—a commitment to trust Him with everything and everyone in your life. A living faith is also demonstrated by a daily confidence that you can trust Him and obey Him. You will never regret placing your trust in Him—in Jesus, the One who bears the name above all names (Philippians 2:9)!

You are helpless and

powerless on your own to

accomplish anything of

eternal value; following the

Lord is the only way of living

life to its fullest.

Deep Roots of Faith

Hebrews 11:1–6 (NLT)

Faith is the confidence that what we hope for will actually happen; it gives us assurance about things we cannot see . . . And it is impossible to please God without faith. Anyone who wants to come to him must believe that God exists and that he rewards those who sincerely seek him.

In what do you place your trust? Do you trust in your own abilities, in others, in your bank account, your career, your intelligence, or attractiveness? To trust in any of these things is like building a foundation on moving sand.

Today, choose to place your confidence in **the Rock** (Luke 6:48, 49). Say to Jesus," I trust You, Jesus, with every fear, doubt, and question." If you sincerely seek Him for comfort, healing, or guidance, He will answer! He will never fail you nor forsake you. When the strong winds of life kick up, you will be able to stand like a strong tower. Every time you choose to trust Him, your foundation grows ever stronger. Will you strengthen your foundation today?

Commitments Define You

The Lord is available to you; He made you to journey through this life with Him as your Gentle, Caring, and Capable Father. He is your Rock of Ages—Solid and Trustworthy. His standard is **Holiness** and apart from Him there is no **righteousness** to be found in you.

Will you take inventory today and examine your habits and your daily busyness? Will you honestly consider the top commitments in your life? Who are the people and what are the things to which you are committed?

Your commitments define you. Do your commitments define you as one of His? Do others see the Glory of the Lord in your life?

If not, make the necessary changes right now. **Repent**, follow the cloud of God's leading that will guide you to a well-ordered life, and leave the wilderness of ungodly concerns and valuations—**idols** of earthly care. Come! Leave the wilderness behind and enter the **Promised Land** of God where you will find meaningful, abundant life.

The Fulfillment of Giving

Proverbs 21:13 (NLT)
Those who shut their ears to the cries of the poor will be ignored in their own time of need.

James 2:15, 16 (NLT)
Suppose you see a brother or sister who has no food or clothing, and you say, "Good-bye and have a good day; stay warm and eat well"—but then you don't give that person any food or clothing. What good does that do?

God hears your every prayer and sees your every need. Because He is a Compassionate and Loving Father, He longs to fulfill your needs. However, the cries of the poor pierce His ears. He sees your ability to help the poor and needy because He provided all you possess. And because God knows your heart, He knows what will bring you the greatest fulfillment—doing His will.

True fulfillment and happiness will coat your heart like a soothing **balm** when you give to someone else. Giving to others is allowing God's own heart to guide you, for He gave His all for you.

Are you shutting your ears to the cries of the poor? Are you closing your ears, your wallet, your schedule, and your heart to those looking to you for help?

Will you ask **Abba** Father to lead you to the ones He would have you help? He will show you. The poor need you. Will you help them? They are crying for help. Can you hear their cries?

Be Thankful

Psalm 50:23 (NLT)

But giving thanks is a **sacrifice** that truly honors me. If you keep to my path, I will reveal to you the **salvation** of God.

Daniel 6:7, 10 (NLT)

"We are all in agreement—we administrators, officials, high officers, advisers, and governors—that the king should make a law that will be strictly enforced. Give orders that for the next thirty days any person who prays to anyone, divine or human—except to you, Your Majesty—will be thrown into the den of lions." . . . But when Daniel learned that the law had been signed, he went home and knelt down as usual in his upstairs room, with its windows open toward Jerusalem. He prayed three times a day, just as he had always done, giving thanks to his God.

Colossians 3:17 (NLT)

And whatever you do or say, do it as a representative of the Lord Jesus, giving thanks through him to God the Father.

Remember, child of God, your heavenly Father hears and sees everything. As your Lord and Creator, He requires of you a **sacrifice** of thanksgiving. He desires that you discipline your conversations to be rich in gratitude. Grumbling, complaining, and negativity dishonor your Lord and demonstrate a self-centered and prideful heart.

Are you thankful? Is your life one of "thanks-living"? Do you acknowledge your Lord's **Sovereign**ty? When you complain, you prove your arrogance and ignorance. God allows difficulties for a divine purpose. He promises you He hears your every cry to Him—every petition for help (Psalm 34:17). He also promises to work everything out for your good (Romans 8:28) in His perfect timing. When you complain, you are telling others and God that He is not doing a good job.

Will you make it your custom to be a thankful voice in a very unthankful world?

When you complain,

you are telling others

and God that He is not

doing a good job.

Ripe for the Harvest

John 4:34–36 (NLT)

Then Jesus explained: "My nourishment comes from doing the will of God, who sent me, and from finishing his work. You know the saying, 'Four months between planting and harvest.' But I say, wake up and look around. The fields are already ripe for harvest. The harvesters are paid good wages, and the fruit they harvest is people brought to eternal life. What joy awaits both the planter and the harvester alike!"

Arise, shine, and sever your heart from the world (1 John 2:15–17)! The world offers empty, short-term pleasures and satisfaction. God offers you real nourishment that never fails to satisfy. When you choose to **glorify** Him through obedience to His call to love others, your soul is nourished by being a channel for His life flowing into the world.

Are you a mouthpiece for Jesus? Are you the hands and feet of Christ? Stop today and fully give yourself to someone who needs a listening ear or helping hand. Demonstrate incredible care for him or her. By your actions and words, let others know they matter because God made them and created them to be a in a nourishing relationship with Him!

Will you show others the way to eternal, abundant life? The fields are ripe for harvest; what joy awaits both the planter and harvester alike! Go and plant some good seed today!!!

Yeshua Calls

Psalm 27:8 (NLT)
My heart has heard you say, "Come and talk with me. "And my heart responds, "Lᴏʀᴅ, I am coming."

John 4:42 (NLT)
Then they said to the woman, "Now we believe, not just because of what you told us, but because we have heard him ourselves. Now we know that he is indeed the Savior of the world."

Abba Father has planted a desire in your heart to know Him—your Creator and your God. Why do you waste so much time and energy chasing the wind (Ecclesiastes 2:11)? He is your **Yeshua**—your **Salvation**. Snuggle up to Him; hold His hand; talk to Him; seek Him and find rest and well-being for your soul.

Not everyone will hear Him calling to them; some do not seek to know the Way, the Truth, and the Life (John 14:6). You, however, hear Him calling you and your heart is responding to Him. The more you give audience to Him the deeper your communication grows and the keener your ear grows to the sound of His voice.

Your **Yeshua** is calling you! Will you sit with Him and talk to Him? He has much to share with you.

In His Image

The moment you believed in Jesus and declared Him Lord of your life, He deposited His Spirit in you as a sign that you are now His. He is now your Lord, your Guide, and your Protector. With the help of His Spirit, you have new understanding when you study His **covenant**s found in His inspired and living Word.

The Holy Spirit within you works in conjunction with God's Word to reveal deeper truths so you can better understand your Lord and His kingdom. He desires you to function in a manner which is best for you—in obedience to His will. When you live in unity with the Lord, with His Spirit directing you, you nourish your soul and you **glorify** your Savior.

Are you becoming more and more like the Lord—changing to reflect His image (2 Corinthians 3:18)? Will you reflect the Glory of the Lord?

Listen to God

Matthew 13:12 (NLT)
To those who listen to my teaching, more understanding will be given, and they will have an abundance of knowledge. But for those who are not listening, even what little understanding they have will be taken away from them.

Philippians 1:9 (NLT)
I pray that your love will overflow more and more, and that you will keep on growing in knowledge and understanding.

A re you prepared to listen to the Lord today? He desires to connect with you every day because He loves you so much. You are deeply valued and treasured by Him. After all, He personally knit you together, fiber by unique fiber, making you the only you to ever live (Psalm 139:13). He has wonderful plans for you; but you must first seek understanding by listening to His Word.

His Word is living and powerful. Knowing His Word can result in life-giving knowledge and insight. However, just as the sun that melts ice also hardens clay, so it is with your Creator's words—they can melt all the hard, cold places in your heart or you can reject them and live as dry, brittle clay.

Will you allow the Word of God to flood your parched soul and mind? Will you receive His Word and choose to grow in life-giving knowledge and understanding of your Creator's plan?

Trust

Psalm 91:1, 2 (NLT)

Those who live in the shelter of the Most High will find rest in the shadow of the Almighty. This I declare about the LORD: He alone is my refuge, my place of safety; he is my God, and I trust him.

There are four simple words that can change your life: "I trust You, Jesus."

Our Lord invites you into a trusting relationship with Him. He can be trusted. Is your journey with Him defined by your unconditional trust? If not, then today is the day to begin! Lay every fear, doubt, and question before Him—leave them before His throne. Ask Him how to proceed, tell Him you will keep your ears and eyes open to His answers while you read His Word and listen to His teachings.

Abba Father is your shelter, your refuge, and your place of safety. But if you never run to Him when doubts and fears threaten, how will you ever know? To place your unquestioning trust in God may be one of the most difficult things you will ever try to do. Ask God to remind you that, no matter what happens, you can trust Him. When your heart grows faint, weary, or troubled, ask Him to give you the ability to say, "I trust You, Jesus! I know You have got this."

Will you rest in the shadow of the Almighty? This is your privilege as His child.

Praise the Lord

Psalm 25:8 (NLT)
The LORD is good and does what is right; he shows the proper path to those who go astray.

Psalm 35:28 (NKJV)
And my tongue shall speak of Your righteousness and of Your praise all the day long.

John 10:11 (NLT)
I am the good shepherd. The good shepherd **sacrifice**s his life for the sheep.

2 Peter 1:3, 4 (NLT)
By his divine power, God has given us everything we need for living a godly life. We have received all of this by coming to know him, the one who called us to himself by means of his marvelous glory and excellence. And because of his glory and excellence, he has given us great and precious promises. These are the promises that enable you to share his divine nature and escape the world's corruption caused by human desires.

When someone brings good into your life, you eagerly share the wonderful news with others. Why do you not share **Abba** Father's Goodness more often? Do you recognize all that He has given you? He tenderly and lovingly cares for your every need; His eye is constantly on you. He is Good! Yes, He is Good all the time.

When you reflect upon His Goodness and praise Him, something beautiful covers your heart—His Peace, His **Shalom**. His **Shalom** is far-reaching and deeper than anything you could ever experience from the world. When you praise Him, He quiets you, He completes you, and He covers you with a deep-seated sense of well-being and safety.

Are you developing the discipline—the determined lifestyle—of praising your God for His goodness? Will you praise Him right now?

When you reflect upon His

Goodness and praise Him,

something beautiful covers

your heart—His peace,

His Shalom.

Peace, Sweet Peace

Psalm 85:10 (NKJV)
Mercy and truth have met together; **righteousness** and peace have kissed.

Hosea 4:1 (NKJV)
Hear the word of the LORD, you children of Israel, for the Lord brings a charge against the inhabitants of the land: "There is no truth or **mercy** or knowledge of God in the land."

Determine today to write God's everlasting truths on the walls of your heart and mind. Allowing God to plant seeds of truth in the soil of your life brings forth a harvest of **mercy** and love for others and yourself. God's Truth is saturated with **Grace** and tender, loving Care. When it takes root in your life, you will be enabled to reveal to the world the nature of the One you serve. Choose to be a true example of Jesus by peeling back the hard corners of your heart and receiving His seeds of Truth and **Grace**.

When your choices reflect his Truth and **Grace** you begin to live life the right way—God's way. When you do, a peace that surpasses all understanding (Philippians 4:6, 7) will envelope your entire being because you are living the way you were created to live.

Will you choose to be a person of truth and **mercy**, **righteousness** and peace?

Relax in His Divine Control

> **Psalm 37:3-7 (NLT)**
>
> Trust in the LORD and do good. Then you will live safely in the land and prosper. Take delight in the LORD, and he will give you your heart's desires. Commit everything you do to the LORD. Trust him, and he will help you. He will make your innocence radiate like the dawn, and the justice of your cause will shine like the noonday sun. Be still in the presence of the LORD, and wait patiently for him to act. Don't worry about evil people who prosper or fret about their wicked schemes.

Keep your eyes on Jesus. He is your Loyal, Wise, Fair, and Perfect Savior. Don't ever give up on Him. Continue to commit your life and your loved ones to Him and relax in His divine control. He can work everything out for you; be patient and wait for Him. God's timing is always perfect; but it may not be the timing you would choose.

When your eyes are focused on Jesus, you will not be looking about at the circumstances of others' lives. Look only to Jesus and do not allow your mind to become tangled in other people's lives. You will not stand before Him for them; you will only give an account for your life. Therefore, trust Him every day with the events of your own life. Praise Him, thank Him, and be good to everyone He brings into your life.

Are you committing everything you do to the Lord? He is a Just God; you can trust Him. Hand over your controlling tendencies and relax in His divine control.

Do You Finally Believe?

John 16:31, 33 (NLT)

Jesus asked, "Do you finally believe? . . . I have told you all this so that you may have peace in me. Here on earth you will have many **trial**s and sorrows. But take heart, because I have overcome the world."

You will not always understand your circumstances. There is a whole world around you your eyes cannot see; it is the spiritual world where an unseen battle rages. There is constant fighting for your life and your family's life between the **angels of God** and the **servants of Satan**. But take heart, the Power at work within you is greater than the power at work against you (1 John 4:4).

When troubles come your way, remember to thank Jesus; not for the troubles, of course, but for His promise of help. Trust His Omnipotence. Rest in knowing He has servants everywhere (angelic and human) whom He calls to action on your behalf simply because you asked Him for help.

You are on a spiritual journey that can be filled with obstacles. Jesus is faithful to come to your aid whenever you seek His help. No matter how small you perceive your faith to be at this moment, step toward Him. Regardless how small that step may be, let Jesus know you are giving Him your circumstances and your trust and you will wait for Him to overcome!

The Great Restorer

> ## Psalm 27:13 (NLT)
> Yet I am confident I will see the LORD's goodness while I am here in the land of the living.
>
> ## Psalm 40:3 (ESV)
> He put a new song in my mouth, a song of praise to our God. Many will see and fear, and put their trust in the LORD.
>
> ## Joel 2:25a (ESV)
> I will restore to you the years that the swarming locust has eaten.

Has your recent path been steep and difficult? Are you weary and a bit bruised and beaten up? Do you wonder what happened? Do you think to yourself, "It was not supposed to end up like this"? Jesus understands. He asked the Father to take His cup of suffering; but chose to trust God's perfect will (Mark 14:36). Jesus submitted to our Father's will and His suffering was great; but the **salvation** of mankind resulted.

Though your own path may be difficult and you may see suffering along the way, you can sing a new song—a song of joy and thanksgiving—because you are delivered and set free in Christ. Others will be astounded by the joy they see in your transformed life—a life that has peace and hope despite difficulties. You can sing a song of rejoicing in even the worst circumstances because you know all things in this "land of the living" are temporary and God is working everything out for good.

Our God is the Great Restorer. He longs to restore to you all that life's difficulties and hardships have taken. He desires to give you a new song to sing! Will you pray, "I trust You, **Abba** Father, for a new day to dawn in my life"?

The Creator's Love

> **Job 10:11, 12 (NLT)**
> You clothed me with skin and flesh, and you knit my bones and sinews together. You gave me life and showed me your unfailing love. My life was preserved by your care.
>
> **Psalm 139:13–15 (NLT)**
> You made all the delicate, inner parts of my body and knit me together in my mother's womb. Thank you for making me so wonderfully complex! Your workmanship is marvelous—how well I know it. You watched me as I was being formed in utter seclusion, as I was woven together in the dark of the womb.

It is hard to fully comprehend the depth of Love your Creator has for you. In His eyes, you are marvelous and wonderfully complex. He loves you simply because you are you and you are part of His family. He loves you no more and no less whether you obey Him and honor Him with your life or not. His Love is unconditional; it is not given based on certain conditions.

You may not feel His Love or nearness. If not, ask yourself if you have moved away from the Lord. He never moves away from you. If you are not feeling His Love, reflect on your recent choices. Have they included Him? Have you been seeking Him with all your heart? His arms are open to receive you. Will you embrace Him today? He gave you life and longs to show you His unfailing Love. Ask Him to give you fresh eyes to see His loving Care for you.

Lean on Him

Remember your Lord today. He is waiting to connect with you. He loves to spend time with you—sharing His thoughts through His Word and listening to you. Seek Him with your prayers. Lean on Him and not your own perceptions or experience of life (Proverbs 3:5, 6). When you lean on Him, you are demonstrating your trust in Him. Leaning on Him grows hope within you for a better tomorrow.

Jesus is a safe shoulder to lean on. Do you remember when John leaned against Him during the Last Supper in the upper room (John 13:23–25)? At that time, John sought answers from Jesus and Jesus revealed to him the truth. When you lean into the **King of kings** with your questions, He will always supply the answers you need. Cling to Him for your peace of mind and security. He has always been there for you and He will always be there for you.

Will you remember Him today? He never forgets you (Isaiah 49:15, 16).

Give Him Everything

Psalm 37:3-5 (NLT)
Trust in the LORD and do good. Then you will live safely in the land and prosper. Take delight in the LORD, and he will give you your heart's desires. Commit everything you do to the LORD. Trust him, and he will help you.

As God's people, we are to walk by faith (2 Corinthians 5:7). This is an ongoing challenge for the children of God. A walk of faith requires a **humble** trust in our Lord.

Over and over in His Word, God assures you that He hears your every prayer. He loves you and desires what is best for you and He is perfectly capable of providing for your every need. He is calling you to Him, asking you to really trust Him. Whatever is causing you anxiety, you can trust **Abba** Father will work it out.

Visualize yourself placing your trouble at His feet. When you lay it before Him, you are demonstrating your trust. Your faith pleases Him (Hebrews 11:6) and He moves on your behalf. Your God is a perfect gentleman and will not interfere until you relinquish your concerns into His care. Once you commit them to Him, don't try to take them back and work them out yourself. Continue to trust Him by praising Him for His care over you and thanking Him for promising to come to your aid whenever you call on His Name (Psalm 28:7).

Your Days are Numbered

Job 12:10 (NLT)

For the life of every living thing is in his hand, and the breath of every human being.

Psalm 39:4 (NLT)

Lord, remind me how brief my time on earth will be. Remind me that my days are numbered—how fleeting my life is.

Proverbs 21:30 (NLT)

No human wisdom or understanding or plan can stand against the LORD.

From dust you were formed and to dust you will return (Genesis 3:19). It's a sobering thought, isn't it? It can make you wonder if your short life on earth really matters. The answer is "Yes;" every moment matters to your Maker. Even though your days on earth are numbered, the real you, the inner you, is an eternal being. You will not cease to exist when your body returns to dust; that is not the issue. The issue is whether you will know eternal, spiritual life in the Presence of God or be eternally separated from Him and all that is good and holy.

As a child of God, your eternal, spiritual life begins with Him when you believe in and receive Jesus as your Lord and Savior—He died on the cross to pay the penalty for your sin and He was raised from death to life on the third day. As God's child, your willingness to live out His words, ways, and will in your everyday choices has eternal value.

Will you ask Him today for the courage to live under His Lordship; the choices you make today will have eternal impact.

Busy, Busy, Busy

Psalm 39:6, 7 (NLT)
We are merely moving shadows, and all our busy rushing ends in nothing. We heap up wealth, not knowing who will spend it. And so, Lord, where do I put my hope? My only hope is in you.

Ecclesiastes 9:10 (NLT)
Whatever you do, do well. For when you go to the grave, there will be no work or planning or knowledge or wisdom.

Ecclesiastes 12:13, 14 (NLT)
That's the whole story. Here now is my final conclusion: Fear God and obey his commands, for this is everyone's duty. God will judge us for everything we do, including every secret thing, whether good or bad.

Are you busy, busy, busy—rushing from here to there? Don't waste these precious, numbered days God has given you. Your days should be defined by giving God His due honor and respect. You do this by knowing His commandments and by devoting your ways to following them.

Your Loving Father desires closeness with you. He longs to demonstrate His care for you. Worship Him, obey Him and watch Him work good into your life—and not just for this earthly existence. God is also preparing a place and a plan for you when you finally see Him and go to live in His heavenly kingdom—with Him forever.

Is your daily busyness and rushing about focused on things eternal and significant? Are your days filled with that which "ends in nothing" or do you live your life for the glory of the Lord?

Choose Freedom

Psalm 46:10a (NLT)
"Be still, and know that I am God!"

1 Corinthians 15:34, 57 (NLT)
Think carefully about what is right, and stop sinning. For to your shame I say that some of you don't know God at all . . . But thank God! He gives us victory over sin and death through our Lord Jesus Christ.

Hebrews 10:22 (NLT)
Let us go right into the presence of God with sincere hearts fully trusting him. For our guilty consciences have been sprinkled with Christ's blood to make us clean, and our bodies have been washed with pure water.

You are God's beloved. He set you free from sin so that you no longer need to live in bondage. You are free! Yes; you are free, indeed (John 8:36)! Embrace your freedom in Christ Jesus. Come to your senses and stop living in your old patterns of self pity, addictions, gossiping, lying, and bad choices. Live as a clean child of God.

Your behavior and words reflect what you believe and whom you serve. Are you still serving yourself? Today can be the day of your breakthrough. Find the life of victory available when you choose to serve the Lord God Almighty. Choose to live for Him by spending time listening to Him in His Word. Be still with Him and know your God!

Have you chosen to believe your Lord? He says He gives you victory over sin through Jesus Christ. St Augustine said, "Love God and do what you want." When you really know Him, you can't help but love Him. And when you truly love God, you will desire to do His will. Knowing Him and following in His ways always results in freedom!

Find the life of victory

available when you choose

to serve the Lord God

Almighty.

Lift Up Your Eyes

Exodus 19:18-20 (NKJV)

Now Mount Sinai was completely in smoke, because the LORD descended upon it in fire. Its smoke ascended like the smoke of a furnace, and the whole mountain quaked greatly. And when the blast of the trumpet sounded long and became louder and louder, Moses spoke, and God answered him by voice. Then the LORD came down upon Mount Sinai, on the top of the mountain. And the LORD called Moses to the top of the mountain, and Moses went up.

Psalm 5:3 (NKJV)

My voice You shall hear in the morning, O LORD; In the morning I will direct it to You, and I will look up.

Psalm 121:1, 2 (NKJV)

I will lift up my eyes to the hills—from whence comes my help? My help comes from the LORD, who made heaven and earth.

Mark 3:13 (NLT)

Afterward Jesus went up on a mountain and called out the ones he wanted to go with him. And they came to him.

Abba Father is calling you daily to climb to the top of the mountain, as Moses did, in order to connect with Him. Though it may not be a literal mountain, you must rise above the circumstances and issues of life in order to focus upon the Lord. He has your daily schedule prepared for you and He has your daily provisions waiting for you. Will you sit with Him in His Word and ask Him to guide your every step? Will you surrender your thoughts and your tongue to Him?

Your Father hears your every word of praise and thanksgiving and is moving on your behalf for every request for help, direction, healing, or guidance. Lift up your eyes and gaze at the One who loves you with an everlasting Love.

Your commitments define you. Make spending time with **Abba** a priority in your life; be committed to knowing Him and holding His hand throughout your days. Continually thank Him for His watchful Care over you and yours.

Lift up your eyes and gaze at

the One who loves you with

an everlasting Love.

Abba, Priority One

2 Chronicles 16:9a (NIV)
For the eyes of the LORD range throughout the earth to strengthen those whose hearts are fully committed to him.

Psalm 3:2-4 (NIV)
Many are saying of me, "God will not deliver him. But you, LORD, are a shield around me, my glory, the One who lifts my head high. I call out to the LORD, and he answers me from his holy mountain."

Psalm 3:8 (NIV)
From the LORD comes deliverance. May your blessing be on your people.

James 4:8 (NIV)
Come near to God and he will come near to you. Wash your hands, you sinners, and purify your hearts, you double-minded.

Are you seeking deliverance in your life? Speak to the Lord about it. He never says "No" to a cry for help. Seek Him by calling out to your Ever-present, All-loving, incredibly Caring, **Abba** Father. Tell Him every detail and ask Him to help you. As 1 Peter 5:7 tells us, "Cast all your anxiety on him because he cares for you" (NIV). In whatever circumstance you find yourself, if you provide the effort (see Ephesians 6:13), He will provide the best results for you when you yield the timing and resolutions to Him.

Don't receive discouraging words from others and don't listen to **the enemy** whispering lies of doubt in your ear. If a way seems blocked before you, remember: rejection and closed doors are often God's way of protection. Say, "Thank you, **Abba**" for His faithful Care; then ask Him to show you the right direction to take.

Will you determine to stay loyal to your **Abba**, no matter what happens? He is moving on your behalf and He is drawing near to you. He stands ready to strengthen you if your life is fully committed to Him.

Are you fully devoted to the Lord? Your commitments define you and reveal your priorities. Does your relationship with **Abba** have top priority in your life? You have Him, does He have you?

Your commitments define

you and reveal your

priorities.

Aim for Harmony

Romans 12:16 (NIV)

Live in harmony with one another. Do not be proud, but be willing to associate with people of low position. Do not be conceited.

Romans 14:19 (NLT)

So then, let us aim for harmony in the church and try to build each other up.

2 Corinthians 6:15 (NIV)

What harmony is there between Christ and **Belial**? Or what does a believer have in common with an unbeliever?

2 Corinthians 13:11 (NIV)

Finally, brothers and sisters, rejoice! Strive for full restoration, encourage one another, be of one mind, live in peace. And the God of love and peace will be with you.

Y ou belong to an eternal family. Your brothers and sisters in Christ are your "forever family." God is calling you to encourage them. **Abba** Father desires you to be in **fellowship** with those who are members of the family of God. Are you spending more time with those outside God's family? While you must obey the **Great Commission** (see Matthew 28:16–20), living life in common with those who embrace the world's priorities can drain you. Even worse, continual **fellowship** with those who do not belong to the family of God can lead you away from God's ways. There is a difference between seeking opportunities to shed God's light on darkened lives and comfortably "doing life" with friends who have no desire for **Abba** or His ways. Remember, you are to be in the world, but not of it (see John 17:14–16). Reach out to those who need to meet **Abba**; but live your life in common with those who love and serve Him—the family of God.

Aim for harmony with your brothers and sisters. Ask God to show you who needs encouragement from you today. Perhaps you need to pray for someone, call someone, lend a helping hand, or offer a caring hug. Perhaps you need to ask for **forgiveness**. With whom do you need to seek harmony today? Who needs your encouragement today? Are you proactively building up your eternal family?

Reach out to those who need

to meet Abba; but live your

life in common with those

who love and serve

Him—the family of God.

Follow Intentionally

Who is like your God? He sits enthroned on high, with angels attending Him while He looks down on earth and all of its inhabitants. Do you not find it utterly amazing that your **Abba** Lord desires to illuminate your life with His perfect plan for you, guarding and shielding your every yielded step?

He not only approves of you as His child, He desires to grant you favor and assistance. You are a son or daughter of the **King of kings**! In His eyes, you are highly distinguished and valued. Follow Him intentionally and trust His leading.

Remember, rejection from man may be God's protection at work. God will always have His way when you seek His will; no person on earth can prevent God's perfect will for you. Have eyes to see all the good He has worked into your life and give Him thanks.

Is your walk intentional? Are you lukewarm or fully committed? No good thing does your Father withhold from those whose walk is right.

Engraved on His Hand

Abba Father is your God. You belong to Him and He watches over you—His eye is on you, moment-by-moment. Why, favored one, do you not share everything with Him? He loves you so much that He holds you forever in the palm of His hand. His desire is to walk daily at your side showing you His amazing Love for you and His favor over you.

He seeks to bless those whose walk is intentional—those who set their will toward knowing and serving Him. He will shower those who commit their ways to Him with His Guidance, Protection, and, most of all, His divine Presence.

Yes, there will be pain here on earth. This is not heaven; but heaven awaits you. Now, while on earth, choose to remember His tender care for you each day. Submit every choice, every word, every thought to Him, your **Abba** Father, and watch as blessings pour in and through your life. Trust God and let Him be Lord of your life. Stop resisting your God.

He is Available

Adored child of your **Abba** Father, are you acquainting yourself with Him? He is not hard to find or difficult to know. He promises to be found by the one who seeks Him.

He longs to pour blessing over and through you. He desires to infuse His wise, healthy insight into your life. He longs to break you free from patterns of sin which cause guilt and distress and rob you of joy. He so loves to hear you laugh and sing with joy.

When you truly know Him and His nature (see Names of God article on pages xv through xviii), there is a protective anointing over your heart, which seals you with a love, peace, and joy that is not of this world. He directly imparts this **Fruit of the Spirit** into you and will infuse your future with hope (Jeremiah 29:11).

Your **Abba** is the Creator of all that is good and the Maker of the heavens, earth, and you! What keeps you from seeking Him? What prohibits you from knowing the One who desires to be found by you?

Call on His Name

The days of a daughter or son of God are not always sunny and bright; the clouds roll in on the just and the unjust. But, dear child of Loving **Abba**, do not be discouraged or afraid when troubled waters threaten to overwhelm you. No believer will always wade through calm waters. **Abba** allows storms in order to demonstrate His Omnipotence and Love for you. He also allows trouble in order to build iron in your soul.

However, as His child, you are carefully tended to and watched over; He is waiting for an invitation to help. Cry out to Jesus, "Help me, Lord!" Yield your fears, troubles, and worries to His care. Continue to call on Him until peace covers your entire being.

If storms of trouble rage through your life, will you call on His Name for deliverance? Will you thank Him for always being with you and taking away all reason to fear?

He Loves You

Psalm 139:13 (NLT)
You made all the delicate, inner parts of my body and knit me together in my mother's womb.

Psalm 149:4 (NLT)
For the LORD delights in his people; he crowns the **humble** with victory.

Jeremiah 31:3 (NKJV)
The LORD has appeared of old to me, saying: "Yes, I have loved you with an everlasting love; therefore with loving-kindness I have drawn you."

Zechariah 2:8b (NLT)
For he said, "Anyone who harms you harms my most precious possession."

D o you have any idea how much **Abba** loves and adores you? He knit you together uniquely and wonderfully; He created you to be the only you. There is not another being like you in this entire universe. He looks upon you with delight because you are, indeed, very special and precious in His sight.

When others hurt you, your Father is also hurt and offended because you are the apple of His eye (Psalm 17:8). Every detail of your life matters to Him. If even a hair falls from your head He takes note (Matthew 10:30). His Love is faithful and trustworthy and always hopeful that you will recognize who you are: His child.

He looks upon you with approval because you belong to Him and you matter. Ask Him to open your understanding of His incredible Love for you.

The Lord is Near

Psalm 56 (NLT)

O God, have **mercy** on me, for people are hounding me. My foes attack me all day long. I am constantly hounded by those who slander me, and many are boldly attacking me. But when I am afraid, I will put my trust in you. I praise God for what he has promised. I trust in God, so why should I be afraid? What can mere mortals do to me? They are always twisting what I say; they spend their days plotting to harm me. They come together to spy on me—watching my every step, eager to kill me. Don't let them get away with their wickedness; in your anger, O God, bring them down. You keep track of all my sorrows. You have collected all my tears in your bottle. You have recorded each one in your book.

My enemies will retreat when I call to you for help. This I know: God is on my side! I praise God for what he has promised; yes, I praise the LORD for what he has promised. I trust in God, so why should I be afraid? What can mere mortals do to me? I will fulfill my vows to you, O God, and will offer a **sacrifice** of thanks for your help. For you have rescued me from death; you have kept my feet from slipping. So now I can walk in your presence, O God, in your life-giving light.

Do not be afraid. Cast your cares and fears upon your **Abba** Father. The real battle is His to fight; He is waiting for your invitation to participate and demonstrate how very much He cares for you. You can trust Him to be a Just and Fair God. He knows how to handle the wicked much better than you do.

He has seen your heartache and watched your tears drop. Oh, child of God, cry out to Him for deliverance and help; He is on your side. Don't worry about the enemies who surround you. What can they really do to you when the Sun and Shield is standing by ready to intercede on your behalf (Psalm 84:11)? Call upon God and be patient after you seek His help; God is moving on your behalf even before your human eyes can see His movement.

When trouble strikes, cry out to God and watch for His loving deliverance; then offer a **sacrifice** of thanksgiving for His constant care over you.

Oh, child of God, cry out

to Him for deliverance and

help; He is on your side.

The God Who Sees You

Your **Abba** Father always hears you when you speak with Him. Will you thank Him? Visualize your Lord on His mighty throne listening to your heart-felt requests. He is **El Roi**—He sees you clearly. He hears you and desires to hold your hand as you journey the paths of life. He is a Rewarder of those who diligently seek Him (Hebrews 11:6). He rewards those who search for His answers, pursue Him, and persevere in clinging to Him. He rewards you when you choose to say "I trust you and I know You see me." And He will never disappoint you when you proclaim, "I know You will guide me in the way I should go."

Will you say to Him," Because I trust You and because You see me, I will wait to hear from you"?

Going Through the Motions

Isaiah 58:2–10 (NLT)

"Yet they act so pious! They come to the Temple every day and seem delighted to learn all about me. They act like a righteous nation that would never abandon the laws of its God. They ask me to take action on their behalf, pretending they want to be near me. 'We have fasted before you!' they say. 'Why aren't you impressed? We have been very hard on ourselves, and you don't even notice it!' "I will tell you why!" I respond. "It's because you are **fasting** to please yourselves. Even while you fast, you keep oppressing your workers. What good is **fasting** when you keep on fighting and quarreling? This kind of **fasting** will never get you anywhere with me.

You **humble** yourselves by going through the motions of penance, bowing your heads like reeds bending in the wind. You dress in burlap and cover yourselves with ashes. Is this what you call **fasting**? Do you really think this will please the LORD? "No, this is the kind of **fasting** I want: Free those who are wrongly imprisoned; lighten the burden of those who work for you. Let the oppressed go free, and remove the chains that bind people. Share your food with the hungry, and give shelter to the homeless. Give clothes to those who need them, and do not hide from relatives who need your help. "Then your **salvation** will come like the dawn, and your wounds will quickly heal. Your godliness will lead you forward, and the glory of the LORD will protect you from behind. Then when you call, the LORD will answer. 'Yes, I am here,' he will quickly reply. "Remove the heavy yoke of oppression. Stop pointing your finger and spreading vicious rumors! Feed the hungry, and help those in trouble. Then your light will shine out from the darkness, and the darkness around you will be as bright as noon."

Oh beloved, stop pretending with the Lord. Are you one who goes to church and puts on an act, pretending your actions are for Him when your motives are self-centered? Is it your goal to please yourself instead of your **Abba** Father? What good is church attendance, prayer, or even **fasting** if you keep on quarreling and gossiping? Remember the Apostle Paul said, "Though I have all faith, so that I could remove mountains, but have not love, I am nothing" (1 Corinthians 13:2; NKJV).

Let today be the day you choose to stop going through the motions and start seeking to please the Lord by using whatever resources He has given you to help others. Stop pointing your finger and start feeding the poor and helping those in trouble. Call a sick or suffering soul and ask how you can help. Take food to a homeless shelter and ask if you can pray with someone there. Send money to an orphanage. Do not hide from family members who need your help.

This is the worship the Lord desires and honors; then you will call to the Lord and He will answer!

Is it your goal to please

yourself instead of your

Abba Father?

Stand in the Gap

Ezekiel 22:30 (NLT)

"I looked for someone who might rebuild the wall of **righteousness** that guards the land. I searched for someone to **stand in the gap** in the wall so I wouldn't have to destroy the land, but I found no one."

The Lord's eyes range throughout the earth looking for anyone who is committed to Him (2 Chronicles 16:9a). He expects you to intercede for others. He delights in showing you His **Mercy**. Your Father wants you to stand strong in the places where the faith of others may falter, providing your strength to uphold them. Will you **stand in the gap** for your family and country today?

The Lord is often described in Scripture as a refuge and shield. This means He will surround you with His protection. Sin results in a gap in the hedge of protection the Lord provides; **the enemy** is able to come in and overpower one whose choices have allowed the entrance of evil. You can **stand in the gap** for a weakened soul just as our spiritual father **Abraham** stood in the gap for **Sodom** (see Genesis 18:16–33).

Though the evil city of **Sodom** was destroyed, **Abraham** also stood in the gap for his nephew, Lot, who lived there. The Lord heard **Abraham**'s prayers and rescued Lot. He was snatched from the great catastrophe that engulfed **Sodom**. (Read the story in Genesis 19:1–29.)

Be known in God's kingdom as a prayer warrior on behalf of the weak. Establish yourself in God's kingdom as one who stands in the gap on behalf of others. You can be used by God to rebuild the walls of **righteousness** and restore the broken homes that surround you. God is looking for someone; will you answer, as Isaiah did (Isaiah 6:8; NKJV), "Here am I, send me"?

The Fountain of Living Water

Your soul needs the nourishment of **Living Water** that God promises to provide! Do not go looking for satisfaction from empty, broken wells. Every day, you need refreshing, long, satisfying drinks of **grace**. **Abba** Father's well of supply is immeasurably greater than you can even imagine.

Thank Him for His provision for you today and sing praises to your God who richly quenches and satisfies your every need. Resist the temptation to grumble; instead sing praise songs. God's well of **Living Water** is accessed through prayer, praise, and His Word. Sit at His well and trust Him to pour His amazing **Grace** over the parched ground of your soul.

The Lord promises peace for us when we actively praise Him. Praise creates a fountain of blessing that rises up to cover those who praise God's Holy Name. Are you truly seeking Him from Whom all blessings flow?

Never Leave; Never Forsake

Psalm 12:1 (NLT)

Help, O LORD, for the godly are fast disappearing! The faithful have vanished from the earth!

Isaiah 64:4, 5a (NLT)

For since the world began, no ear has heard and no eye has seen a God like you, who works for those who wait for him! You welcome those who gladly do good, who follow godly ways. But you have been very angry with us, for we are not godly.

Isaiah 65:1 (NLT)

The LORD says, "I was ready to respond, but no one asked for help. I was ready to be found, but no one was looking for me. I said, 'Here I am, here I am!' to a nation that did not call on my name."

People will fail you at times; but your Sweet Jesus will never neglect a cry for help. Is He the first One to whom you run for help? Oh, why not, apple of His eye? His ears are attentive to "Help me, Lord!" He waits for you. Even if you don't see Him moving immediately, the second you pray, He is working everything out for your good. He promises to work everything out for good for those who love Him and call upon Him (Romans 8:28).

Will you continue trusting Him and thanking Him for all that, He is doing for you? Fear not, child of God, He will never forsake you and He is helping you. Will you determine to never leave nor forsake Him?

He Feeds His Flock

Psalm 23:1-3 (NKJV)

The LORD is my shepherd; I shall not want. He makes me to lie down in green pastures; He leads me beside the still waters. He restores my soul; He leads me in the paths of **righteousness** for His name's sake.

Psalm 73:21-26 (NLT)

Then I realized that my heart was bitter, and I was all torn up inside. I was so foolish and ignorant—I must have seemed like a senseless animal to you. Yet I still belong to you; you hold my right hand. You guide me with your counsel, leading me to a glorious destiny. Whom have I in heaven but you? I desire you more than anything on earth. My health may fail, and my spirit may grow weak, but God remains the strength of my heart; he is mine forever.

Song of Solomon 2:16 (NKJV)

My beloved is mine, and I am his. He feeds his flock among the lilies.

John 10:11-16 (NKJV)

"I am the good shepherd. The good shepherd gives His life for the sheep. But a hireling, he who is not the shepherd, one who does not own the sheep, sees the wolf coming and leaves the sheep and flees; and the wolf catches the sheep and scatters them. The hireling flees because he is a hireling and does not care about the sheep. I am the good shepherd; and I know My sheep, and am known by My own. As the Father knows Me, even so I know the Father; and I lay down My life for the sheep. And other sheep I have which are not of this fold; them also I must bring, and they will hear My voice; and there will be one flock and one shepherd."

God is yours and you are His. You can be certain of this and still lose sight of God's provision. You can know you belong to Him and that your soul is secure for all of eternity with Him, yet still be torn up inside with His peace eluding you. You may wonder why you don't feel His Love and Guidance. Where is He? He is feeding His own among the lilies; He is tending His flock in green pastures.

Jesus is found among His followers. Enter into **communion** with those who love Him and seek Him. Ask the Lord to give you a fellow believer(s) with whom you can pray. Ask Him to guide you to a life-affirming, Bible-teaching church led by Truth and living out **Grace**.

The Good Shepherd longs to nourish you among your brothers and sisters leading you to a glorious destiny. He is yours forever. Are you fully His?

Jesus is found among

His followers.

The War for Souls

Romans 14:8 (NLT)
If we live, it's to honor the Lord. And if we die, it's to honor the Lord. So whether we live or die, we belong to the Lord.

Philippians 3:13b, 14, 16, 20a (NLT)
Forgetting the past and looking forward to what lies ahead, I press on to reach the end of the race and receive the heavenly prize for which God, through Christ Jesus, is calling us . . . we must hold on to the progress we have already made . . . we are citizens of heaven, where the Lord Jesus Christ lives.

If your real home is in heaven, why does the Lord keep you on earth? You are still here because you have a purpose on this earth. You have been accepted into the Lord's army and He is calling you to battle. Earth is not a playground; it is a battle ground for the Christian. A war is being waged for the souls of every man, woman, and child. **The enemy**, Satan, roams the earth seeking lives he can devour (1 Peter 5:8). But Jesus died for every one of them. Every person matters to the Lord. Every person in your life is an opportunity for you to share the hope you have in Christ—to be a soldier in the army of the Lord bringing freedom to the captives and breaking the yoke of slavery from those **the enemy** has kept bound.

Today is the day to stand strong as a soldier of the Lord and come to the aid of those whom **the enemy** has deceived. Pray the Lord will enable you to fight well on their behalf by praying for them and telling them God's truth. No matter what obstacles you face or resistance you encounter, press on like a good soldier in the Lord's army.

Are you AWOL on the couch or are you engaging where the Lord has assigned you?

Remember God's Deeds

Psalm 77:11, 12 (NIV)
I will remember the deeds of the LORD; yes, I will remember your miracles of long ago. I will consider all your works and meditate on all your mighty deeds.

Psalm 109:21 (NLT)
But deal well with me, O **Sovereign** LORD, for the sake of your own reputation! Rescue me because you are so faithful and good.

Psalm 126:3 (NLT)
Yes, the LORD has done amazing things for us! What joy!

Abba Father has done great things for you! Have you allowed Him to put a new song on your lips (Psalm 40:3)? Do you have eyes to see His Goodness? Deep down in your heart, do you believe He is a Good God; but has your personal experience been otherwise?

No doubt, life gets hard and we all must endure many trails and disappointments this side of heaven; but **Abba** has always come to your aid and will continue to deliver you because of His great Faithfulness and **Mercy**. When doubt overtakes you, recall all the times God has faithfully delivered you. Recall His past Goodness to encourage your heart as you wait for His hand to move in your present circumstance. Your **Abba** Father has preserved you to this day and He has shown you His favor and honor. He has protected you countless times! Walk intentionally with Him and focus on His Goodness rather than the difficulty. Determine that, the deeper your troubles, the louder you will thank Him for His Goodness and Faithfulness. Your **Abba** Father withholds no good thing from you (Psalm 84:11).

Treasures Await You

Joshua 1:8 (NLT)
Study this Book of Instruction continually. Meditate on it day and night so you will be sure to obey everything written in it. Only then will you prosper and succeed in all you do.

2 Timothy 2:15 (KJV)
Study to shew thyself approved unto God, a workman that needeth not to be ashamed, rightly dividing the word of truth.

There is great treasure awaiting every follower of Christ, including you. However, as with the treasures of gold and silver, you must dig and mine until you find the riches. Our Loving **Abba** invites you to sit with Him and diligently study and meditate on His Word. His eyes range throughout the earth to strengthen those whose hearts are fully committed to Him (2 Chronicles 16:9a).

Can you conceive the incredible treasure—the glistening promise of a strengthened heart and mind and the shimmering hope of prosperity you will find with Him? You will succeed in discovering treasure beyond telling when your motive is to bring glory and honor to your Holy God.

Do you know God's Word of Life? Are you rightly dividing the Word of Truth (2 Timothy 2:15)?

Use Your Voice

Speak for Jesus today; if necessary, use your words.

The Lord has already equipped you with everything you need to be a **witness** for Him. His Spirit lives in you; guiding you, comforting you, convicting you, and reminding you of all His words He has planted in the soil of your soul.

Do not be afraid of what people will say about you. Consider it a compliment if they slander you because you trust in Jesus. The Lord is holding your hand and His shield goes before you and behind you, protecting you, (Isaiah 52:12). You are never too young in physical years or spiritual years to share the hope of His calling—the calling He has given you.

Will you ask Him to put His words in your mouth and help your actions speak the Truth of His kingdom?

The Soil of Your Heart

Jeremiah 4:3, 4 (NLT)
This is what the LORD says to the people of Judah and Jerusalem: "Plow up the hard ground of your hearts! Do not waste your good seed among thorns. O people of Judah and Jerusalem, surrender your pride and power. Change your hearts before the LORD, or my anger will burn like an unquenchable fire because of all your sins."

Matthew 5:3 (NLT)
God blesses those who are poor and realize their need for him, for the Kingdom of Heaven is theirs.

Matthew 5:3 (NKJV)
Blessed are the poor in spirit, For theirs is the kingdom of heaven.

Your heart is like soil from which fruits of **righteousness** or thorns of sin grow (see Matthew 13:3–9, 18–23). Plow up the hard, unnourished clumps of clay in the ground of your heart. Plant seeds of Truth and **Grace** today. Change your heart and change your life.

You can change your heart by continually telling your **Abba** Father you surrender your will to His will; tell Him you surrender your control and seek His control. Surrender your hopeless and proud ways and seek God's hope and blessing-filled ways.

Admit to **Abba** your desperate need for His Presence, His Love, His virtues, His guidance, His **salvation**, and His **redemption**. Cultivate the soil of your heart and plant a crop of good seed; then relax in God's divine control, knowing the good seed you have planted will bring forth a harvest of blessing, both now and forever.

Good Fruit

John 15:7, 8 (NLT)

"But if you remain in me and my words remain in you, you may ask for anything you want, and it will be granted! When you produce much fruit, you are my true disciples. This brings great glory to my Father."

Colossians 1:9, 10 (NLT)

So we have not stopped praying for you since we first heard about you. We ask God to give you complete knowledge of his will and to give you spiritual wisdom and understanding. Then the way you live will always honor and please the Lord, and your lives will produce every kind of good fruit. All the while, you will grow as you learn to know God better and better.

Your **Abba** Father does not accept a life lived based on good intentions or feelings; rather He requires His children to be intelligent followers. The fear of the Lord is the beginning of wisdom (Psalm 111:10). Understanding He is God and you are not lays the foundation for true discernment and insight. However, having good knowledge without a life that honors and pleases the Lord will profit you nothing.

You will know you are growing in spiritual wisdom when your love for others increases—when you demonstrate patience, kindness, gentleness, and **forgiveness**—for then you are producing every kind of good fruit. The more you give in to God's ways, the more fruit of love and **grace** you will produce. This will firmly implant your roots into a deeper understanding of your amazing Lord.

Are you getting to know your God better and better? Is your love for others growing?

Known by Love

> ## Lamentations 3:22-24 (NLT)
> The faithful love of the LORD never ends! His mercies never cease. Great is his faithfulness; his mercies begin afresh each morning. I say to myself, "The LORD is my **inheritance**; therefore, I will hope in him!"
>
> ## 2 John 1:3 (NLT)
> **Grace, mercy,** and peace, which come from God the Father and from Jesus Christ—the Son of the Father—will continue to be with us who live in truth and love.

Your **Abba** Father has given you all He has to give. What more could a Loving Father **sacrifice** than His only Son? And the flow of His Love has not ceased. His Mercies never fail; the **Mercy** of our Great and Faithful God begins anew every morning.

Beloved child of God, if you are unable to extend **grace** and **mercy** to those in your life, the Lord is asking you to receive His unending Love into your hurting heart. Lift your eyes to **Abba** and allow His healing **Mercy** to flood your soul. Yield your hurts, **trial**s, doubts, bitterness, and unforgiveness into His hands and thank Him for His faithfulness. He will give you everything you need to get through each day. You must choose to receive God's amazing **Grace** before you can extend it to others. You cannot give what you have not chosen to receive. **Abba**'s desire for you is to be a person of **grace**. Are you? You cannot be until you fully trust Him and put your hope in Him.

Truth is good, but it is incomplete without **Grace**. Remember, the world will know you are a Christian by your love.

Good and Faithful Servant

Colossians 2:6, 7 (NLT)

And now, just as you accepted Christ Jesus as your Lord, you must continue to follow him. Let your roots grow down into him, and let your lives be built on him. Then your faith will grow strong in the truth you were taught, and you will overflow with thankfulness.

Matthew 25:23 (NKJV)

His lord said to him, "'Well done, good and faithful servant; you have been faithful over a few things, I will make you ruler over many things. Enter into the joy of your lord.'"

Come; enter into the joy of the Lord. Seeds of thanksgiving planted in the soil of your life spring up a harvest of joy. You plant seeds every time you choose to trust Jesus and thank Him for His protection and provision. Those planted seeds help you to stay rooted in His ways and His Truths.

As you follow the Lord, the eyes of your heart become clearer and more focused on His Faithfulness and Love. As a result, gratitude—the mother of all virtues—naturally grows in abundance from the soil of your heart. A sure mark of a maturing Christian is a thankful attitude despite any difficulties being encountered. You can be thankful because you know your Lord and you trust His Faithfulness.

Temple of the Holy Spirit

1 Corinthians 3:16 (NIV)

Don't you know that you yourselves are God's temple and that God's Spirit dwells in your midst?

Let the building continue! The Lord Himself has begun a mighty work, right within your heart and soul. It is He who builds your spiritual temple. His Spirit is at work, polishing the rough cut stones from which you are formed, causing you to stand strong and shine for Him. It is He who builds the foundation of your soul and sands you, trims you, and refines you in preparation for your eternal home in His glorious presence.

He began a good work in you the moment you believed; and because of His amazing **Grace**, He will continue to work within you until He is ready to receive you on the other side of this life. Your calling is to accept His Truth and Love; to trust and obey Him with your life. He does all the work—all the transformation and all the preparation of your soul.

Do you know you are God's temple and His Spirit dwells inside you? Would anyone else know by watching your life?

Half-baked is Worthless

> **Hosea 7:8 (NLT)**
> The people of Israel mingle with godless foreigners, making themselves as worthless as a half-baked cake.
>
> **2 Corinthians 6:14 (NLT)**
> Don't team up with those who are unbelievers. How can **righteousness** be a partner with wickedness? How can light live with darkness?

A re you a "half-baked cake"? Are you someone who has not allowed God's Truth and **Grace** to permeate your entire being? Have you refused to allow the warmth of His presence to complete His work in you? Are you half-baked?

Do you realize that you are a temple in whom God lives (1 Corinthians 3:16)? Can right and wrong join forces within you? Can light and darkness coexist in the same space? Have you allowed dark areas to remain in certain rooms of God's temple?

God is moving within you—His temple. Do not close doors on Him; invite Him to shed light on areas of compromise and corruption that may remain within you.

Don't remain half-baked; allow the heat of His presence to complete you, bringing you His wholesome Truth and delicious **Grace**.

Do not team up with wickedness. Seek to mingle with true followers of Christ and don't link your heart or mind with un**righteousness**. To do so always leads to regret and pain, when all is said and done.

Choose the Right Path

Are you weary and exhausted? Are you restless and stressed?
Are you faced with a choice and have no idea what to do?
Go stand at the crossroads and look around. Visualize Jesus holding your hand and ask Him to guide you down the right path. He is
not a God of confusion (1 Corinthians 14:33), nor does He want to
play games with you. He has great plans for you and desires you to
know His will for your life. Ask Him to show you His way and then
move on out. You will discover God's perfect plan for your life.

As you travel the path God reveals, will you press on when the
way grows rough? When you approach new crossroads, will you
continue asking Him the next turn to take? Your open ears will
hear Him say, "This is the way you should go." Travel His path and
find rest for your soul.

Are you on the path He has chosen for you? If you are not sure,
keep moving forward until He closes the pass and opens a new
way. Ask and then listen for your Father's voice. He is Faithful; you
will receive His guidance.

Saved for a High Calling

Colossians 3:5 (NLT)

So put to death the sinful, earthly things lurking within you. Have nothing to do with sexual immorality, impurity, lust, and evil desires. Don't be greedy, for a greedy person is an **idol**ater, worshiping the things of this world.

Colossians 3:16 (NLT)

Let the message about Christ, in all its richness, fill your lives. Teach and counsel each other with all the wisdom he gives. Sing psalms and hymns and spiritual songs to God with thankful hearts.

2 Timothy 1:9 (NLT)

For God **saved** us and called us to live a holy life. He did this, not because we deserved it, but because that was his plan from before the beginning of time—to show us his **grace** through Christ Jesus.

You have been **saved** for all of eternity by believing Jesus was crucified for you, rose on the third day, and now sits at the right hand of the Father, interceding for you. You have been **saved** because you have made Him Lord of your life. He has given you this gift of **salvation**—abundant life (John 10:10) now and eternal life to follow physical death.

This complete cycle of saving your soul comes with a call to live a holy life now. Those who are **saved** hear God's Holy Spirit within them lovingly and tenderly calling them to a new life. God is inviting you to leave your old life behind; He wants you to allow a new day to dawn, to be who you were created to be in Christ. This is one of the delicious secrets to life: to discover who you really are, a holy loved child of God. Your present **salvation** from this world's ways is evidence of your future **salvation** in heaven.

Living Above Your Circumstances

> ## Jeremiah 10:10a (NLT)
> But the LORD is the only true God. He is the living God and the everlasting King!
>
> ## Colossians 3:23 (NLT)
> Work willingly at whatever you do, as though you were working for the Lord rather than for people.
>
> ## Colossians 4:2, 6 (NLT)
> Devote yourselves to prayer with an alert mind and a thankful heart. Let your conversation be gracious and attractive so that you will have the right response for everyone.

You are a child of the King—a prince or princess of God's kingdom. You have ready access to God Almighty, the **Omnipotent** One! As a member of His royal family, He gives you the desire and the power to reign over your **fleshly lusts**. As heaven, your true home, is above this earth, so you must choose, moment-by-moment, to live above your earthly circumstances and desires.

Your Father is Alive and Powerful and His eye is on you. He patiently awaits your invitation for His involvement in your day. He lavishly fills you with His Power to live to your full potential—to **glorify** Him. God enables you to live for Him by choosing to be in constant communication with Him, always thanking Him for hearing you and moving on your behalf.

We are members of God's family and should represent our Father well. Our God is Love (1 John 4:8). So He delights in our gracious care over others as we share Truth wrapped in Love, considering the needs of others and setting our hearts toward blessing them as our Father blesses us.

Wait Upon the Lord

Psalm 107:7-9 (NIV)

He led them by a straight way to a city where they could settle. Let them give thanks to the LORD for his unfailing love and his wonderful deeds for mankind, for he satisfies the thirsty and fills the hungry with good things.

Isaiah 40:31 (NKJV)

But those who wait on the LORD shall renew their strength; they shall mount up with wings like eagles, they shall run and not be weary, they shall walk and not faint.

Are you waiting for answers from your **Abba** Father? Have you grown weary waiting for His direction? He is much more concerned about your growth than your comfort. As you ask Him for directions and wait patiently, remember to develop the discipline of thanking Him continually for His tender care of you. As you wait, He is strengthening you and preparing you for your heavenly destination and future **trial**s here on earth. Trust in His timing and His Faithfulness.

Your **trial**s are meant to strengthen your trust in Him. When trouble comes and your strength is zapped, you can be sure your Lord will come to your aid. A new day of calmness, energy, and strength is on the horizon for you when you put your trust in Him.

Will you wait on the Lord and allow Him to renew your strength?

Stand Firm

Daniel 3:16–18 (NIV)

Shadrach, Meshach and Abednego replied to him, "King Nebuchadnezzar, we do not need to defend ourselves before you in this matter. If we are thrown into the blazing furnace, the God we serve is able to deliver us from it, and he will deliver us from Your Majesty's hand. But even if he does not, we want you to know, Your Majesty, that we will not serve your gods or worship the image of gold you have set up."

Mark 8:36 (NLT)

And what do you benefit if you gain the whole world but lose your own soul?

When difficulties confront you, stand firm, knowing your Great **Advocate** (1 John 2:1), Jesus is supporting you. There is a deep, delicious contentment planted in the fiber of your being when you refuse to "sell out." When you choose to stand for Truth and **Grace** above popular opinion and refuse to compromise your integrity as a son or daughter of the King, you are demonstrating great faith in your **Advocate**. The lasting result will be a clean conscience, which is worth more than all the gold in the world!

Oh, to have peace with God! His Peace brings a contented heart even if suffering accompanies your way. Your **Advocate** will hold your hand through it all. Trust Him. Do not compromise who you are in Christ. You are royalty for eternity. What can you possibly benefit if you gain the whole world but compromise your eternal soul?

Significance

Are you calling on Jesus? Does He have priority in your life? Do you even think about Him during your day? Oh, child of God, He longs to "do life" with you. He has wonderful plans for you—plans to prosper you and not to harm you. His plans are full of hope for your future; but you must seek Him in order to experience this supernatural hope.

There is no sweeter place to be than in the center of His will for us. There is a comforting weight of significance that engulfs our beings when we are seeking Him and living for His purposes. We feel empty when we are not impacting the kingdom. When the weight of God's Truth is not written on our hearts and Truth and **Grace** are not heard on our lips or seen in our actions, we have no weighty, significant impact on this life.

If the Good Lord weighed your life on His balances today, would your actions measure up?

God's Nourishing Word

Jeremiah 15:16 (NLT)

When I discovered your words, I devoured them. They are my joy and my heart's delight, for I bear your name, O LORD God of Heaven's Armies.

Colossians 2:8 (NLT)

Don't let anyone capture you with empty philosophies and high-sounding nonsense that come from human thinking and from the spiritual powers of this world, rather than from Christ.

Hebrews 5:12, 13 (NLT)

You have been believers so long now that you ought to be teaching others. Instead, you need someone to teach you again the basic things about God's word. You are like babies who need milk and cannot eat solid food. For someone who lives on milk is still an infant and doesn't know how to do what is right.

Y ou feed your soul with something every day. Is it empty nonsense that comes from human thinking? Human thinking changes and is unreliable; at one time, even the smartest scientists believed the earth to be flat. Man's thinking is ever-changing; God's Word never changes.

Gods Truth is not empty, fluffy, non-nourishing, whipped cream; it is a delicious, weighty sustenance that feeds your soul. His nourishment influences right living, which results in joy and significance in your life. Don't be tempted to devour the lovely, sweet, whipped cream of this world's nonsense. It will leave you empty and wanting every time.

Will you devour God's Truths and ask Him how you can apply them to your life? Are you a God-nourished soul?

Words of Influence

Jeremiah 15:19 (NLT)

This is how the LORD responds: "If you return to me, I will restore you so you can continue to serve me. If you speak good words rather than worthless ones, you will be my spokesman. You must influence them; do not let them influence you!

Philippians 1:27 (NKJV)

Only let your conduct be worthy of the **gospel** of Christ, so that whether I come and see you or am absent, I may hear of your affairs, that you stand fast in one spirit, with one mind striving together for the faith of the **gospel**.

Out of the overflow of your heart your mouth speaks (Matthew 12:34). What flows from your heart? Is it streams of patience, consideration, **forgiveness**, goodness, harmony, gentleness, truth, and love? Or do worthless words pour from your lips?

Our conversations have a deep and lasting impact. Our words can affect others as much as our behavior. Words can cut and damage as deeply as a sword thrust into the soul. On the other hand, words can encourage and help others build up their lives in Christ. Do your words bring peace and clarity to listening ears? Our God is not a God of confusion but a God of clarity. Are others confused by your Christianity? Do you claim to love the Lord but speak as one who loves the world?

The Lord boldly proclaims Truth in His Word. Do your words proclaim His Truth? The **gospel** is Loving and full of **Grace**.

Do your words have worth? As a spokesman for Jesus, pray to speak in a manner worthy of your **heavenly citizenship**.

Thistles and Thorns

> **Proverbs 19:3 (NKJV)**
> The foolishness of a man twists his way, and his heart frets against the LORD.
>
> **Hebrews 11:6 (NKJV)**
> But without faith it is impossible to please Him, for he who comes to God must believe that He is, and that He is a rewarder of those who diligently seek Him.

A re you weary and burdened? Fretting against the Lord is like attempting to forge a path through a land filled with thistles and thorns. Stop trying to forge your own trail and trust the Lord. When you fail to follow the path the Lord has for you, unwise choices and painful consequences usually follow.

If you have not invited God into past decisions and are left with disappointments and failures, don't waste another moment fretting, complaining, and worrying. Stop blaming God for past frustrations and start seeking Him. **Confess** your choice of doing life your own way instead of seeking His perfect way. Then grab His hand and move forward with Him.

Your **Abba** Father takes great delight in rewarding His children who trust Him and diligently seek Him. This diligence requires perseverance. Don't give up until you see the Lord moving. It is His promise to work everything out for the good of those who love Him and call upon Him (Romans 8:28).

Heavy Loads Removed

Psalm 81:6, 7a (NLT)

Now I will take the load from your shoulders; I will free your hands from their heavy tasks. You cried to me in trouble, and I **saved** you.

Blessed are you who put your trust in the Lord (Proverbs 3). Say, this moment and every moment, "Jesus, I trust You." Make Him your hope and confidence. Cry out to Him and be **saved**. Do not stumble off the ancient highway of Truth and **Grace** and walk in muddy paths of **humanism**.

When we place our trust in limited human beings and rely on their wisdom and strength, we are forfeiting divine, supernatural **Grace**, Guidance, and Power.

Ask **Abba** Father to take the world off your shoulders. Ask Him to lead you out of the bad place into which you have walked. He will free you from burdens and enable you to walk unshackled into tomorrow.

Will you let Him save you today and forever?

Pride Before a Fall

> **2 Chronicles 32:31 (NLT)**
> However, when ambassadors arrived from **Babylon** to ask about the remarkable events that had taken place in the land, God withdrew from Hezekiah in order to test him and to see what was really in his heart.
>
> **Proverbs 16:18 (NLT)**
> Pride goes before destruction, and haughtiness before a fall.
>
> **1 Thessalonians 5:18 (NLT)**
> Be thankful in all circumstances, for this is God's will for you who belong to Christ Jesus.

What is really in your heart? Ask God to open the eyes of your heart in order to really see the Truth. Recognizing your own weaknesses and seeing areas prone to sin will help you lean into your God of amazing **Grace** for help.

King Hezekiah received many blessings from God; yet, when God withdrew the **veil** covering his heart, Hezekiah demonstrated pride in himself rather than in God. Pride always leads to problems. Our Lord is the Giver of all gifts, including this day and each breath we take.

God lovingly reminds us in His Word to always be thankful. It is impossible to become prideful if we understand all that we have and all that we are is from the Gracious, Merciful hand of our **Abba** Father.

Are you thankful in all circumstances? Are you recognizing and intentionally dealing with any pride in your heart before destruction comes to you?

Be an Encourager

Proverbs 27:17 (NLT)
As iron sharpens iron, so a friend sharpens a friend.

Ephesians 4:29b (NLT)
Let everything you say be good and helpful, so that your words will be an encouragement to those who hear them.

1 Thessalonians 5:11 (NLT)
So encourage each other and build each other up, just as you are already doing.

Be a true friend to those in your life. As a member of God's holy family, you are called to have relationships according to God's high standard. He is honored when you encourage others and build them up in Christ. He is pleased in your conversations that are centered on Truth and **Grace**. He is pleased when friends lovingly encourage (speak courage into) others. It is your privilege as a member of God's family. The most incredible thing happens when you honor God by encouraging others; you are yourself greatly inspired by **witness**ing another's freshly-infused, Holy Spirit courage.

We have so little time on earth together; and what we say here matters for all of eternity. Our time here is short and our days are numbered. We must ask ourselves if we use each day as an opportunity to build others up according to their needs. Do not waste a second on the dull nonsense of the world. Grind out life issues with the ones the Lord has placed in your life. Make the most of every opportunity to join with others and take issues before your **Abba** Father, thanking Him for His willingness to hear you and to be involved.

Living Water

This verse from Zechariah can be hard to comprehend. It can be understood to speak of the living, nourishing waters that began flowing from Jerusalem when the Holy Spirit was poured out on believers (Acts 2:1–4). Filled and empowered by the Holy Spirit, these early believers spread the **Good News** of Jesus throughout the land—it flowed from Jerusalem to the East and to the West. Wherever the truth of Jesus' death and resurrection go, the **Grace** gift of **salvation** goes; and therein flows **Living Water** (John 7:38).

Summers and winters will come and go as days of your life go by. With each new season, you may change, but God never changes. He is always a prayer breath away, overflowing with Love and Concern for you. His nourishing, **Living Water**s flow throughout summer droughts and winter frosts.

He longs to lead you to His quiet waters; His reviving, renewing, clean, refreshing and sustaining waters. Why do you drink from the muddy streams of **Babylon**—the godless world that surrounds you? Turn from such worthless, polluted streams; take long, nourishing, satisfying refreshment from **Abba**'s overflowing rivers of Love and **Grace**. Will you?

God is Able

> **Numbers 11:23 (NLT)**
> Then the LORD said to Moses, "Has my arm lost its power? Now you will see whether or not my word comes true!"
>
> **Jeremiah 32:27 (NIV)**
> "I am the LORD, the God of all mankind. Is anything too hard for me?"

O h, the rich promises God gives you, His intentional follower! He has summoned you by name; you are His! He promises, when you pass through rough waters, He will be with you; and when you walk through fire, the flames will not set you ablaze (Isaiah 43:2). He has engraved you on the palm of His hand (Isaiah 49:16). Imagine! Almighty God, All-Knowing, Ever-present, All-Powerful God has your back! Is anything in your life too difficult for this God you worship?

You must stop entertaining unbelief and doubt. Ask **Abba** to help your confidence in Him grow. Will you **confess** at those times when you focus on your need instead of on Him? Turn your eyes to Him and ask for strength for the journey while you anticipate seeing His promises come true. He is your **Abba** Father. He is the Lord your God! Is anything too hard for Him? You can be sure that He can handle anything in your life . . . if you let Him.

The Gift that Keeps Giving

Psalm 46:1 (NLT)

God is our refuge and strength, always ready to help in times of trouble.

Your God is your refuge. Will you enter into His shelter and find protection from the storm? Will you live in His armor of truth and **salvation** and ward off the dangers of this world (Ephesians 6:13–17). Will you place your trust in God's protection and defend your soul from lies?

He is your strength. He is the Source of your boldness. It is the Lord Who exalts the **humble** with Might and Majesty. He is your Ever-present help in trouble. He is instantly available to you as your Gift of help and strength.

Regardless of your trouble, adversity, heartache, hardship, frustration, illness, hurt, bad news, tribulation, disappointment, or distress, He is the Lifter of your head (Psalm 3:3).

He is the One Who lifts your head high.

Will you thank Him and receive His gift of help and strength? The more you receive, the more He desires to give. He is the Gift that keeps on giving.

Seek No Vengeance

Proverbs 20:22 (NLT)
Don't say, "I will get even for this wrong." Wait for the LORD to handle the matter.

Romans 12:19 (The Message)
Don't hit back; discover beauty in everyone. If you've got it in you, get along with everybody. Don't insist on getting even; that's not for you to do. "I'll do the judging," says God. "I'll take care of it."

Stop fretting and stop feeding the wild tiger of vengeance in your mind. What would happen if you released a wild tiger in your home? Nothing good, for sure! The tiger would only wreak havoc and destruction. You release a wild tiger in your mind every time you hit the rewind button and repeatedly play a wrong committed against you—reliving it time after time.

When an injustice comes to mind, visualize yourself before **Abba**'s mighty throne with Jesus sitting at His right hand. Next, say, "Jesus, I give you this injustice. Thank You for being my Great **Advocate** and for promising to defend me, rescue me, and give me victory over my troubles." Finally, commit to trusting Him for His perfect timing. Wait for your **Abba**; He will take care of everything. He will avenge the wrong in the perfect way, in His perfect time.

Honor God

Psalm 90:8 (NLT)

You spread out our sins before you—our secret sins—and you see them all.

Psalm 139:7 (NLT)

I can never escape from your Spirit! I can never get away from your presence!

Jeremiah 32:19 (NLT)

You have all wisdom and do great and mighty miracles. You see the conduct of all people, and you give them what they deserve.

Are you the same person in public that you are in private? As a follower of Christ, if you habitually practice sin because you think no one else knows, you don't know **Abba** very well. Where can you hide from His eyes that range throughout the earth (2 Chronicles 16:9)? He is everywhere—He is **Omnipresent**. Do you really think you can hide from Him in any secret place?

God made you in His own image; therefore, you are supposed to reflect His image. Will you surrender every choice, every addiction, and every thought to Him? Will you choose Him over your sin? He knit you together and He knows everything about you. Allow your **Abba** to search you and test you. Invite Him to point out anything in you that offends Him, and ask Him to lead you along the path of everlasting life.

He made all the delicate inner parts of your body. You are wonderfully complex; His workmanship is marvelous! Every day of your life is recorded in His book (Psalm 139:16); therefore, don't squander away even one day.

Will you live your precious, numbered days honoring Him?

Chaff or Wheat

Seek solid, nourishing Truth. Be careful of what you allow yourself to hear. Does the supposed messenger of Truth to whom you listen speak the whole Truth? As followers of Christ, **Abba** does not give us the option to pick and choose which parts of His Word we receive. All Scripture is God-breathed and is useful for teaching us what is true and to make us realize what is wrong in our lives (2 Timothy 3:16).

Your heart and mind grow and transform when nourished. You can't nourish your soul with **chaff** or straw, which the winds of life blow away. Attempting to sustain your life with the **chaff** of this world—its beliefs, customs, and practices—will leave you poorly supplied with the vital nutrients for sound health and growth.

The Word of God provides life-giving nourishment and sustenance. He is the **Bread of Life** (John 6:35); He supplies us with grain that is purified from all **chaff**.

The world-view of man is like **chaff**—here today and blown away tomorrow. God's rich nourishment is the same yesterday, today, and forever!

From Information to Application

God's words found in the Bible are consecrating Truths. His Truths, when whole-heartedly embraced, make you different—alive to His purposes and plans. His Truths induct you into a sacred devotion to His divine purposes. When your ears hear God's Truths, when your heart chooses to receive Truth, and when your motive is to apply His Truths in your daily thinking and living, you transform! Will you ask your **Abba** to help you take His information and use it for application?

When you accepted Jesus Christ as your Lord and Savior, **Abba** Lord deposited His Spirit within you. His Holy Spirit helps you believe the Truth your ears hear. The Holy Spirit is a Powerful Force Who moves to connect Truth with action in your life. The Truth is the sanctifier and consecrator. The Holy Spirit at work within you to bring understanding and insight of God's Word prepares and purifies you for God's divine purposes.

You have been marked in Christ with a seal—the promised Holy Spirit (2 Corinthians 1:21, 22). Will you set yourself to learning His Truths and allow the Spirit within to enable your understanding? The Holy Spirit will give you the ability to know and apply the Word of God.

Spirit to Spirit

> ## 1 Corinthians 2:14 (NLT)
> But people who aren't spiritual can't receive these truths from God's Spirit. It all sounds foolish to them and they can't understand it, for only those who are spiritual can understand what the Spirit means.
>
> ## 1 Timothy 4:1, 2 (NLT)
> Now the Holy Spirit tells us clearly that in the last times some will turn away from the true faith; they will follow deceptive spirits and teachings that come from demons. These people are hypocrites and liars, and their consciences are dead.

Spirit can be known only by spirit—God's Spirit and your spirit in open **communion**. As a follower of Christ, you have Jesus' very own Spirit dwelling within you (1 Corinthians 6:19). Without Jesus living in your heart, you cannot receive spiritual Truths and understand His teachings. Jesus' Holy Spirit discerns Truths from God and lies from **the enemy**. The Holy Spirit helps you receive divine revelations and gives you the desire to follow the true faith.

Some may say they are "spiritual," but whose spirit is dwelling in them? Does it belong to Jesus, the Prince of Peace (Isaiah 9:6) or the **prince of this world** (Ephesians 2:1–3)?

Will you ask Jesus to transform the thoughts and intents of your heart? You are spiritually alive in Christ; therefore, you have access to everything God's Spirit desires you to know and to do. Will you seek Him today and follow Him in every way?

His Grace is Greater

> **Psalm 51:1 (NLT)**
> Have **mercy** on me, O God, because of your unfailing love. Because of your great compassion, blot out the stain of my sins.
>
> **Psalm 86:5 (NLT)**
> O Lord, you are so good, so ready to forgive, so full of unfailing love for all who ask for your help.

Sin separates you from **Abba** Father; but every time you get yourself in trouble, **repent** and He will forgive! Allow Him to wash away your guilt. Allow Him to wipe away the stains of sin with His cleansing cloth of **Grace**. His **Grace** is greater than any sin.

Abba Father's Mercies never fail. The stain of sin need not be permanent because His great Mercies are new every morning; great is His Faithfulness (Lamentations 3:22, 23)! There is no sin that can bar the way to **Abba**'s unfailing Love. He eagerly awaits your **repent**ance and longs to shower you with His Merciful **forgiveness**.

Your heavenly Father understands how weak you are; He made you from dust! Yet, His Love for you abounds. Will you take all your sins and lay them before Him—admitting your failure and **repent**ing with a sincere heart? Remember, as a child of God, even fear, doubt, and worry are sins; through these reactions to life you profess a belief that God Almighty can't handle the **trials** of your life. However; the God you worship is Good, Caring, Compassionate, and Forgiving. He is a big, Tender-hearted God who seeks a deep relationship with you. He is ready to forgive you; you only need to ask.

Forgive and Be Forgiven

Matthew 6:14, 15 (NLT)

"If you forgive those who sin against you, your heavenly Father will forgive you. But if you refuse to forgive others, your Father will not forgive your sins."

1 Timothy 1:15, 16 (NLT)

This is a trustworthy saying, and everyone should accept it: "Christ Jesus came into the world to save sinners"—and I am the worst of them all. But God had **mercy** on me so that Christ Jesus could use me as a prime example of his great patience with even the worst sinners. Then others will realize that they, too, can believe in him and receive eternal life.

God's **Grace** is greater than sin. His **Grace** covers any sin you could ever commit and His **Grace** covers any sin committed against you. Sins committed against you can cut deep causing you to bleed profusely. When someone hurts you, you must remember how Jesus bled for your sins. When you choose to forgive, you choose to absorb the offense just as Jesus does with you. This act of absorption connects you to your Savior in a very profound sense because you are demonstrating your understanding of His incredible **Grace** and **forgiveness** toward you.

You also demonstrate your level of faith in the Lord when you trust Him to deal with one who has sinned against you. You only need to forgive and allow your Fair and Just God to deal with the offender. He will work everything out for your good and for the good of the one who has sinned against you. Will you do your part and forgive?

Led by Truth

P salm 25:9 says God "leads the **humble** in doing right, teaching them his way" (NLT). You demonstrate true humility by choosing to have a teachable spirit. Ask the Lord to teach you His Ways. Will you trust Him with your life? Ask Him to give you listening ears in order to hear Him. Will you follow His commands? He is the God who **saved** you for all of eternity; He can certainly save you today and tomorrow from making bad choices and traveling wrong paths; you only need listen and obey.

Abba Father longs for your invitation to hold your hand. Are you calling on Him constantly? Are you submitting to His Truth? Are you asking Him to teach you and lead you? Will you put your hope in Him each day?

The Season of Sorrow

Proverbs 25:20 (NLT)
Singing cheerful songs to a person with a heavy heart is like taking someone's coat in cold weather or pouring vinegar in a wound.

Ecclesiastes 3:1, 2, 4 (NLT)
For everything there is a season, a time for every activity under heaven. A time to be born and a time to die. A time to plant and a time to harvest . . . A time to cry and a time to laugh. A time to grieve and a time to dance.

If your heart is heavy, go ahead and cry all night because joy comes in the morning (Psalm 30:5)! When you cry out to **Abba**, taking your pain to Him, His **Grace** never fails. As surely as a new day dawns after the darkness of night, God will send a new day of Comfort and Strength. While you live in this **fallen world**, there will be sad days. Recognize different seasons will come and go, in your life and in the lives of others. But **Abba**'s love will sustain you through them all.

You are called to be God's messenger of **Mercy** to those in a season of pain and grief. Allow them the **grace** to walk through the dark valley; but encourage them to move forward toward the breaking dawn. There is a time to laugh and a time to cry; for everything there is a season.

Faithful Abba

Psalm 89:8 (NIV)
Who is like you, LORD God Almighty? You, LORD, are mighty, and your faithfulness surrounds you.

H as someone you loved been unfaithful to you? Has some-one you trusted betrayed you or stabbed you in the back? Pray for them. Pray Almighty God will open the eyes of their heart and show them their sin so they will **confess**, clean up, and be led down His righteous, everlasting path.

Though people may betray you, your **Abba** Lord never will. Praise Him for His Faithfulness and Loyalty toward you; He always has your back and your best interests in mind. You will never find anything or anyone quite like Him. The holy angels are in awe of Him. He owns the cosmos and everything in it. **Righteousness** and Justice are the roots of His authority; Love and Truth are its fruits.

You will be blessed if you know and practice a lifestyle of praise; the very presence of God will be ushered in (Psalm 22:3, 4). Shout out praises to Him! He is forever Faithful to you. All you have and all you are you owe to your Loving **Abba**. Praise your Ever-Present, Loyal Shepherd today. He is your Faithful Lord Almighty!

No Gossiping

You have a wonderful opportunity to **glorify** Your Lord when you are in the presence of a gossiper. You must discourage this sinful practice by extinguishing the fire the sparks of gossip create. The gossiping tongue will stop when it is met with the refusal to participate. The sparks are quenched when you suggest prayer for the person being slandered.

Your watchful, Loving **Abba** is not pleased when you do not protect your brothers and sisters in Christ. It is your duty as a member of God's eternal family to protect the ones He loves. Love always protects.

The sin of gossip, if encouraged, burns a destructive path. Do not allow another's tongue to set your soul afire with the sin of a hateful tongue. Will you fight against the temptation to participate and practice true Godliness by refusing to engage in a conversation that tears down one whom Christ loves? When we resist the temptation to enter in, the carrier of gossip will often become aware of his or her wrong-doing—they experience **conviction** over their sin.

Ask the Lord for His strength and courage in this area; your courage will keep you clean and might encourage another from walking a destructive path.

Care for Your Family

John 19:26, 27 (NLT)
When Jesus saw his mother standing there beside the disciple he loved, he said to her, "Dear woman, here is your son." And he said to this disciple, "Here is your mother." And from then on this disciple took her into his home.

1 Timothy 5:8 (NLT)
But those who won't care for their relatives, especially those in their own household, have denied the true faith. Such people are worse than unbelievers.

If you bear the name Christian, you are called to follow Christ and behave as He would behave . . . toward everyone . . . even family. Jesus cared for His earthly family. God Himself placed you in the earthly family of His choosing. Your family, no matter how difficult, is a gift from God.

God has commanded you to care for your family. This is important to Him; therefore, it must be important to you. He expects you to provide for the needy with your own resources. It is your honor to care for the destitute. How much more so when those in need are members of your own family? God does not desire you to be exploited; but He is clear that anyone who neglects to care for family members in need repudiates his or her faith. Are you denying your faith?

Gifted to Serve

Romans 12:6-8 (NLT)

In his **grace**, God has given us different gifts for doing certain things well. So if God has given you the ability to prophesy, speak out with as much faith as God has given you. If your gift is serving others, serve them well. If you are a teacher, teach well. If your gift is to encourage others, be encouraging. If it is giving, give generously. If God has given you leadership ability, take the responsibility seriously. And if you have a gift for showing kindness to others, do it gladly.

1 Timothy 4:14 (NLT)

Do not neglect the spiritual gift you received through the prophecy spoken over you when the elders of the church laid their hands on you.

1 Peter 4:10 (NLT)

God has given each of you a gift from his great variety of spiritual gifts. Use them well to serve one another.

All gifts are from the hand of God. You did nothing to deserve any gift you possess; they are gracious enablings from the Lord for the display of His Splendor.

When you received Jesus Christ as your Lord and Savior, He deposited one or more spiritual gifts within you. You find meaning and your purpose in this life when you discover your gift(s) and use it to build up God's **chosen people**. Read God's Word and grow in His Truth and **Grace**. As you grow and walk out your faith, your gift(s) will become obvious to you and others. (You may want to find a spiritual gifts test and take it for confirmation.)

Be who you were made to be; do not compare yourself to others or wish you had a different gift. Embrace who you are in Christ. Ask Him to help you identify your special spiritual gift(s) and thank Him for blessing you.

Will you dedicate your gift(s) to Him by serving others whole-heartedly and with cheerfulness? Do not hold back and do not neglect your God-given gift. Give it freely as a good steward (Luke 16:1–13) of God's amazing **Grace**. Are you serving others with your gift?

Be who you were made to

be; do not compare yourself

to others or wish you had a

different gift.

Jesus is the Truth

John 8:44b-47 (NIV)
"He [the **devil**] was a murderer from the beginning, not holding to the truth, for there is no truth in him. When he lies, he speaks his native language, for he is a liar and the father of lies. Yet because I tell the truth, you do not believe me! Can any of you prove me guilty of sin? If I am telling the truth, why don't you believe me? Whoever belongs to God hears what God says. The reason you do not hear is that you do not belong to God."

John 14:6 (NIV)
Jesus answered, "I am the way and the truth and the life. No one comes to the Father except through me."

Ephesians 4:15 (NLT)
Instead, we will speak the truth in love, growing in every way more and more like Christ, who is the head of his body, the church.

Jesus is the Truth. Satan is the father of all lies. Seek to fill yourself with Truth as a starving child devours a meal. When you plant seeds of Truth in your mind, everything about you changes. The soil of your heart softens and is divinely cultivated to desire more Truth. Your thoughts begin to transform from being centered on yourself to genuinely caring for others. The hardships of others, which once left you unmoved, now move your eyes to tears and your hands to action.

When you seek Truth, your tongue begins to desire harmony, peace, and resolution. Your words encourage and build others up; you are no longer comfortable with slander and negativity—an indication that you are spiritually maturing. Of course, this growth occurs only as you allow the Holy Spirit full access to your heart.

The Holy Spirit is the Spirit of Revelation Who helps you understand God's Truth. He is the Connector between head knowledge and heart response—between information and application. Are you inviting the Holy Spirit to move God's delicious Truths from your head to your heart?

The Holy Spirit gives you that check in your spirit when you are not sharing Truth wrapped in Love. Truth spoken in Love requires care in recognizing the dignity and value of the person to whom you speak. Maturity in Jesus is marked by a follower who knows the Truth and speaks it with kindness, gentleness, patience, and self-control. This does not mean the person hearing the Truth will be pleased. You are not called to be a people pleaser; you are called to love others. This includes sharing Truth.

To whom is God asking you to speak Truth in Love and **Grace?**

When you plant seeds

of Truth in your mind,

everything about you

changes.

Seek Living Water

Would you consider your life as one planted in fertile soil? Are you well nourished with abundant, **Living Water**? If you have been wandering aimlessly through life without purpose or meaning, stop trying to plant yourself in the dry, rocky soil of this world. Plant yourself, instead, beside the streams that flow from the Throne of **Grace**.

Your Lord and Savior will grow you like a tiny, willow seedling into a strong and beautiful tree. The roots of a willow tenaciously seek abundant water and the roots rapidly grow when nourished. The willow tree, although strong and tough, is a soft and pliable tree. So will you grow when you have your roots deep in the fertile soil that is nourished by the **Living Water**s of the Lord.

Jesus is offering you His abundant **Living Water**! Today is the day! Will you stop wandering in the desert and plant yourself like a willow by streams of **Living Water**? Tenaciously seek Him and grow in strength and power as you develop a soft and pliant heart for Him and others.

Holy, Holy, Holy

Holy, Holy, Holy is the Lord God Almighty! God is not a mere mortal; He is the Holy One in your midst. He is absolute pureness; there is not a trace of sin or ugliness found in Him. It is hard for your brain to fully comprehend such a perfect Holy, Holy, Holy God. No one you have ever known comes close to comparing to Him. There is only One True God. There is only One **Omniscient, Omnipresent, Omnipotent I AM** (Exodus 3:14). He is the One "who was and is and is to come" (Revelation 4:8; NKJV). Do you worship Him with adoration and praise?

In the kingdom of God, the angels continually sing His praises, calling to one another "Holy, Holy, Holy is the Lord Almighty! The whole earth is full of His Glory." Will you join them in singing a song of praise to Him? Will you live with thankfulness in your heart for the blessed opportunity to worship the One True Holy God Who is Ever-present and active in your life?

No Fear

2 Timothy 1:6, 7 (NLT)

This is why I remind you to fan into flames the spiritual gift God gave you when I laid my hands on you. For God has not given us a spirit of fear and timidity, but of power, love, and self-discipline.

God gave you a spiritual gift or perhaps two or three. Are you fanning your gift(s) into flames of fire? When you neglect burning embers, they soon cool off and die out. Do not let your gifts grow cold; do not let them grow dim and die away. He deposited a special gifting in you so you could bless others and be the person He created you to be. Your love and closeness to Jesus grows deeper when you serve in the places He's called you. Discover and enjoy the personal gift God has deposited in you. If you are not sure what your spiritual gift may be, ask **Abba** Father. He will reveal it to you.

However, you may be like Timothy who knew what his gift was, but needed courage and strength to put it to use. Fear is a great obstacle to usefulness for the Lord. Are you afraid to step out in boldness because others may ridicule you or ostracize you? Jesus understands; many made fun of Him and rejected Him. He gives you a delicious promise that He has delivered you from the spirit of fear, and has filled you with Power, Love, and self-discipline. When fear begins to extinguish the flame of your calling, turn up the heat by declaring in your heart, "Jesus is my Helper. What can mere humans do to me? He will protect my soul now and forever." Will you say with confidence, "I will not fear" and step out in boldness to serve the Lord with gift(s) He reserved just for you?

The Power of Humility

Psalm 131 (NLT)

LORD, my heart is not proud; my eyes are not haughty. I don't concern myself with matters too great or too awesome for me to grasp. Instead, I have calmed and quieted myself, like a weaned child who no longer cries for its mother's milk. Yes, like a weaned child is my soul within me. O Israel, put your hope in the LORD—now and always.

Will you stop fretting and trying to figure everything out in your life? Relax in God's divine control. Whatever it is that causes you angst, He's got it covered. Only pride considers human effort to be of greater value than trusting in the Lord. Remember, "Blessed are the poor in spirit" (Matthew 5:3; NKJV)—those who do not think more highly of themselves than they should. Blessed are you when you slide over from the driver's seat and give the wheel to Jesus. At first, it is very scary and uncomfortable to stop trying to be the boss of your own life; but oh, the peace that comes with giving Him control.

And stop worrying about and interfering in everyone else's life. Cultivating within yourself a quiet heart of contentment is enough to occupy you. As you learn to place more hope in Jesus and less hope in your own efforts and ideas, your heart will settle like a well-fed baby, snuggled in his mother's arms. Will you stop trying and start trusting? Will you set out to discover the power of a **humble** heart?

Press On

John 16:33 (NLT)

"I have told you all this so that you may have peace in me. Here on earth you will have many **trial**s and sorrows. But take heart, because I have overcome the world."

2 Timothy 2:3 (NLT)

Endure suffering along with me, as a good soldier of Christ Jesus.

2 Timothy 2:12a (NLT)

If we endure hardship, we will reign with him.

Y ou are living on earth; you are not in heaven . . . yet. Heaven is your hope and your future. As a believer, you know everything is going to be okay; if not this side of heaven, then certainly when you cross over to your eternal home. But that hope is for some distant tomorrow; what about today?

In this life, you will have **trial**s, hardship, and sorrows. Do not give in to self-pity, doubts, or other lies from **the enemy**. You have the blessed assurance that you are never alone in your suffering. Friends and family may judge you or abandon you; but take heart; you can grab your Mighty Savior's hand and walk with Him through any dark valley. You can endure any **trial** with Jesus by your side.

2 Timothy 2:3 calls you to be "a good soldier of Christ Jesus" (NKJV). Will you remain as faithful and obedient as a good soldier while suffering? Sustain your unyielding trust in the One who has overcome the world. Your reward will be peace on earth and riches in heaven. You are destined to reign (Revelation 2:26, 20:6) with Him; so press on, good and faithful soldier!

Do You Really Trust Him?

James 1:2, 3 (NLT)
Dear brothers and sisters, when troubles come your way, consider it an opportunity for great joy. For you know that when your faith is tested, your endurance has a chance to grow.

God will never tempt you (James 1:13), but He will test you. When troubles come your way, He is testing your faith. He is asking you, "Do you trust Me?" He is always using people and circumstances to ask you, "Do you really trust Me?" It is important for you to know the answer. You cannot grow into maturity if you won't trust Him. God's desire is to be in a deep, trusting relationship with you.

Everything that happens to you is Father-filtered; nothing gets by Him. He wants to demonstrate His Loving and Virtuous problem-solving skills to you; so when the next trouble comes, you won't hesitate to run into His arms for help. He is building you up in Christ, developing your godly character. You demonstrate Christ's character when you respond to persecution and trouble by choosing to trust Him and by reacting in joyful thanksgiving (Philippians 4:6, 7) instead of self-pity and bitterness.

How did Jesus respond when He suffered at the hands of those who sought His life (1 Peter 2:21–23)? He did not retaliate; when He suffered, He made no threats. Instead, He entrusted Himself into the hands of His Loving Father.

Trust Him

Job 13:15 (NKJV)
Though He slay me, yet will I trust Him. Even so, I will defend my own ways before Him.

Jeremiah 24:6a (NIV)
My eyes will watch over them for their good.

Job endured the loss of all he valued and all he loved (see Job 1:13–22). In one day, He went from prosperity and plenty to poverty and want. Yet, he demonstrated incredible trust in his **Abba** Lord. Even in his miseries, Job determined to trust God, even unto death. Deep in his heart, through all his sorrow, He believed God's eye was still watching over him; even though his circumstances were anything but good, he believed God was somehow working good in his life.

Is your **Abba** Lord asking you to trust Him though your eyes see no good thing? Do you feel as though God is no longer on your side in some area of your life? If so, you are at a crossroads. You can stop trusting and walk away from God; or like Job, you can determine to trust Him, believing He will always watch over you.

The enemy is constantly whispering in your ear that God is not good and does not desire good for you. That is not Truth. Simply say "**Devil**! March!" The Truth is, God's eye is on you and you can trust He is moving on your behalf. Will you place your hope in Him?

Sing For Joy

Psalm 92:4 (NLT)

You thrill me, Lord, with all you have done for me! I sing for joy because of what you have done.

Will you sing for joy because your **Abba** Lord's works are magnificent?

Ask **Abba** to open the eyes of your heart to all that He has done for you! A melody of thanksgiving resonating through your life will produce a symphony of joy. It is exciting to realize all the blessings your Lord has bestowed upon you.

The Lord delights in your cheerful countenance because it makes you an attractive **witness** to others. Joy is appealing and captivating to the lost. Joy is also supernatural, because it is not dependent on perfect circumstances; joy is dependent only on your trust in your Perfect Provider. Will you ask the Lord to open your eyes to His hand in your life?

The Lord's works are wonderful and His Love for you is unfailing. Sing to the Lord! Sing a new song of praise! Sing for joy because of what He has done!

Flourish in the Lord

> ## Psalm 92:12-14 (NIV)
> The righteous will flourish like a palm tree, they will grow like a cedar of Lebanon; planted in the house of the LORD, they will flourish in the courts of our God. They will still bear fruit in old age, they will stay fresh and green.

As an intentional follower of Jesus, you are declared righteous by Him. You are a planting of the Lord (Isaiah 61:3) for the display of His Splendor. You do not grow and transform into a strong tree by your own doing. You are planted by the Lord Himself in His rich, fertile, eternal soil. According to God's **Grace**, He provides you with the necessary nutrients—His Word and His Holy Spirit. Both are needed for you to grow strong and produce eternal fruit.

His Holy Spirit nourishes your understanding of Truth seeds planted by God in the soil of your heart. The more you open your heart to the Holy Spirit of Jesus, the more **Grace** He gives you to help you apply His Truths in your life. You have a glorious future with Jesus. What good is a tree that does not produce? With Jesus, your life will be fruitful, indeed. What are the fruits of **righteousness**? They include a sold-out devotion to Jesus and a willingness to care for others.

Have you noticed, as people age, they either wither and dry up, or become more radiant and lovely? Those who have not been nourished by God's Word and the Holy Spirit, become like a barren land. Those whose lives are "planted in the house of the Lord" will flourish. The flow of God's **Grace** does not slow down with age; it increases if the individual allows it. The last days of your life should be your very best fruit-bearing days. The righteous will "bear fruit in old age; they will stay fresh and green."

Consider Him

Consider Jesus. Who is He? What does He mean to you? He was God clothed in flesh and bone; although Holy and Pure, He walked among mean, ugly, and unreceptive humanity. His eyes saw behavior that brought forth tears. His ears heard men say they represented Him while they spoke lies about Him and tried to lead others away from Him. And yet, He endured.

He was rejected, laughed at, excluded, slandered, beaten, spat upon, and hurt by the people He so desired to save and bless. When insults and lies were spoken of Him, He endured. When marched off to be beaten almost to death, He endured. When forsaken by those who said they loved Him, He endured. When betrayed by trusted friends, He endured. While hanging in pain on a wooden cross, He endured. When the burden of your sin was upon Him, He endured. When separated from God, His Father, He endured.

Why did He endure such pain? He endured because He loves you that much. Consider Him.

Endure to the End

Matthew 5:10 (NIV)
Blessed are those who are persecuted because of **righteousness**, for theirs is the kingdom of heaven.

Matthew 13:21 (NIV)
"But since they have no root, they last only a short time. When trouble or persecution comes because of the word, they quickly fall away."

What does light have in common with darkness? What does truth have in common with lies? (See 2 Corinthians 6:14.) What does right have in common with wrong? Nothing! When you live in the Light, sharing Truth, and making right decisions, darkness, lies, and wrong thinking will diminish in your life.

If you live for the Lord, you will be persecuted just as He was. The first Christians who followed Him were persecuted—attacked by lions in public forums while crowds cheered in evil delight. You will not be thrown into the lion's den, but you may sustain claw marks etched down your back because you choose the way of Jesus over the way of the world. Guard the Truth you have received and don't go weak. You belong to your Loving, Righteous Creator; He will strengthen you for the journey.

This life is a test; it is just a test. The real you is being tested and prepared for your eternal home with Jesus. He will heal all the oozing claw marks and wipe away every tear. Blessed are you when you are persecuted, for the kingdom of heaven is yours (Matthew 5:10). **Amen!**

Unfailing Love

Psalm 94:18, 19 (NLT)

I cried out, "I am slipping!" but your unfailing love, O LORD, supported me. When doubts filled my mind, your comfort gave me renewed hope and cheer.

Cry out to Jesus; He will quiet you with His Love. Friends and family may fail you; but He never will. He is your **Omnipresent** Protector and Provider. What support do you need today? Ask Jesus to lend His big, Gracious hand of support. He loves to defend you. You are His.

It is natural to doubt, but don't entertain these thoughts. The second doubts enter your mind; say "Thank You, Jesus, for helping me." Calm your heart by reminding yourself that He will never leave you nor forsake you (Hebrews 13:5). Say "Thank You, Jesus, for tending to me and exchanging my anxieties and worries for a peace that surpasses all understanding" (Philippians 4:7).

Will you thank Jesus for His unfailing Love that supports and sustains you? Will you seek Him for support if you feel you are slipping? When doubts fill your mind, will you go to Him and ask Him for His Comfort, Hope, and Cheer?

His unfailing Love will never fail to support and comfort you.

Wolves in the House

B e careful, ears, what you hear. There are wolves dressed as good shepherds who claim to profess Christianity; however, their words are not from **Jehovah**. He is the One True God. There is One Truth, but there are two powers at work: the Father of all and the father of lies (John 8:44). Those who do not proclaim the truth of God's Word are of their father, the **devil**.

False teachers do not teach the Truth made clear in the Bible because they don't believe the Truth. They follow their own desires with complete disregard to God's desire and His will. They have never trusted Jesus with anything. Run from teachers who seek to entertain rather than to reveal God's Word.

Are your ears alert to trendy opinions and "feel good" teachings? God's Word is living and powerful; it is not to be trifled with, changed, added to, or watered down. To manipulate God's Word is to reject His Truth.

Beware of false, slick teachers; they are wolves spreading lies that lead to death rather than God's Truth that leads to life.

Consecrated to the Lord

In Old Testament days, altars of worship were to be built according to God's design and instruction. Any sign of human effort used to improve upon God's instructions made the altar unholy and unacceptable to the Lord. And now, thousands of years later, God's people still are tempted to "improve" upon God's design.

You may be tempted to offer God Almighty a helping hand in the outworking of your life; instead, guard the Truth He has entrusted to you. Keep it pure and undefiled, fit for use by Him. Your mind becomes unfit for Holy use when you seek understanding according to human logic and reasoning. Your heart becomes unfit for Holy use when it tells you to earn God's approval based on your natural gifts and talents.

The tools of **legalism** and pride shape stones used in altars to **false gods**. In humility and surrender, remember you stand clean and fit for use only because of the blood of Jesus, not because of anything you could ever offer at the altar. He alone is to be the center of your worship, keep your mind fixed on Him and seek His understanding, guidance, provision, purpose, and fulfillment with all your heart; this will keep you fit for Holy use.

Do They Know?

Do others know you are a chosen child of God? Your love is the proof of who you really are. Do they know you are a Christian by your love? Words are easy to say; it is behavior that demonstrates whether you are living as a true disciple of Jesus. Are you the hands and feet of Jesus to others?

In 1 Corinthians 13:3–7, Paul explains the nature of true love: "Love never gives up. Love cares more for others than for self. Love does not strut. Love does not have a big head. Does not force itself on others. Isn't always "me first." Does not fly off the handle. Does not keep score of the sins of others. Does not revel when others grovel. Takes pleasure in the flowering of Truth. Trusts God always. Always looks for the best" (The Message).

They will know you are Christian by your love. Do they know?

Invite Him In

Zephaniah 3:17 (NKJV)

The LORD your God in your midst, The Mighty One, will save; He will rejoice over you with gladness, He will quiet you with His love, He will rejoice over you with singing.

Zephaniah wrote this verse to those who recognized their sinful state and need of **redemption** and restoration. He was writing to those who were willing to trust in the Name of the Lord. His words are just as applicable to us today.

Oh, Jesus follower, what a delicious promise Zephaniah proclaims—God is with you! The Mighty One who bears the Name above all names will save you. Your Lord is a God of Justice and **Righteousness**, but also a God of incredible Joy and Beauty. He rejoices over you! He celebrates your faith in Him with jubilant songs. There is joy in heaven because of you today. And you will someday partake in lavish banquets, feasting at the banqueting table with your Mighty Savior. (See Luke 14:15–24; Revelation 19:9.)

As you look forward to your incredible future, will you allow the Lord's affection and devotion toward you to calm your restlessness, soothe your hurts, and quiet your heart? He saves you and quiets you with His Love. Will you invite Him into all your days?

Hear and Obey

2 Kings 5:10-13 (NLT)

But Elisha sent a messenger out to [Naaman] with this message: "Go and wash yourself seven times in the Jordan River. Then your skin will be restored, and you will be healed of your leprosy." But Naaman became angry and stalked away. "I thought he would certainly come out to meet me!" he said. "I expected him to wave his hand over the leprosy and call on the name of the LORD his God and heal me! Aren't the rivers of Damascus, the Abana and the Pharpar, better than any of the rivers of Israel? Why shouldn't I wash in them and be healed?" So Naaman turned and went away in a rage. But his officers tried to reason with him and said, "Sir, if the prophet had told you to do something very difficult, wouldn't you have done it? So you should certainly obey him when he says simply, 'Go and wash and be cured!'"

Luke 11:28 (NLT)

Jesus replied, "But even more blessed are all who hear the word of God and put it into practice."

Your God makes it very clear what He expects from you in this life. He tells you in Romans 10:9, "If you **confess** with your mouth that Jesus is Lord and believe in your heart that God raised him from the dead, you will be **saved**" (NLT). Eternal **salvation** is handed to you as a gift from the Almighty hand of God. You simply believe, **confess**, and receive.

Salvation is a gift, but it is important that we prove our belief through an obedient life. Jesus said in John 14:23 "All who love me will do what I say" (NLT). A life surrendered to the will of God demonstrates love for Jesus. God's Word makes it clear, obedience is more desirable to Him than even **sacrifice** (1 Samuel 15:22).

You may be tempted to equate pomp and circumstance with blessings from God. You may be frustrated that He has not given you what the world would view as a "big calling" or a large platform. Recognition and awe from others will not bring you the deep satisfaction you are seeking. It is obedience to God that will cause blessing to flow in and through your life (James 1:25).

Will you release your will to God's will? Will you make daily choices that reflect obedience to His ways? If you will, you will be blessed in ways you never could have hoped or even imagined!

Salvation is a gift,

but it is important that we

prove our belief through an

obedient life.

Name Bearer

Jeremiah 15:16 (NLT)
When I discovered your words, I devoured them. They are my joy and my heart's delight, for I bear your name, O LORD God of Heaven's Armies.

Romans 6:17 (NLT)
Thank God! Once you were slaves of sin, but now you wholeheartedly obey this teaching we have given you.

God's Word promises that if you seek the Lord you will find Him (Deuteronomy 4:29). That promise is for you. But, where are you looking for Him? Do you seek Him in your own heart and common sense? The Lord says the human heart is deceitful and cannot be trusted (Jeremiah 17:9). Are you seeking to connect with Him through others? Second-hand knowledge of God has never transformed anyone's life. He wants you to sit with Him in His Word. His Word was written just for you. He wants to spend time with you—just you and Him. He has much to tell you.

When you encounter God's Word, meditate on it, chew on it, and devour it! It is divine nourishment that can change you forever. Nothing could sit better in your soul than God's Word of Truth and **Grace**; it richly satisfies and fulfills.

The Holy Spirit within you encourages you to live according to God's Word (John 14:26). You are an ambassador of your Lord and Savior—you represent Him in this **fallen world** (2 Corinthians 5:20). You must not represent Him with words only; your actions of kindness, **grace**, and love will speak more loudly to those who remain slaves to sin.

As a Christian, you are no longer a slave to sin. Will you choose to be His willing servant? Will you bear His Name?

Gateway to Your Soul

> **Psalm 101:3a (NLT)**
> I will refuse to look at anything vile and vulgar.
>
> **Matthew 6:22 (NLT)**
> Your eye is a lamp that provides light for your body. When your eye is good, your whole body is filled with light.

Your eyes are a gateway to your soul. You have the volition and control regarding what your eyes allow into your being. Whatever enters your mind through the gateway of your eyes, lays the foundation for who you are and how you perceive life. If your eyes are healthy they are good—single-focused on sound Truth and **Righteousness**. Healthy eyes refuse to consider or look at immoral acts, degrading practices, destructive behaviors, or evil ways. If your eyes focus on Jesus and anything that brings glory to Him, your whole body will shine forth the Light of godly character.

Satan disguises himself as the angel of light and he packages darkness in wrappings of light. His goal is to deceive you and cause you to focus unwittingly on the "vile and vulgar." His intention is to gain access to your soul by causing your vision to be captured by his disguised darkness. He will deceive your mind to accept humanistic views as good. He will delude your heart by enticing you to desire worldly "treasures" that promise happiness and satisfaction, but deliver sorrow and disappointment. He uses your eyes to gain access to your mind and heart. He delights when you compromise godly boundaries and allow darkness access into your being.

Will you turn your eyes from all darkness—anything that would cause Jesus sadness—and focus your eyes on His Truth, **Grace**, and Goodness? The Light shines before you as bright as the noonday sun; step into it and absorb its warmth and radiance. Will you allow the Light of the Lord to guard and guide your life? Will you take great care with what you allow your eyes to see? Remember, when your eyes are good, your whole body is filled with light.

Whatever enters your mind

through the gateway of your

eyes, lays the foundation for

who you are and how you

perceive life.

Follow the Leader

God loves you immeasurably more than you can even imagine! He provided the way for you to live in absolute freedom through the blood of His Son. It is for freedom you have been set free (Galatians 5:1), not for continued bondage to sin. Sin—the choice to operate in ways outside of God's perfect design for you—is not good for you. Sin will never bless you nor benefit you.

The enemy (Satan) packages sin in sparkly, attractive, and enticing ways; yet, in the end, sin always leads to destruction and pain. **The enemy** will even speak through those who claim to love the Lord. They will paint false pictures that lead to false hopes and away from Truth and **Grace**. In the end, you will find yourself in self-imposed exile from the presence of **Abba**.

God has great plans and purposes for you. His plans are to prosper you and to give you hope and a bright future (Jeremiah 29:11). He does not want you living in the pits; rather, He desires you to soar on the wings of eagles. The real you is meant to soar in the freedom of Christ Jesus.

In Matthew 15:8, we learn that Jesus said some people honor Him with their lips, but their hearts are far from Him. Leave them; they are blind guides and both they and their followers will fall into a pit (Matthew 15:14). Are you sure the teacher you are following is following Jesus?

Starving Children

Lamentations 2:19 (NLT)

Rise during the night and cry out. Pour out your hearts like water to the Lord. Lift up your hands to him in prayer, pleading for your children, for in every street they are faint with hunger.

What has happened? Our children are starving. They come from broken homes and schools that have forsaken our God. They are told at every turn He does not exist; and the further they walk from Him, the emptier they feel. On every street of our nation, our children are faint with hunger—they have no spiritual nourishment—they are not fed from God's Word; they do not know the **Bread of Life** (John 6:35).

Fall on your knees, lift up your hands! Pour out your heart like water for the sake of the children of the land! Lift up your hands in prayer pleading for their eternal souls. Will you invite God to move on your city streets, on your country lanes, and on your suburban roads? Our children are starving. Please pray for opportunities to share God's Truth and **Grace** with them. Pray for Christians to find their voice and reach out to the children of our land.

God hears your every prayer and moves on these young ones' behalf. Will you please pray for **Abba** Father to lead the lost children home? They are faint with hunger.

Refresh a Parched Soul

Philemon 1:7 (NLT)
Your love has given me much joy and comfort, my brother, for your kindness has often refreshed the hearts of God's people.

God is asking you to show kindness to a fellow believer today. Care and love given to a struggling believer can make them feel renewed, encouraged, and reenergized. Words and acts of kindness have the power to help others re-route hopeless feelings. The simple act of a phone call or shared cup of coffee can refresh a parched soul. Words of encouragement can join with the Holy Spirit in your loved one's heart and stimulate new hope. Uplifting words can open eyes to hidden joys. Tender, caring words can be as comforting as a soft, warm blanket on cold shoulders.

Ask the Holy Spirit to guide you to someone who needs comforting today. You were made to demonstrate kindness in order to bless others. When you honor Jesus with a loving heart, your bond with Him deepens and you have yet more to give to those who are in need.

Whose heart is God asking you to refresh today?

Hopeful Anticipation

> **Lamentations 3:25, 26 (NKJV)**
> The LORD is good to those who wait for Him, to the soul who seeks Him. It is good that one should hope and wait quietly for the **salvation** of the LORD.

Are you depending on the Lord? Do you seek Him and desire to submit to Him? Oh, the goodness that awaits you if you are! Psalm 145:9 tells you the Lord is Good to all; He has compassion on all He has made. You know this is true; He gives you the air you breathe and calls up the sun each day and the moon at night. He calls forth the rain for the righteous and the unrighteous (Matthew 5:45).

Our Father is especially good to those who wait for Him—those who quietly linger in His presence while they await His timing. We should wait for His answers with hopeful anticipation, knowing His timing is always perfect. Anticipate His Wise leading. He hears you; He knows what to do; and He has your very best interests in mind.

How do you seek Him in the waiting? Do you ask Him to reveal His perfect will for you? Do you look for answers in His Word? Do you perk your ears to trusted teachers on the radio or Internet? Do you surrender your petitions at the foot of His mighty throne, visualizing Jesus sitting at **Abba** Father's right hand, interceding for you?

Will you thank the Lord for hearing your every prayer and tell Him you wait with hopeful anticipation for His answers in His time? The earlier you learn to seek and wait on the Lord, the easier you make your life, and the more mature you will grow. Will you seek Him for all you're worth? **Abba** is Good and He will reward you when you diligently seek Him (Hebrews 11:6).

You Belong to Him

Lamentations 3:55-57 (NKJV)

I called on Your name, O LORD, from the lowest pit. You have heard my voice: "Do not hide Your ear from my sighing, from my cry for help." You drew near on the day I called on You, and said, "Do not fear!"

Y ou belong to **Abba** Father, The One who sees everything. Your God hears everything and is Powerful and Loving enough to change everything for your good. Do you feel overwhelmed? Are you in a pit of despair? Do not fear. Cry out to Jesus! Call on the Name above all names (Philippians 2:9). Ask Him to forgive you for your sins and your doubts, and then tell Him everything. Tell Him how overwhelmed and out of control you feel. Tell Him every hopeless detail of your situation. Ask Him for help.

Will you invite the Lord into your circumstances? Will you include Him in every detail and hold nothing back from Him? Visualize yourself laying it all at the foot of His throne; leave all your cares right there with Him. He is your **Jehovah Shammah**, the Lord Who is There with you. He will not leave your side. When you call to Him, He is already there. Do not fear. He is moving on your behalf.

Every time fear creeps into your mind say, "Thank you, Jesus, for helping me and loving me." Do not linger in your fear; it dishonors your **Abba** Father. Move forward through your fear, holding the hand of Jesus; you belong to Him.

Worthy of Praise

Hebrews 2:17 (NLT)

Therefore, it was necessary for him to be made in every respect like us, his brothers and sisters, so that he could be our merciful and faithful **High Priest** before God. Then he could offer a **sacrifice** that would take away the sins of the people.

I t was for you that Jesus chose to leave holy, perfect, glorious heaven and be born as a human baby—flesh and bone—to live among sinners and share in their pain and sorrow. It is essential that Jesus knows, in every aspect, the experience of being human. He experienced a growling, hungry stomach, physical aches and pains; He knew joy and laughter and suffered betrayal from friends and lies from enemies. He entered into the details of human life.

Jesus was tempted by **the enemy** (Matthew 4:1) in all the ways Satan tempts us (Hebrews 4:15). Yet, unlike us, Jesus never sinned. Because He was sinless, though fully man, He was able to die on behalf of all men. His **sacrifice** on our behalf paid the penalty—His blood covers the sin of mankind.

Jesus was fully man; He is also fully God. He sits at the right hand of the Father as your Sympathetic and ever-so-Faithful **High Priest** (Hebrews 4:15), ready to cleanse you. His **Grace** is greater than any sin you can commit.

Will you praise Him for His Loyalty? Will you praise Him for His Goodness? Will you praise Him for His **sacrifice**? Will you praise Him for His **forgiveness**? Will you praise Him? He is Worthy; oh, so Worthy of your praises!

A Better Way

Psalm 103:14 (NIV)

For he knows how we are formed, he remembers that we are dust.

Hebrews 2:18 (NIV)

Because he himself suffered when he was tempted, he is able to help those who are being tempted.

Jesus understands your struggles. He lived as a man and experienced all the **trial**s this life can inflict. He is deeply touched by your sad, tempted soul. Jesus was pierced and afflicted by temptations and sorrow. He identifies with your **trial**s.

As a human, you will never be completely free from temptations and sorrows. However, the hope you have is incredible! Jesus stands ready to help and strengthen you when you are tempted. He understands you are only human and, therefore, weak and volatile; but you have His supernatural Power at work within you (Ephesians 3:20). Call upon His Power to help you! He will come to your aid in ways you could never imagine.

When you are tempted toward sin, ask Jesus to help you withstand. He will give you strength to avoid sin. He is the way (John 14:6) and He is able to help you. Will you ask Him?

Open Wide Your Heart

Hebrews 3:6–8a, 12–14 (NLT)

But Christ, as the Son, is in charge of God's entire house. And we are God's house, if we keep our courage and remain confident in our hope in Christ. That is why the Holy Spirit says, "Today when you hear his voice, don't harden your hearts." . . . Be careful then, dear brothers and sisters. Make sure that your own hearts are not evil and unbelieving, turning you away from the living God. You must warn each other every day, while it is still "today," so that none of you will be deceived by sin and hardened against God. For if we are faithful to the end, trusting God just as firmly as when we first believed, we will share in all that belongs to Christ.

Dearly loved child of God, are your eyes fixed on Jesus? He is the center of every important truth you believe. What you believe about Him is the most important thing about you.

Many of your spiritual ancestors tried His Patience by refusing to trust and follow Him. Sadly, as a result they never fulfilled their true purpose on earth and never enjoyed God's rest, peace, and joy.

You are an eternal member of the house of God. Today, please listen to the Holy Spirit within you; don't harden your heart to the Spirit's leading. Ask Jesus to help you with your unbelief and disobedience. Choose today to listen to God through His Word and believe in your heart that you can trust Him!

Will you place your confidence and hope in Jesus? Will you tell Him you are choosing to fix your thoughts on Him instead of your worries and fears? Today, when you hear His voice, please do not harden your heart; open it wide to Him.

Confirm Your Calling

Are you committed to your walk with Jesus? In order to have a good relationship with anyone, you must persistently devote personal attention to that person. Relationships require an investment. Jesus invested all He had to give in order to have a relationship with you. When you accepted His invitation to receive Him as your Savior and Lord of your life, He gave you His Holy Spirit and you became a recipient of His eternal promises for His divine interaction in your life. Do not waste a second; build on what you have been given. "Commit your way to the Lord" and enjoy your rich, kingdom **inheritance** (Psalm 37:5).

Diligently build the foundation of your life on the Solid Rock (2 Samuel 22:2). Add to your faith by asking Jesus to help you be a person of moral goodness—a person of integrity, honesty, decency, compassion, and kindness. Commit to getting to know Him better. He longs for you to know Him, because when you know Him, you will trust Him more and more. Knowing Jesus intimately will sharpen your understanding of good and evil, right and wrong; it will help you know whether to turn to the left or the right, and when to say "yes" or "no." As you pursue Him, you grow in Him; and as you grow in Him, your love for others deepens and transforms you into a productive and effective child of God.

Don't wait another second to commit your life to Jesus. Make every effort to confirm and honor God's calling; after all, He chose you! If you accept Him and choose to live for Him, you are promised a rich welcome into the eternal kingdom of our Lord and Savior Jesus Christ.

Relationships require an

investment. Jesus invested

all He had to give in order to

have a relationship

with you.

Nothing But a Test

You are blessed in this life with joy, peace, and spiritual fullness when you recognize how insignificant your ways, understanding, and wisdom are compared to those of God Almighty. You are blessed by trading in your will for His will. In return, you are promised the kingdom of heaven! Consider this great promise. You are guaranteed heaven forever! If you endure in Christ, you will rule and reign with Him in your eternal home (2 Timothy 2:12). This is your God-given destiny.

This world is temporary and your time here is only a test that will prepare you for your eternal purpose. God has uniquely designed your life to be the perfect training ground for your position in your heavenly destination. Your life on earth is your opportunity to grow into the person God intends for you to be.

Jesus presents you with opportunities to grow your soul by continually choosing to die to this world (Colossians 3:5). You die with Him every time you deny your flesh and your will in order to **glorify** Him. You die with Him by exchanging the comfort zone for the Jesus danger zone (Romans 8:35, 36). You die with Jesus when you are persecuted because of **righteousness** (Matthew 5:11, 12). Jesus blesses you with His favor when people slander you and persecute you because of your commitment to Him. When this world persecutes you, be joyful because your reward in heaven is strong and intense. What is temporary discomfort in this world compared to the glorious kingdom awaiting you? Its streets are paved with gold and there will be no more tears, suffering, or sorrow (Revelation 21:4).

Press on, son or daughter of the King; your heavenly home is being prepared for you (John 14:2, 3). Are you preparing to reign with the **King of kings**?

This world is temporary and

your time here is only a test

that will prepare you for

your eternal purpose.

No Fear in Death

1 Corinthians 15:54, 55 (NIV)
When the perishable has been clothed with the imperishable and the mortal with immortality, then the saying that is written will come true: "Death has been swallowed up in victory. Where, O death is your victory? Where, O death is your sting?"

Philippians 1:21 (NIV)
For to me, to live is Christ and to die is gain.

While you live on this earth, you are to be an ambassador for Christ (2 Corinthians 5:20). To live as His ambassador is an exhilarating ride; what can be more thrilling than experiencing God Almighty moving in your life and **witness**ing His answers to prayers? To live in Christ is to never be alone, never feel abandoned, empty, or hopeless; is to be in constant conversation with your **Jehovah Shammah**—the Lord Who is There. But the day is coming when each of us will cross over to the other side—into eternity—and we will live with Him; we will see Him, touch Him, and hear Him!

When you have left this physical world, you gain the glory of eternity. Death is not to be feared by one who belongs to the Lord. Jesus defeated death when He rose from the dead . . . so will you! Your hope goes beyond the grave right into His arms! There, your corruptible, mortal being will be changed into a pure, imperishable, and immortal being (1 Corinthians 15:50–53)! When you cross over, you will immediately feel as though you are home. Death will be swallowed up in your victorious entry into heaven!

Therefore, do not fear death. You are **Abba**'s precious child and He is always with you. He will never leave nor forsake you, especially while you are crossing over to Him.

Never Turn Back

Pigs do not wallow in the mud because they like being dirty; they wallow in the mud to cool and satisfy their flesh. How sad when those who have learned of our Lord return to wallowing in the filth of this world. To be ruled by fallen flesh is a dangerous thing.

Your **Abba** Lord is exhorting you to be careful with your life. He has freed you from the corruption of the world and all its pollution. Deny your fleshy desires to wallow in the mud of this world and keep moving forward on God's path—trusting Jesus, getting to know Him better, and choosing to honor Him. You must not become weary in doing good; in God's perfect timing, He will pour out blessings beyond your imagining if you keep yourself unstained by the world (James 1:27).

Do not be lured back to a lifestyle of corruption. You now know the Truth, and the Truth has set you free (John 8:32)!

Be Who You Were Created To Be

You are marvelously and wonderfully made. You were knit together from the very hand of God and made in His own image. He knows every detail about you. He has been with you from the very beginning of you—from even before your conception. He has all your days written in His Book of Life (Psalm 139:16; Philippians 4:3). Think on these Truths. How valuable you are to Him! Praise Him for His incredible workmanship. He who formed you deserves your honor.

Honor Him by growing into the being He created you to be. Do you know where you came from? You came from the hand of God! Thank Him. Do you know who you are? It is said the two most important days in your life are the day you were born and the day you figure out why. You were made to live in an intimate relationship with your Creator.

Do you know where you are going? There are only two

choices—heaven or hell. God made you to live forever with Him; but He loves you too much to force you to choose eternity with Him. He leaves the choice up to you. "This is how much God loved the world: He gave his Son, his one and only Son. And this is why: so that no one need be destroyed; by believing in him, anyone can have a whole and lasting life" (John 3:16; The Message).

Will you be who you were created to be, both now and forever?

You were knit together by

the very hand of God and

made in His own image.

Are You Willing?

Do you struggle with feeling unworthy of God's **Grace**, Love, and **Salvation**? Every human falls short of the Glory of God (Romans 3:23). You are not worthy of the incredible honor of being called His precious and dearly-loved child. You are not worthy of the specific calling He has on your life. Thank goodness it is not a question of your worthiness; but of your willingness and His Worthiness. Jesus simply invites you to come to Him, warts and all, and He receives you with open arms.

Are you willing to trust Jesus with every aspect of your life? Are you willing to trust Him with today's worries and tomorrow's fears? He knows His plans and purposes for you will be the only way you will find fulfillment in this life. And He has every answer to every question. Are you willing to seek Him, listen to Him, and then live for Him? If you are willing, Jesus is willing to do immeasurably more than you could ever ask or even imagine (Ephesians 3:20)!

Surgery is Required

> **Romans 12:2 (NLT)**
> Don't copy the behavior and customs of this world, but let God transform you into a new person by changing the way you think. Then you will learn to know God's will for you, which is good and pleasing and perfect.
>
> **Hebrews 4:12 (NLT)**
> For the word of God is alive and powerful. It is sharper than the sharpest two-edged sword, cutting between soul and spirit, between joint and marrow. It exposes our innermost thoughts and desires.

A re you "Spirit" led or "feelings" led? Feelings are a gift from God; but when you allow your feelings to direct your decisions, they can be detrimental. Your feelings can lead you to make wrong choices. If you have not planted God's Word in your mind, your feelings are driven by your fleshly desires, by **the enemy**, and by the world, not by God. Your choices and feelings are directed by what you think. Do you think godly thoughts? Has your mind been transformed and renewed? Do you know God's living and powerful Word? It is like a sharp sword that cuts though nonsense, lies, and doubts.

Your mind is the battlefield where life's battles are fought. **The enemy** of your soul (Satan) wants to convince you to follow fleshly desires; He will fight hard to lead you to make wrong choices. What victories await you when you allow the Spirit to lead you! God's Word is so powerful that it can convict the hardest heart and comfort the deepest hurt. God's Word has supernatural abilities to cut away sinful reactions, ignorance, and disobedient desires. It operates deep within your mind where surgery is most required.

Just as your body requires daily nourishment, your mind

requires daily renewing by ingesting God's living and powerful Word. Will you let God transform you into a new person by changing the way you think and feel? Are you learning His will for you and setting your will to living it out?

If you have not planted

God's Word in your mind,

your feelings are driven by

your fleshly desires, by the

enemy, and by the world,

not by God.

Roots of Bitterness

Psalm 73:21, 22 (NLT)
Then I realized that my heart was bitter, and I was all torn up inside.
I was so foolish and ignorant—I must have seemed like a senseless
animal to you.

Hebrews 12:15 (NLT)
Look after each other so that none of you fails to receive the **grace**
of God. Watch out that no poisonous root of bitterness grows up to
trouble you, corrupting many.

Failing to receive the **Grace** of God cultivates soil for seeds
of bitterness to grow and quenches the flow of God's Spirit
in your life. (Failing to receive the **Grace** of God refers to rejecting
God's merciful Kindness; it means rejecting Jesus' Holy influence
upon your soul and to fail to increase in Christian knowledge.)
Do you recognize bitterness when it seeks to plant itself within
your heart? When you resist the Spirit's direction, poisonous fruit
springs up within you that is toxic to you and others. Your insides
are torn up and you say and do foolish things. Your vision is blind-
ed and the good God has done for you in the past becomes darkened and hidden from you. You lose perspective and your eyes do
not see His **Grace** for today or His Hope for tomorrow. A bitter
spirit does not believe God is Good (certainly not good to him or
her) because it refuses the **Grace** of God.

A Spirit-filled believer does not allow seeds of bitterness to take
root. Your life, directed by the Holy Spirit within, produces everlasting fruit of kindness, goodness, gentleness, and self-control
(Galatians 5:22, 23). Oh, child of the King, do not miss the **Grace**
of God at work in your life. Receive His **Grace** so no bitter root
grows up to cause trouble and defile many!

Temporary Home

God is preparing you for your eternal home. Earth is your temporary home; this is not your destiny. Earth is a training ground where you are being prepared for your glorious, heavenly home. As you are being prepared to enter your eternal dwelling place with God, Jesus is preparing to receive you into His kingdom (John 14:2)

God has so fashioned the world, that it gives you glimpses of heaven. When you see an amazing sun set or feel a fresh, cool breeze caress your face, or notice the magnificent beauty of nature, you are experiencing just a small taste of what awaits you.

Take Jesus by the hand; allow Him to guide you and comfort you. Your trust in Him prepares your soul for home. God's Holy Spirit is your assurance for what and Who awaits you (Ephesians

1:13, 14). Even though your outer shell will return to the dust from which it was formed, a new, glorious, radiant, perfect, and eternal body awaits you.

You belong to Jesus. Will you hold His hand every day, listen to His Wise counsel, and anticipate your glorious destiny?

Earth is a training ground

where you are being

prepared to enter your

glorious, heavenly home.

Temporary vs. Forever

Psalm 73:26 (NKJV)

My flesh and my heart fail; but God is the strength of my heart and my portion forever.

Isaiah 40:6-8 (NLT)

A voice said, "Shout!" I asked, "What should I shout?" "Shout that people are like the grass. Their beauty fades as quickly as the flowers in a field. The grass withers and the flowers fade beneath the breath of the LORD. And so it is with people. The grass withers and the flowers fade, but the word of our God stands forever."

The real you exists temporarily inside a fading and fragile tent called a human body. Your heart and flesh are going to fail you. Left on your own, you are as unstable and weak as grass underneath the lawn mower. One swipe by the mower and the grass is cut and gone. But, the Word of the Lord stands forever. It is the same yesterday, today, and tomorrow.

The connection you have with your Jesus in His Word will guide you and strengthen you when your youth, beauty, and physical strength begin to fail you. He is your strength and portion forever. Imagine God Himself as your portion—He is everything you will ever need! Nothing this world has to offer can compare to the wonders He has in store for those who love Him (1 Corinthians 2:9).

All the things of this earth will come to an end—they will fade and die. But the beauty, peace, joy, strength, and glory to be found in our God will never fade away!

Magnify the Lord

1 Chronicles 9:33 (NKJV)
These are the singers, heads of the fathers' houses of the Levites, who lodged in the chambers, and were free from other duties; for they were employed in that work day and night.

Psalm 18:49 (NKJV)
Therefore I will give thanks to You, O LORD, among the Gentiles, and sing praises to Your name.

Psalm 29:2 (NKJV)
Give unto the LORD the glory due to His name; worship the Lord in the beauty of **holiness**.

Psalm 34:3 (NKJV)
Oh, **magnify** the LORD with me, and let us exalt His name together.

Fill your heart with the Name above all names. Think on the nature of your God; sing praises to Him, and give thanksgiving to Him. Give Him the honor due Him. Be as the four living creatures mentioned in Revelation 4:8 (NKJV)—continually proclaim: "Holy, Holy, Holy, Lord God Almighty, Who was and is and is to come!"

Your God allowed King Solomon to build an earthly Temple of worship modeled after our heavenly Temple (1 Kings 6:1–9). In the Temple, were singers and musicians from the **house of Levi** (one of the twelve tribes of Israel) who praised the Lord day and night. They lived in the chambers of the Temple in order to ensure constant songs of praise arose to our Magnificent and Glorious God (1 Chronicles 9:33; NKJV). They gave unto the Lord the Glory due His Name (Psalm 29:2).

Do you, beloved saint of God, give glory to His Mighty Name? You were created to worship Him; this is good for your soul (John 4:23). Will you **magnify** Him? Will you exalt His very nature and attributes before others? Will you make a new habit of praising Him when you open your eyes in the morning, throughout your day, and when you lay your head on your pillow at night? There is an incredible blessing of peace that will **anoint** your mind and heart when you focus on this amazing God Who has called you His own. His Love never fails (Psalm 36:7)! His Mercies are new every morning (Lamentations 3:22, 23)! How amazing is His **Grace**! Will you praise Him? Will you give all glory and honor and praise to the **King of kings**—the Great **I AM** (Exodus 3:14)!

There is an incredible

blessing of peace that will

anoint *your mind and*

heart when you focus on

this amazing God Who has

called you His own.

For His Name's Sake

Psalm 23:3 (NKJV)

He restores my soul; He leads me in the paths of **righteousness** for His name's sake.

Psalm 31:3 (NKJV)

For You are my rock and my fortress; therefore, for Your name's sake, lead me and guide me.

Do you know this God Whom you worship? His Name is above all names. His Name is Holy, Holy, Holy. There is no impurity found in Him. His Name is Love, **Grace**, **Mercy**, Omniscience, Omnipotence, Omnipresence, Justice, **Righteousness**, Truthfulness, Eternal, **Immutable**, and **Sovereign**. He is your refuge in times of trouble (Psalm 9:9). He is your solid Rock of Truth and **Grace** and He is the Great Redeemer—the only One Who can restore your soul (Psalm 19:14). He is Wisdom and knows the right path for you.

Since He has the Power to save your soul for all eternity, He certainly can save you from wrong decisions and troubles in this life. Seek Him and you will find Him if you seek Him with all your heart (Jeremiah 29:13). Ask Him to lead you to the paths of right living (Psalm 23:3). You belong to Him. For His Name's sake, He delights in guiding His children.

You can pray for God's guidance with great confidence knowing He will open and close doors for you in His perfect timing. Are you allowing Him to lead and guide you?

God Can Be Trusted

Genesis 22:1-4, 9-13 (NLT)

Some time later, God tested **Abraham**'s faith. "**Abraham**!" God called. "Yes," he replied. "Here I am." "Take your son, your only son—yes, Isaac, whom you love so much—and go to the land of Moriah. Go and **sacrifice** him as a burnt offering on one of the mountains, which I will show you." The next morning **Abraham** got up early. He saddled his donkey and took two of his servants with him, along with his son, Isaac. Then he chopped wood for a fire for a burnt offering and set out for the place God had told him about. On the third day of their journey, **Abraham** looked up and saw the place in the distance . . . When they arrived at the place where God had told him to go, **Abraham** built an altar and arranged the wood on it. Then he tied his son, Isaac, and laid him on the altar on top of the wood. And **Abraham** picked up the knife to kill his son as a **sacrifice**. At that moment the angel of the LORD called to him from heaven, "**Abraham**! **Abraham**!" "Yes," **Abraham** replied. "Here I am!" "Don't lay a hand on the boy!" the angel said. "Do not hurt him in any way, for now I know that you truly fear God. You have not withheld from me even your son, your only son." Then **Abraham** looked up and saw a ram caught by its horns in a thicket. So he took the ram and **sacrifice**d it as a burnt offering in place of his son.

Hebrews 6:11, 12 (NLT)

Our great desire is that you will keep on loving others as long as life lasts, in order to make certain that what you hope for will come true. Then you will not become spiritually dull and indifferent. Instead, you will follow the example of those who are going to inherit God's promises because of their faith and endurance.

It is easy for you to become lazy and indifferent in your walk with Jesus. Your relationship and walk will not grow without your intentional care and attention. The Book of Hebrews gives you the solution to your spiritual laziness and indifference. The passage above shares how you can make certain your hope for today and for eternity will come true.

First, love God and love others. Show kindness, consideration, and hospitality to your brothers and sisters in Christ. You demonstrate your love for God whenever you love others. Looking for ways to bless others keeps you from being lazy and dull. Ask God to show you how you can love your eternal family better.

Next, believe God will not forget your acts of love. When your circumstances become difficult, it is easy for you to believe God has forgotten you. God never forgets you. Serve others for Him; He sees everything and He always remembers.

Your spiritual father, **Abraham**, struggled with doubts and human weaknesses just like you; however, he pressed on toward the goal. **Abraham** trusted **Abba** Father and he persevered, even when God called him to do the unthinkable. **Abraham** did not allow his discouragement and heartache during the journey to stop him from responding to God. He would not give up on God and he did not take his eye off his eternal destiny. You see, God had promised **Abraham** that his descendants would number more than the stars of the sky (Genesis 22:17). Isaac was given to **Abraham** and his wife long after their child-bearing years had ended (Genesis 21:1–7); the promise of God depended on their only son. So **Abraham** knew he could trust God with Isaac, even if He did not understand what God was asking of him. He trusted God enough to obey because he had complete faith in God's promise.

Do not be discouraged; God can be trusted. Press on, keep your eyes focused on Him and keep loving others. You will be blessed; your hope will come true.

Anchored by Hope

Hebrews 6:17–19 (NIV)

Because God wanted to make the unchanging nature of his purpose very clear to the heirs of what was promised, he confirmed it with an oath. God did this so that, by two unchangeable things in which it is impossible for God to lie, we who have fled to take hold of the hope set before us may be greatly encouraged. We have this hope as an anchor for the soul, firm and secure. It enters the inner sanctuary behind the **curtain**.

Who is God encouraging in these verses? He is encouraging those who have fled from the world's sinful, empty promises to take hold of the Hope of Jesus Christ and His promises. You are a vessel of the Holy Spirit of God set upon the river of life. Your journey will include both smooth sailing and rough waters. Storms and turbulent waters will strive to shipwreck you or run you ashore, rendering you ineffective on life's journey.

Your hope is found in God's Word to you—His incredible promises of provision, protection, and strength for the journey. Your hope is a firm and secure anchor hooked into **the Rock** of Ages Himself—Jesus Christ! He is an unbreakable, spiritual lifeline to God. He sits at the right hand of the Father interceding and cheering for you.

Fix your hope upon your Trustworthy Rock; He is a Loyal and Safe Guide, firm and secure regardless of the wind, waves, and turbulent seas you may encounter.

To what or to whom have you anchored your life?

Carefully Consider

You only get one earthly life; are you carefully considering your steps as you walk through it? You must be careful whose words you consider and follow. Do not be easily enticed and persuaded by everything you are told. Test everything you are told by the faithful truth of God's Word. Ask the Holy Spirit for discernment. Ask Him to give you a check in your spirit if you are placing your confidence in false teachers or false doctrines. Be wise and cautious! It is so easy to follow your fleshly desires and look for teachers who will tell you what your itching ears want to hear. You belong to God Almighty! You are not a simpleton; you are royalty—a child of the **King of kings**.

Abba Father has good, sound teachings to guide you and grow you. Will you ask your Father for wisdom and discernment and then carefully consider your steps? In doing this, you will avoid much trouble and danger in this life.

Be Generous

1 Timothy 6:17, 18 (NIV)

Command those who are rich in this present world not to be arrogant nor to put their hope in wealth, which is so uncertain, but to put their hope in God, who richly provides us with everything for our enjoyment. Command them to do good, to be rich in good deeds, and to be generous and willing to share.

To whom much is given, much is expected (Luke 12:48). You were made to give and to be generous. God is the Giver of all Good things; and if He has given you riches, He has given you opportunity to bless others. Jesus encourages His followers by assuring them they are more blessed when giving than receiving (Acts 20:35). His ways are counter-intuitive to our ways, for it would seem the more we give the less we will have. But God is always trustworthy. His Word tells us, "Give, and it will be given to you. A good measure, pressed down, shaken together and running over, will be poured into your lap. For with the measure you use, it will be measured to you" (Luke 6:38; NIV). Your generosity toward others opens many opportunities for blessings. You set an example for other brothers and sisters and encourage them to share; and along the way, God will repay your generosity in His own special way. And you build up your soul by demonstrating your thanksgiving to God for His blessings.

When you demonstrate your trust in Jesus by giving (rather than by hoarding temporary riches), you will greatly strengthen your faith. Also, your generosity compels those in need to thank God for providing through you. You will be enriched with a deep-seated satisfaction by your willingness to share the blessings God has given you.

Jesus had much to say about giving to and caring for those in need. "Then the King will say to those on His right hand, 'Come, you blessed of My Father, inherit the kingdom prepared for you from the foundation of the world: for I was hungry and you gave Me food; I was thirsty and you gave Me drink; I was a stranger and you took Me in; I was naked and you clothed Me; I was sick and you visited Me; I was in prison and you came to Me.' Then the righteous will answer Him, saying, 'Lord, when did we see You hungry and feed You, or thirsty and give You drink? When did we see You a stranger and take You in, or naked and clothe You? Or when did we see You sick, or in prison, and come to You?' And the King will answer and say to them, 'Assuredly, I say to you, inasmuch as you did it to one of the least of these My brethren, you did it to Me'" (Matthew 25:34–40; NKJV).

You will be enriched with a

deep-seated satisfaction by

your willingness to share the

blessings God has given you.

Enter the Pleasant Land

> ## Leviticus 20:24 (NLT)
> "But I have promised you, 'You will possess their land because I will give it to you as your possession—a land flowing with milk and honey.' I am the LORD your God, who has set you apart from all other people."
>
> ## Psalm 106:24, 25 (NLT)
> The people refused to enter the pleasant land, for they wouldn't believe his promise to care for them. Instead, they grumbled in their tents and refused to obey the LORD.

You are invited to enter the pleasant land of comfort, care, love, guidance, **forgiveness**, confidence, and goodness of God. Your **Abba** God is the Father of Compassion and the God of all Comfort (2 Corinthians 1:3, 4). He eagerly awaits opportunities to comfort you in all your troubles. His Love for you abounds, embrace His Love with open arms of trust. Because of His great Love for you, He made you alive with Christ even when you were dead in sins (Ephesians 2:4, 5). It is by His amazing **Grace** you are freed from bondage (Galatians 5:1) to live in the pleasant lands. Please do not dishonor Him by complaining and refusing to see His **Grace** in your life. Will you choose to believe His promise to guide you always, to satisfy your every need, and to give you strength for the journey? (See Isaiah 58:11.)

Entry into the pleasant land requires that you deal properly with sin. First, you must acknowledge your sin and seek God's **forgiveness**. David, whom God considered a man after His own heart (Acts 13:22), understood this; he said to the Lord, "I said to myself, 'I will **confess** my rebellion to the LORD.' And you forgave me! All my guilt is gone" (Psalm 32:5; NLT). Secondly, you must allow **forgiveness** to flow through your life to others. Jesus said, "If you forgive those who sin against you, your heavenly Father will forgive you" (Matthew 6:14; NLT). Follow the wisdom of God's Word and walk in freedom! Stay out of the wasteland of a hard, unforgiving heart.

Do you walk in the pleasant lands or the grumbling wastelands? The best way to keep from wandering into the wilderness of grumbling is to receive God's promises of Goodness for your life. The LORD is Good to those whose hope is in Him, to those who seek Him (Lamentations 3:25). Commit your mind to knowing His promises and believe in your heart that, in all things, He is working Good into your life because you have chosen to enter the pleasant land of God.

Follow the wisdom of God's

Word and walk in freedom!

Be Strong in the Lord

Daniel 11:32b (HCSB)
The people who know their God will be strong and take action.

You have been offered an amazing opportunity to know God! He is Perfect, **Omniscient**, **Omnipotent**, **Omnipresent**, Eternal, Pure, and Holy and He makes Himself available to you—a mere mortal. What a gift of **Grace**! Do not make light of this incredible opportunity.

Knowing God opens incredible doors for you. The more time you spend in His Word getting to know Him, the more readily you trust Him and the deeper your love for Him grows. Knowledge of Him opens the eyes of your heart to see Him moving in your life. You will notice transforming changes in your attitude and behavior as you come to know your God. Instead of falling apart under stress and bad news, you learn to cling to the strong arm of God. You come to recognize His very presence and begin to sense His guidance. The more you seek Him the more you perceive Him; and this will result in increased spiritual strength.

Will you start taking action by sharing everything with Him and accepting His Peace, which transcends all understanding (Philippians 4:7), because you know He can be trusted to work everything out for good (Romans 8:28)?

Do you know Him? You can experience His divine Strength when you come to know the **Omnipotent** One. Don't let anything keep you from knowing Him!

Belief vs. Trust

Romans 3:30, 31 (NLT)
There is only one God, and he makes people right with himself only by faith, whether they are Jews or Gentiles. Well then, if we emphasize faith, does this mean that we can forget about the law? Of course not! In fact, only when we have faith do we truly fulfill the law.

James 2:19 (NIV)
You believe that there is one God. Good! Even the demons believe that—and shudder.

If you are a true child of **Abba** God, you are forgiven! You are clean. You are called a saint—a chosen child of God. Does this mean you can forget **God's laws**; no, of course not. Those who say they are Christian but live in habitual patterns of sin have not believed in Jesus. Sure, they may say, "Yes, I am a Christian. I believe." However, there is a big difference between "believing" and "believing *in*." I may believe the fire extinguisher sitting in my bedroom will put out a fire; but unless I use the fire extinguisher to put out the fire, it does me no good whatsoever. When you believe *in* God you demonstrate true faith. You trust Him with everything and everyone in your life. This real faith in Him places your trust in His Word and in His way. Your trust in Him shifts your life and desires.

When you are walking close to God your focus is not on following rules, your focus is on Him. Your mind and heart become in tuned with Father God. As He works within you, your love for Him grows. The more time you spend with Him, the more you think and act like Him; obeying Him becomes a natural outcome and desire.

Psalm 16:5, 7 (The Message) says, "My choice is You, GOD, first and only; and now I find I'm your choice. . . . The wise counsel GOD gives when I'm awake is confirmed by my sleeping heart. Day and night I'll stick with GOD, I've got a good thing going and I'm not letting go."

Is God your first choice? Are you holding fast to Him and refusing to let go? Do you say, "Sure, I believe"; or do you say with confidence and boldness "I believe in and trust in Jesus"?

When you believe in God

you demonstrate true

faith. You trust Him with

everything and everyone in

your life.

Move Forward in Freedom

> **Romans 5:19 (NLT)**
> Because one person disobeyed God, many became sinners. But because one other person obeyed God, many will be made righteous.

As a follower of Christ, you are an earthly child of Adam (the first man and your ancestor) and a spiritual child of God. Adam disobeyed God and caused sin to flourish. Jesus obeyed God and opened the door to **righteousness**; Jesus' "yes" to God triumphed over Adam's "no." **Grace** is greater than sin. You are declared righteous because you believe in Jesus. You are right with God! Of course, sinful choices are available to you; but the Holy Spirit residing in you stands by ready to empower you to choose life over sin.

Before you were a child of God, you lived as child of Adam—everything was all about you. You were not too concerned about **righteousness** or right living. How did living for yourself bless you? Were you joyful, peaceful, or content? When you look back, are you proud of the choices you made? Of course not! Why would you ever entertain that old way of thinking? Move forward, living in the freedom of Christ Jesus. His ways are higher and better than the world's ways. His yoke is easy (Matthew 11:30) and you will be most satisfied when your eyes are on Him, following Him.

Your "yes" to Jesus results in a completely new life; not a cleaned up life, but an actual new life. Oh, follower of Christ, you have a deposit of God's very Spirit in you. Ask the Holy Spirit to help you choose the rich, abundant life He has for you—the righteous life you were made to live!

The King's Pathway

Matthew 7:13, 14 (NLT)
You can enter God's Kingdom only through the narrow gate. The highway to hell is broad, and its gate is wide for the many who choose that way. But the gateway to life is very narrow and the road is difficult, and only a few ever find it.

The wide, open highway of life is tempting. It is the easy, popular way that requires little effort. Many will invite you to wander it with them, taking wrong turns that lead away from God. On this spacious, comfortable, attractive road, you can do what you want and receive other's approval. But this way always leads away from life and toward destruction.

Jesus' teachings will provide you with direction. Chapters 5, 6 and 7 of Matthew contain one of Jesus' teachings called the Sermon on the Mount. In this sermon, Jesus gives insight into how to choose the narrow pathway of God. He encourages you with this Sermon to keep asking Him for guidance. He exhorts you to continue seeking Him—the Author of Truth and Giver of **Grace**.

Jesus teaches that you must be careful as you travel through life. Even if a road claims His Name, never forget **the enemy** is the father of lies—he will never stop trying to deceive you and lead you away from God's path for you. Many wolves (Matthew 7:15) will talk like Christians but really don't know Jesus at all; and they certainly do not follow His teachings. Run! Please do not travel one mile with those who travel the highway to destruction.

You will be tempted to pick and choose from Jesus' teachings. Instead, commit to the King's Pathway. Continually seek Him, listen to Him, and embrace every word that proceeds out the mouth of God Almighty. He promises to hold your hand throughout the entire journey until you are safely at your journey's end—secure in your heavenly home.

Intimately Connected

How do we know if we are right with God? Romans 3:30 tells us, "[God] makes people right with himself only by faith" (NLT). Our trust in Him makes us children of **Abba** Father's. Not everyone receives this incredible Truth of **Grace**. Many will call Him Lord, attend church, even know Scriptures, but never cross the line into placing their trust in Him. Oh, what a sad tragedy! Here is an incredible truth: the more we get to know God the easier it is to trust Him. The more we trust Him, the deeper our love for Him and the greater our desire to obey Him.

God is incredibly Patient with us. He will extend as much **Mercy** and **Grace** as each of us needs to encourage and help us do His will. Not everyone who calls Him "Lord, Lord" will enter the kingdom of heaven. This is not because God has favorites. It is because He has intimates—those who have entered into a close relationship and an ongoing dialogue with their Savior.

Are you intimately connected to your Savior?

Lord Means Master

Matthew 7:22, 23(NLT)

"On **judgment day** many will say to me, 'Lord! Lord! We prophesied in your name and cast out demons in your name and performed many miracles in your name.' But I will reply, 'I never knew you. Get away from me, you who break **God's laws.**'"

I never knew you." Oh, what sorrow and despair that simple sentence from Jesus would evoke. Does He know you? You may call Him "Lord," but it means nothing if you have not made Him your Master. An outward proclamation is empty without an inward declaration of the heart. Romans 10:9 states clearly that "if you **confess** with your mouth that Jesus is Lord and believe in your heart that God raised Him from the dead, you will be **saved**" (NLT). Once you receive His **salvation**, you can be sure He knows you (John 10:14).

In order to bless His children, God may enable an unbeliever to perform flashy works. The **devil** himself or his demons may perform miraculous works, speak in tongues, or even seem to drive out demons. People may be impressed with works from a heart not surrendered to Jesus; but Jesus is not the least bit impressed and will tell them plainly, "I never knew you; away from me, you evildoers!"

Will you seek God and discover how to live your new life? This is the way to live that is acceptable to God. Hebrews 12:14 says we should "work at living in peace with everyone, and work at living a holy life, for those who are not holy will not see the Lord" (NLT). **Grace** and Love are God's approved ways of life. One may speak in the tongues of men or of angels, fathom all mysteries, have incredible knowledge, and give all to the poor, but without a heart that loves Jesus, nothing is gained (1 Corinthians 13:1–3)!

Have you fallen in love with **Abba**? Does He know you?

You Must Choose

1 John 2:15 (NLT)

Do not love this world nor the things it offers you, for when you love the world, you do not have the love of the Father in you.

Do you love the world or the Father? You cannot love both (Matthew 6:24). You are either living for Him or you are living for the world.

What does love for the world mean? King Solomon, whose wisdom is acclaimed, wrote about this in Ecclesiastes. During a part of his life, he believed fame, fortune, beautiful women, fine wine, intelligence, and all the comforts of this world would bring him happiness and fulfillment. But, at the end of his life, this wise man looked back at his foolish choices to love the world and concluded it was all meaningless, like chasing the wind (Ecclesiastes 1:14). Here is his final conclusion: fear God and obey His commands, for this is the duty of all mankind (Ecclesiastes 12:13).

To live the world's way is to make life all about you. You are the center point from which you make all your decisions. Whatever feels good to you seems right. You want everything for yourself and you want to appear important. You want, want, want and find yourself like King Solomon—chasing the wind.

There is no room for what Jesus wants for you when you love the world. Do not be deceived by the emptiness the world offers compared to what Jesus offers. He offers purpose in this life, true joy, peace, contentment, guidance, and love throughout your days, and eternal bliss in His presence forever. The things of this world are temporary and pale in comparison to the riches of God's kingdom; the things of God are satisfying and lasting.

Do you love and live for the world or for **Abba** Father?

Rise with Him

Jesus is worthy of your adoration, worship, trust, and loyalty. He is the only One in all of human history who claimed to be God (John 10:30) and then proved it before many **witness**es. Jesus performed unbelievable miracles that amazed those who saw; but to actually die and rise from the dead was His final proof to all that He alone deserves the title of Lord and Savior. No one can approach the Father except by believing in Jesus Christ (John 14:6).

Jesus was not just a good man or simply a wise prophet. He was God in flesh and bone. And He poured out His life, shedding His blood until He died on the cross for you. He was not stolen off the cross before dying, and His body was not stolen from the tomb. He died an excruciating death on the cross; then He did what only God could do—He rose from the dead and lived again!

He died and was resurrected to bring **salvation** and abundant life to every nation and every tongue. He alone has the power to give **forgiveness** and offer new life for all—for male and female, for the educated and uneducated.

Repent—change your mind and direction and turn toward God. Recognize how sin brings death and destruction and open your heart to Jesus; He offers you a new life filled with the same power that resurrected His body from the tomb. Jesus rose from the dead and you can know the same victory over death. Jesus rose to a new life; you can, too!

Jesus was not just a good

man or simply a wise

prophet. He was God in flesh

and bone.

It is Finished

Before Jesus, priests of God offered **sacrifice** after **sacrifice** for the **remission** of sin (Hebrews 9:22). The blood of goats, sheep, cattle, turtledoves, or pigeons was shed; their lives were **sacrifice**d and their blood "covered" a person's sins for a time. But sin continued to grow and grow. People simply could not follow **God's Law**—the only way to God before Jesus came to earth as **Messiah**. (This is known as the **Old Covenant**.) Sinful people were simply not capable of obeying **God's Law**; they were simply not that good. So God sent Jesus to be our **High Priest**—to offer the perfect **sacrifice** once and for all—to enact a **New Covenant**.

Jesus, the perfect, sinless Son of God and **Son of man**, chose to spill His life—to become the **sacrifice** that would cover all sin for all time. His clean blood was shed in order to perfect imperfect you. Jesus did away with the old system of offering continual **sacrifice**s for sin. His death on the cross finished it! No more **sacrifice**s required.

When you accept Jesus' **sacrifice** on your behalf; when you accept Him as your Savior, He gives you His Holy Spirit as a guarantee in your soul (2 Corinthians 5:5). The Holy Spirit confirms God's words of Truth and **Grace**, writes them on your mind, and solidifies them in your heart (John 14:26).

Jesus forever wiped out your sins when you believed in Him; God will remember them no more (Hebrews 8:12). Through Jesus, you have been made clean—sinless in the eyes of God.

Will you hold on tightly to your Lord without wavering from the Hope you have in Jesus (Hebrews 10:23)? God promises you can have eternal life through His Son (John 3:16); and **Abba** God can be trusted to keep His promises.

Jesus, the perfect, sinless Son

of God and Son of Man,

chose to spill His life—to

become a sacrifice that

would cover all sin

for all time.

Develop Endurance

Romans 5:3, 4 (NLT)

We can rejoice, too, when we run into problems and **trials**, for we know that they help us develop endurance. And endurance develops strength of character, and character strengthens our confident hope of **salvation**.

Philippians 1:6 (NLT)

And I am certain that God, who began the good work within you, will continue his work until it is finally finished on the day when Christ Jesus returns.

Because you believe in Jesus, He views you as His perfect child. When you have trusted Him with your life and believed in His death and resurrection, you are clothed in Jesus' **righteousness**; when God looks at you He sees the perfection of His Son (2 Corinthians 5:21).

However, you are going to make mistakes this side of heaven. Things you think and say may keep you from feeling like a child of God. You may doubt, feel hopeless, and know times of struggle. During those times, you must endure! Press on (Philippians 3:13, 14), asking Jesus for help, strength, and guidance. Perseverance will produce godly character within you (Romans 5:3, 4). As you develop strength of character, you become more confident of whom you are in Christ. No matter what, will you choose to keep on holding Jesus' hand?

God is working in you, strengthening your relationship with Him. Will you let Him continue to work in you—building your character and establishing endurance in your soul?

God has started a very good work in you; will you allow Him to bring it to completion (Philippians 1:6)?

You are Presentable

Hebrews 10:20-22 (NLT)

By his death, Jesus opened a new and life-giving way through the **curtain** into the Most Holy Place. And since we have a great **High Priest** who rules over God's house, let us go right into the presence of God with sincere hearts fully trusting him. For our guilty consciences have been sprinkled with Christ's blood to make us clean, and our bodies have been washed with pure water.

Go to **Abba** God for everything with a sincere heart, fully trusting Him. Do not hesitate to run to Him because you feel unworthy or guilty. You are "presentable" to Him because you are cleansed by the blood of Christ.

Jesus' perfect, holy **sacrifice** of His life for you secures your eternal **redemption**. (To redeem means to be released from, delivered from, or ransomed from.) He paid for your release from sin's captivity. His new way for you does not include living with a guilty conscience. You have been offered His amazing gift of freedom: freedom to live a better life, freedom to live the way you were created to live, free to live in **fellowship** with Jesus. You honor Him when you hold tightly to His promise of **salvation**. He can be trusted!

Will you encourage others to keep trusting Him? Will you persevere in loving fellow brothers and sisters and think of new ways to "motivate one another to acts of love and good works" (Hebrews 10:24; NLT)?

Produce Godly Fruit

Matthew 7:16-18 (NIV)
"By their fruit you will recognize them. Do people pick grapes from thorn bushes, or figs from thistles? Likewise, every good tree bears good fruit, but a bad tree bears bad fruit. A good tree cannot bear bad fruit, and a bad tree cannot bear good fruit."

Matthew 21:43 (NIV)
"Therefore I tell you that the kingdom of God will be taken away from you and given to a people who will produce its fruit."

Hebrews 10:35, 36 (NLT)
So do not throw away this confident trust in the Lord. Remember the great reward it brings you! Patient endurance is what you need now, so that you will continue to do God's will. Then you will receive all that he has promised.

There are two different kinds of spiritual "fruit trees" that produce vastly different "fruit." There is the wonderful fruit the Holy Spirit produces when you allow Him to guide your life—this fruit nourishes your soul and, in turn, allows you to nourish others. But **the enemy** can also cause you to produce fruit; he delights in stirring up your sinful nature and producing his poisonous fruit in you. You have the power and freedom to choose which fruit is produced in your life.

You are constantly presented with choices. Will you worry and fret, producing poisonous fruit; or will you cast your cares upon Jesus (1 Peter 5:7) and allow His Spirit to produce the fruit of peace and well-being? In difficult relationships, do you ask the Lord for His heart toward the difficult ones and treat them as you would like to be treated; or do you spray poison with your impatient, cutting words? In seemingly impossible situations, do you allow **the enemy** to lure you into despair; or do you do as Zephaniah 3:16, 17 reminds you; "Cheer up! Don't be afraid." God is with you and He is a Strong Warrior.

Will you thank Him for His ability to save you and help you? Will you praise Him for His Faithful Love and ask Him to calm your heart with His Love. Your confident trust in the Lord produces nourishing fruit which is healthy for you today and rewarding for you for all of eternity. From whose fruit tree are you partaking?

You have the power and

freedom to choose which

fruit is produced in your life.

Dressed in Righteousness

Isaiah 61:10 (NLT)

I am overwhelmed with joy in the LORD my God! For he has dressed me with the clothing of **salvation** and draped me in a robe of **righteousness**. I am like a bridegroom in his wedding suit or a bride with her jewels.

You are lavishly clothed because of your faith in Jesus; by God's amazing **Grace**, He has covered you with **salvation**. He has **saved** you forever and stands by to save you from all your questions, doubts, and troubles. He outfitted you in a robe of **righteousness**. You are special and greatly valued to Him. You are as beautiful and as cleaned up as a bride or bridegroom on their special day. There is absolutely no condemnation found in you. He sees you as His holy, perfect, acceptable, and righteous child. You may not feel holy and righteous; but you are draped in a robe of **righteousness**. You do not look like your old self to God. You look like Jesus. Your robe of **righteousness** is a gift to be received and worn; it is not something you can earn. It is a gift. Receive it and wear it.

You are either right with God or you are not. You are seen by Him as righteous or unrighteous. There is no middle ground, it is an either/or situation. Romans 10:9, 10 (NASB) says, "if you **confess** with your mouth Jesus as Lord, and believe in your heart that God raised Him from the dead, you will be **saved**; for with the heart a person believes, resulting in **righteousness**, and with the mouth he **confess**es, resulting in **salvation**."

Have you believed, fully trusted in, and relied on Jesus as your Savior? Will you ask Him to help you fully trust Him today? Will you rejoice as your spiritual ancestor, Isaiah, rejoiced? Are you dressed with the clothing of **salvation** and draped in a robe of **righteousness**?

What Do You Carry?

Abba Father has a plan and purpose just for you. He has clothed you in a wonderful comfortable robe of **righteous-ness**. He tells you clearly in His Word how to live for Him. Do not weigh yourself down with unnecessary burdens. His yoke (or way to live) is light and easy to bear (Matthew 11:30) and His burdens are never more than you can endure (1 Corinthians 10:13). Do not carry with you heavy weights of unbelief and distrust; your walk will be slow and wearisome. Do not add to His perfect robe of **righteousness**.

Will you choose to walk in the freedom of belief? Will you flee from temptations and sin? **The enemy** loves to lure you to enter the sinful paths. These paths are filled with trouble and are not meant for you, righteous child of God. Run from sin, ask for direction, and move one foot of trust in front of the other. Praise Jesus in your heart for never leaving you or forsaking you (Hebrews 13:5). Keep your focus on Him, thanking Him for His provision, strength, and protection for each day. Prepare for tomorrow with Him, but don't *worry* about tomorrow; tomorrow will take care of itself (Matthew 6:34).

Will you choose to hold fast to the hand of Jesus while you run this race of life? He promises He will always be running right by your side.

Coat of Many Colors

> **Colossians 3:12, 13 (NLT)**
> Since God chose you to be the holy people he loves, you must clothe yourselves with tenderhearted **mercy**, kindness, humility, gentleness, and patience. Make allowance for each other's faults, and forgive anyone who offends you. Remember, the Lord forgave you, so you must forgive others.

What does your robe of **righteousness** look like? Your robe should be formed of the glorious colors of compassion, kindness, humility, gentleness, patience, and **forgiveness**. Did you forget you were wearing it for all to see?

Your robe of **righteousness** clothes you in love for others; but it provides for your own well-being, as well. There is no better place to be than in God's perfect will for you. This is the place where you find true meaning and contentment in life. The Lord Jesus Himself set the perfect example for you and then gave you robes of **righteousness** to wear. But whether you wear them or not is up to you.

Do not neglect to put the right clothes on today! Will you ask the Holy Spirit within you to guide you in all Truth and **Grace**? Will you ask Him to help you by giving you His thoughts of compassion, kindness, humility, gentleness, patience, and **forgiveness** toward others? Will you ask Him to give you the desire to demonstrate **righteousness** toward others?

You are **Abba** Father's chosen, **saved**, and dearly-loved child. Are you clothed properly as a child of your Holy King?

Judge Only Yourself

Romans 8:1 (NLT)

So now there is no condemnation for those who belong to Christ Jesus.

Romans 14:10-12 (NLT)

So why do you condemn another believer? Why do you look down on another believer? Remember, we will all stand before the judgment seat of God. For the Scriptures say,

"As surely as I live," says the LORD, "every knee will bend to me, and every tongue will **confess** and give praise to God." Yes, each of us will give a personal account to God.

As a follower of Jesus, there is no condemnation for you! Hallelujah! You do and will stand cleansed and righteous before the Father.

One day, you will stand before the Father to give an account for your life (2 Corinthians 5:10). (Please remember, you will give an account for you and no one else, so do not be a busybody. Focus on your own life and how you are living. Do you mind your spiritual business?) For the follower of Christ, the Judgment Seat (also known as the **Bema Seat**) is not a place where sins will be judged. You are in Christ Jesus, therefore, there is no condemnation awaiting you (Romans 8:1). The **Bema Seat**, for you, will be a place where you are rewarded for trusting Jesus with your life. You will also be rewarded for your life of serving Him and giving to others in His Name.

Paul, in the Book of Timothy, tells you there is a crown awaiting those who live by God's rules and a crown of **righteousness** for those who eagerly look forward to His appearing (2 Timothy 4:8). The Book of James says the crown of life will be given to the one who perseveres under **trial**s and is faithful to God (James 1:12). The Apostle Peter says the crown of glory awaits godly leaders who diligently and lovingly care for their flocks (1 Peter 5:3, 4). There may be many more crowns not mentioned in God's Word. But you can be sure there are many rewards awaiting God's faithful ones.

Will you press on, ambassador for Christ (2 Corinthians 5:20)? There is a glorious awards ceremony planned just for you. Oh, how He loves you!

One day, you will stand

before the Father to give an

account of your life.

Witness for Christ

> **1 Corinthians 15:4–6a (NLT)**
> Christ died for our sins, just as the Scriptures said. He was buried, and he was raised from the dead on the third day, just as the Scriptures said. He was seen by Peter and then by the Twelve. After that, he was seen by more than 500 of his followers at one time.

What are the absolute essentials of our Christian faith? Paul tells us that Christ died for our sins. This was prophesied for hundreds of years before He lived, died, was buried, and was raised from the dead on the third day. The fact of His resurrection was **witness**ed by more than 500 people. This is no fairy tale and it is not possible to say Jesus was just a great prophet. There are too many **witness**es and too many documented details proving Jesus was on earth, died, and was resurrected!

In *The Case for the Real Jesus,* author Lee Strobel shares this point: "In terms of ancient manuscripts writings, less than 200 years after the event are considered very reliable. Paul wrote many of his letters less than 40 years after Jesus' death."[1]

We have over 24,000 manuscripts of the New Testament and several non-Christian sources all giving the same accounts of Jesus. Although there is overwhelming evidence for the life of Jesus on earth, the greatest evidence for Jesus is all the Christians—many thousands who chose to die for Him rather than to deny Him. People will die for what they know in their heart is truth, but they will not exchange their life for a lie.

Do you know the Truth? Are you a reliable **witness** for Christ?

1. Strobel, Lee. *The Case for the Real Jesus: A Journalist Investigates Current Attacks on the Identity of Christ.* Grand Rapids, MI: Zondervan, 2009. Print.

Citizen of Heaven

1 Corinthians 15:22, 30, 32 (NLT)

Just as everyone dies because we all belong to Adam, everyone who belongs to Christ will be given new life . . . And why should we ourselves risk our lives hour by hour? . . . And what value was there in fighting wild beasts—those people of Ephesus—if there will be no resurrection from the dead? And if there is no resurrection, "Let's feast and drink, for tomorrow we die!"

Paul believed in Jesus' death and resurrection. He believed Jesus died so that all who put their trust in Him will live forever with Him. Paul understood the "real Paul" was an immortal soul and this earth was only his temporary home.

Paul lived at a time when it was very dangerous to be a Christian. In his day, Christians constantly faced the threat of death. Paul himself was whipped five times with 39 lashes, three times he was beaten with rods, and once he was even stoned! He was often thrown in prison where he was beaten and starved. And he spent endless days under house arrest—unable to lead his life in freedom.

Paul was a respected student of the Word of God as a young man. Why would He forsake a highly-esteemed, comfortable position to face discomfort, ridicule, hatred, and physical suffering? Why not be like everyone else and eat, drink, and be merry? Paul risked it all because he knew, like you, that his real citizenship was not here on earth. Paul was convinced of his new life to come.

You are a citizen of heaven. You will be resurrected to a glorious new life with every joy and comfort you can imagine. Does your new life to come undergird your choices today? Do you know the incredible future that awaits you?

Double-Minded Mistake

Hebrews 13:8, 9a (NLT)

Jesus Christ is the same yesterday, today, and forever. So do not be attracted by strange, new ideas.

James 1:5–8 (NKJV)

If any of you lacks wisdom, let him ask of God, who gives to all liberally and without reproach, and it will be given to him. But let him ask in faith, with no doubting, for he who doubts is like a wave of the sea driven and tossed by the wind. For let not that man suppose that he will receive anything from the Lord; he is a double-minded man, unstable in all his ways.

Man's knowledge is always changing. People used to think the earth was flat; and doctors once thought sickness could be cured by allowing leeches to suck out the bad blood. New research and technology have taught us better.

Jesus' teachings, however, never change. They were true yesterday, they are true today, and they will still be true tomorrow. The truth of God is the only thing we can trust. So we should seek God's truth above all. He alone is **Omniscient**. He knows everything; of course He does, because He created everything and put it in its place.

God wants you to know Truth and He loves to share His Wisdom with you. He encourages you to seek Him, promising you will find Him when you seek Him with all your heart (Jeremiah 29:13). When you find Him, you will have found the Source of all wisdom. James 1:5 encourages you to ask your Generous **Abba** Father for wisdom (which includes guidance and discernment) and He will give it to you! The Message translation puts it this way: "If you don't know what you're doing, pray to the Father. He loves to help. You'll get his help, and won't be condescended to when you ask for it. Ask boldly, believingly, without a second thought. People who "worry their prayers" are like wind-whipped waves. Don't think you're going to get anything from the Master that way, adrift at sea, keeping all your options open."

Do not be the Christian who is adrift in stormy seas. Set your mind that you will believe your **Abba**'s every word and hold tight to God's never-changing Word of Truth. He has given you everything you need to be wise on this earth. Will you stop letting the winds of this world toss you about? Will you diligently seek **Abba** and grow in His wisdom?

God wants you to know

Truth and He loves to share

His Wisdom with you.

Harvest with Shouts of Joy

> **1 Samuel 1:2, 7, 11, 19b, 20 (NLT)**
>
> Elkanah had two wives, Hannah and Peninnah. Peninnah had children, but Hannah did not . . . Year after year it was the same—Peninnah would taunt Hannah as they went to the Tabernacle. Each time, Hannah would be reduced to tears and would not even eat . . . And [Hannah] made this vow: "O LORD of Heaven's Armies, if you will look upon my sorrow and answer my prayer and give me a son, then I will give him back to you. He will be yours for his entire lifetime, and as a sign that he has been dedicated to the Lord, his hair will never be cut" . . . the LORD remembered her plea, and in due time she gave birth to a son. She named him Samuel, for she said, "I asked the LORD for him."

You may encounter trouble and sorrows as you faithfully seek the Lord. Some in your own family may insult you, slander you, and harass you because you follow Jesus. Some in your own church or other so-called Christians may try to provoke you because of your commitment to Jesus. **The enemy** usually uses those closest to you or those whom you would least expect to try to hinder your walk. Your frustrations and hurts may reduce you to tears.

Oh, child of God, a better day is coming. Your **Abba** Lord does not miss a thing; He sees every tear that falls from your eye and as your Protector and **Advocate** He is working on your behalf. Will you turn to Him when you are in need?

Psalm 126:5, 6 says, "Those who plant in tears will harvest with shouts of joy. They weep as they go to plant their seed, but they sing as they return with the harvest" (NLT). God is producing a harvest through you! Will you keep planting His seeds of Truth and **Grace** in your soul, even through tears? If you do, a bountiful harvest awaits you!

Vision and Wisdom

Proverbs 29:18 (KJV)
Where there is no vision, the people perish: but he that keepeth the law, happy is he.

Perhaps you have heard the acronym for BIBLE: Basic Instructions Before Leaving Earth. You need direction, you need truth, you need love and **grace**, and you need a vision for the course of your life—God's vision. God designed you with these needs; you need His vision and His wisdom to succeed in life. Proverbs 1 asks how long will fools hate knowledge and despise wisdom and instruction. Proverbs 1:32 says that simpletons turn away from God to death. Fools are destroyed by their own complacency. The fear of the Lord is the beginning of wisdom.

Jesus taught in John 6:63 that His words are Spirit-filled and life-making. His words, when heeded and planted, change lives. When you trust in Jesus, fall in love with Him, and follow His words, everything changes. Your life changes, your dreams change, your purposes change, your thinking changes, and your vision for the future changes. Your eternal vision begins to develop and your desire to serve **Abba** Father and others deepens. You are no longer like **dry bones**, aimlessly wandering in the desert (see Ezekiel 37:1–14).

Will you taste and see that the Lord is Good? Will you devour His Word and ask Him to place His vision in you today? People perish for lack of vision.

Soul Rest

You will experience different seasons: in this life: there will be times to laugh and times to cry, times to rest and times to work hard (Ecclesiastes 3:1–8). Your walk with Jesus will include days of testing and temptations. You will always have challenges this side of heaven.

But, as a Christian, do not run *from* your **trial**s; run *to* Jesus. Will you tell Him you are casting your cares upon Him (1 Peter 5:7)? Can you visualize yourself handing over your troubles and then asking Him for wisdom and thanking Him for moving on your behalf? When challenges arise, your trust in Jesus is forced into the open for you to see. This is an opportunity to trust Him more, take His hand, and relax in His divine control. The more you resist, the more difficult you make your own circumstances. You were made to be close to Jesus; He is drawing you into a deeper, more trusting relationship. He longs to quiet you with His Love (Zephaniah 3:17). Will you allow Him?

Will you hang unto Him with all your strength? If you will, you will see His Goodness and your soul will be at rest again . . . because His Love never fails (Lamentations 3:22).

Holy Spirit Guidance

As a believer in Jesus Christ, you have a deposit of His Spirit in you! You have the Holy Spirit; He is the Spirit of Truth and can guide you in **Grace** and Truth. He transforms your thinking by instructing you in God's higher ways and leading you to the paths of righteous living. You have the HOLY SPIRIT OF GOD; but, does the Holy Spirit have you? Are you asking Him for guidance? Are you seeking His instruction or do you think you know better? Who is in control of the details of your life; is He?

When you give yourself to God and invite His Spirit to guide your life, the Holy Spirit exhibits His Fruit (Galatians 5:22, 23) in your surrendered, seeking, and soft heart. On your own, you cannot produce sustaining divine fruit; it must come from its Source—**Abba** Father. His nourishing fruit is the opposite of the poisonous fruit your flesh produces—the fallen and sinful flesh produces impurity, jealousy, sexual immorality, quarreling, worry, pouting, bitterness, ungratefulness, drunkenness, and lust.

When you invite the Holy Spirit to guide you, His divine fruit will eventually manifest itself as love, joy, peace, patience, kindness, goodness, faithfulness, gentleness, and self control. You have the Holy Spirit; will you let Him have you?

Restoration

Ezekiel 37:5, 6 (NLT)

"This is what the **Sovereign** LORD says: Look! I am going to put breath into you and make you live again! I will put flesh and muscles on you and cover you with skin. I will put breath into you, and you will come to life. Then you will know that I am the LORD."

Joel 2:25, 27 (NKJV)

"So I will restore to you the years that the swarming locust has eaten, the crawling locust, the consuming locust, and the chewing locust . . . Then you shall know that I am in the midst of Israel: I am the LORD your God and there is no other."

John 20:22 (NKJV)

And when [Jesus] had said this, He breathed on them, and said to them, "Receive the Holy Spirit."

Romans 6:4 (NKJV)

Therefore we were buried with Him through baptism into death, that just as Christ was raised from the dead by the glory of the Father, even so we also should walk in newness of life.

You were once spiritually dead but you have been resurrected to a new life! In Ephesians 1:13, God's Word tells you how this happens: you heard and really listened to His life-giving Word; having believed, you accepted His Breath of Life, the promised Holy Spirit. Then, as you seek to know and understand Him more, your loyalty and obedient service increases. You will begin to experience His renewed, abundant life!

As you take more and more steps with the Holy Spirit leading, and as you choose to receive God's **Grace** and **Mercy**, which He liberally extends to you, He will restore the wastelands the locusts have eaten—He will return to you all **the enemy** has stolen. He will take the ashes of your former life and fill your future with beauty and hope (Isaiah 61:3). As you learn to trust your All-Powerful, All-Knowing, and Ever-Present, Loving **Abba**, your wasteland of what once was will transform into a well-watered garden of **righteousness**, beauty, truth, and **grace**.

Will you refuse the seeds of doubt, self-pity, anger, worry, and fear borne of the past devastation of **the enemy** and plant seeds of praise, thanksgiving, and trust deep within your heart? As Charles Spurgeon asked, "Will you plant seeds of thanksgiving in the soil of your soul and allow Him to reap sheaves of **grace**"? You can experience **Abba**'s Breath of Life blowing through your soul and be empowered by the Holy Spirit of Truth and **Grace** to walk in "newness of life." You can watch as **Abba** restores to you all **the enemy** has stolen.

Will you seek to really know your **Abba** Lord?

He will take the ashes of

your former life and fill your

future with beauty

and hope.

The Power of Words

Luke 6:45 (NLT)

A good person produces good things from the treasury of a good heart, and an evil person produces evil things from the treasury of an evil heart. What you say flows from what is in your heart.

James 1:26 (NLT)

If you claim to be religious but don't control your tongue, you are fooling yourself, and your religion is worthless.

There is a tight connection between a soft, surrendered heart toward God and a gracious, loving tongue. Jesus said the greatest Commandments God gave are to love Him and to love others (Matthew 22:36–40). Your tongue can express to others how much you love God. It is true, kind words can show the nature of God—they can heal and help; but cutting words wound and maim. Words can pierce deeper than a sword and cause more damage than a knife to the soul. Words can kill dreams, self-esteem, love, and peace. Your tongue is a powerful force.

God gave you the ability to communicate as a gift for good, not as a weapon for harm and evil. Choose to receive His amazing **Grace** and endless Mercies so your words can be a force of life for others (Proverbs 18:21). You cannot give what you have not received, so open your heart to all God wants to pour in and through you. James 3:9, 10 reminds you, "with the tongue we praise our Lord and Father, and with it we curse human beings; who have been made in God's likeness. Out of the same mouth come praise and cursing. My brothers and sisters, this should not be" (NIV). Do not say you are a Christian and, with the same tongue, hurt others made in the very image of God! By the words your tongue speaks, others will know if your religion is worthless or worthy.

Is your tongue under the control of the Holy Spirit?

Don't Fool Yourself

James 1:22 (NLT)
But don't just listen to God's word. You must do what it says. Otherwise, you are only fooling yourselves.

D o not be fooled by **the enemy**'s lies that you can be **saved** by going to church, Bible study, or even by doing good deeds. Do you remember what Jesus will say to the "religious" ones who simply call Him, "Lord, Lord?" He will say, "Away from Me. I never knew you" (Matthew 7:21–23). These people are ones who possess a form of godliness, but do not receive its power. They have head knowledge that never enters their hearts. They know, but fail to do. Only the ones who do the will of the Father will enter heaven. Dead faith—faith without actions (see James 2:20)—does not save.

You can listen to God's Word and even agree with it; but saving faith is demonstrated in a changed life. How you live reflects what you believe. Your good works are not the *cause* of your **salvation**; your good works are the *result* of your **salvation**. It is not enough to say you believe in Jesus, yet never change. This reflects dead faith. Saving faith requires giving your entire being over to Jesus; this results in a new heart and a new spirit. Ezekiel 36:26, 27 says God will remove your heart of stone and give you a soft heart toward Him. He will put His Spirit within you, and cause you to walk in His ways, careful to obey Him.

True faith in Jesus is always demonstrated by new choices and a new heart, which desires Him and His ways. Faith without works is a dead faith because it comes from a heart that has not truly surrendered and trusted in Jesus.

Jesus stands by, waiting for the invitation to give you a new heart and a new spirit. Will you open your life to Him and receive His amazing **Grace**?

Visible Faith

John 13:35 (NKJV)

"By this all will know that you are My disciples, if you have love for one another."

James 2:17 (NLT)

So you see, faith by itself isn't enough. Unless it produces good deeds, it is dead and useless.

Paul tells us in Romans 11:6 and Galatians 2:16 that we are **justified** (made right) with God through trusting in Him and not by the things we do (works). Yet James says faith is not enough; faith must be accompanied by actions (works). Does this issue point to a discrepancy in God's Word? Absolutely not!

You see, it is important to read Scripture passages in context. Paul writes in Ephesians 2:8, 9 that God **saved** you by His **Grace** when you believed in Him. You cannot take any credit for you **salvation**; it is a gift from God. **Salvation** is not a reward for good things you have done, so no one can brag about receiving it. However, Paul goes on to say, "we are [God's] workmanship, created in Christ Jesus for good works, which God prepared beforehand that we should walk in them" (Ephesians 2:10; NKJV). Obviously, faith must be lived out in order to be real.

If you truly are in Christ, you are a new person (2 Corinthians 5:17). If you truly received God's **salvation**, your trust in Jesus will result in a changed life that exhibits good works. And these good works are a product of the love Jesus pours into the hearts of those who belong to Him (Romans 5:5). As a Christian, you are called to represent Jesus to the world. They cannot see Him, they can only see you—His child and a member of His body on earth (1

Corinthians 12:27). The works of love you perform reveal Jesus to a lost and hurting world.

We cannot save ourselves, nor can we save others. Only Jesus is the Way to **Abba** Father (John 14:6). But we can show Jesus' Love through our good works and draw others to His incredible, life-giving Love. In Jesus' own words: "Your love for one another will prove to the world that you are my disciples" (John 13:35; NLT).

If you truly received God's

salvation, *your trust in*

Jesus will result in a changed

life that exhibits good works.

Through His Eyes

You used to run wild before you belonged to Jesus. Now, as a member of His family, you should seek Him and His guidance. As you seek Him, it is important that you leave your past mistakes at the foot of His gracious throne (Hebrews 4:16). He remembers your sins no more (Hebrews 10:17) and He wants you to remember them no more; yesterday is history.

God is calling you to move forward with Him. Are you feeling purposeless? Do you have unfulfilled dreams? Do you know the plans God has for you? If you are calling upon the Holy Spirit, He will, in His perfect timing, impart a vision for your future. If your future seems purposeless and without direction, you most likely are not seeking **Abba** Father's will for you.

As you spend time with Him in His Word, God will communicate to you His amazing and perfect will for your life. He has very specific purposes for you. Why would you blindly move forward without seeking to see your life through His eyes?

Will you slip your hand into His and accept His divine guidance? You cannot even imagine all the incredible moments He has planned for you (Jeremiah 29:11).

The Intentional Life

Philippians 2:12 (NIV)

Therefore, my dear friends, as you have always obeyed—not only in my presence, but now much more in my absence—continue to work out your **salvation** with fear and trembling.

Philippians 3:12–14 (NIV)

Not that I have already obtained all this, or have already arrived at my goal, but I press on to take hold of that for which Christ Jesus took hold of me. Brothers and sisters, I do not consider myself yet to have taken hold of it. But one thing I do: Forgetting what is behind and straining toward what is ahead, I press on toward the goal to win the prize for which God has called me heavenward in Christ Jesus.

Philippians 2:12 is often misinterpreted to suggest it is possible to lose your **salvation** in Christ. If you have given Him your life, you can sleep well knowing you are eternally secure in Jesus. The words "work out" in this passage mean to press on, to keep fighting for, and to stay intentional. Paul (who wrote the Book of Philippians) understood he did not have it all together; but he kept pressing on, determined to keep going and reaching out for Christ—his "goal" and "prize." He chose to focus his eyes forward and to let the past go. He pressed on—running the race wherever God called him.

The phrase from Philippians 2:12 that can seem a bit confusing is "work out your **salvation** with fear and trembling." Does this mean we should fear and tremble, hoping to find **salvation**? No! The word "fear" in this verse means a deep respect and reverence for God Almighty. "Trembling" is the Greek word "*tromos,*" which means to distrust one's own abilities to meet all requirements, causing a state of dependency upon God. Paul is exhorting us to press on, growing closer and closer to Jesus through His Word, leaning on Him for guidance and strength while acknowledging He is God and we are not.

How intentional is the race you are running? Do not turn back; press on toward your heavenly prize promised by God in Christ Jesus.

If you have given Him

your life, you can sleep well

knowing you are eternally

secure in Jesus.

Flowing Waters

In watering others, you are watered. This means when you allow God's **Living Water** (John 7:38) to flow through you to others, you too, are refreshed. You are more blessed in giving than in receiving. When you give, you get so much more in return; when you seek to bring waters of love and laughter to one who suffers, your own cup overflows. When you seek the spiritual good of others, your own spirit is nourished. God made you to be a person of **grace** and goodwill—a generous soul. When you seek to bless others, a wonderful, little miracle happens in you—the eyes of your heart are opened to God's Holy Spirit working through you, giving you tender words you did not know you possessed. He gives you strength you never experienced and a caring heart moved to make a difference in another person's life. When you seek to comfort the sick and hurting, you will often walk away feeling as though you were the one comforted and built up.

A self-centered, isolated person is a malnourished soul. Will you ask **Abba** God for opportunities to reach out to someone in need today? You cannot out give God. Water others and be well-watered yourself.

Run from Temptation

Genesis 37:18, 21, 22a, 26, 27a, 28 (NLT)

When Joseph's brothers saw him coming, they recognized him in the distance. As he approached, they made plans to kill him . . . But when Reuben heard of their scheme, he came to Joseph's rescue. "Let's not kill him. Why should we shed any blood? Let's just throw him into this empty cistern here in the wilderness" . . . Judah said to his brothers, "What will we gain by killing our brother? We'd have to cover up the crime. Instead of hurting him, let's sell him to those Ishmaelite traders" . . . So when the Ishmaelites, who were Midianite traders, came by, Joseph's brothers pulled him out of the cistern and sold him to them for twenty pieces of silver. And the traders took him to Egypt.

Genesis 39:6–12 (NLT)

So Potiphar gave Joseph complete administrative responsibility over everything he owned. With Joseph there, he didn't worry about a thing—except what kind of food to eat! Joseph was a very handsome and well-built young man, and Potiphar's wife soon began to look at him lustfully. "Come and sleep with me," she demanded. But Joseph refused. "Look," he told her, "my master trusts me with everything in his entire household. No one here has more authority than I do. He has held back nothing from me except you, because you are his wife. How could I do such a wicked thing? It would be a great sin against God." She kept putting pressure on Joseph day after day, but he refused to sleep with her, and he kept out of her way as much as possible. One day, however, no one else was around when he went in to do his work. She came and grabbed him by his cloak, demanding, "Come on, sleep with me!" Joseph tore himself away, but he left his cloak in her hand as he ran from the house.

Joseph endured such hardship! He was betrayed by those closest to him, his very family! Not only was he betrayed, but he was sold like an invaluable piece of cloth to Ishmaelite traders, who marched him off to a foreign land. Yet, Joseph clung to **Abba** Father. He knew God would never leave him nor forsake him, although his family had.

Be alert! **The enemy** (Satan) hates it when you are loyal to **Abba** God. During difficult times, he will do all he can to tempt you to be unfaithful to your heavenly Father. When he could not overcome Joseph with troubles, he tempted him with soft, lustful pleasures. And so our enemy will attack you with his lies; he will do all he can to undermine your relationship with **Abba**.

But Joseph remained faithful in the face of **the enemy**'s scheme. Joseph and Potiphar's wife were alone. Who would ever have known if he slept with her? Joseph believed in God; and because he was in an intimate relationship with God, he understood **Abba** God was in the room with them. Joseph knew God would **witness** how he handled this temptation. Joseph could not betray his Lord. Joseph was able to resist the little goodie Potiphar's wife offered because he knew it was really not a "goodie" at all. He knew falling for the temptation would only lead to destruction and trouble. He understood the choice of whether to please God or a human is really no choice at all. Potiphar's wife stole Joseph's cloak, but she could not steal his virtue.

Will you do as Joseph did when presented with an opportunity to sin; will you RUN?

Give God Control

Do you consider yourself as more or better than you actually are? Do you evaluate yourself by comparing yourself to others? Your viewpoint and the actions of others are not the standards; God's Truth is the standard. The world does not set the standard for you, child of God, God's Word does.

If you must evaluate and compare, then compare yourself to your Holy God; then you will realize how far short you fall of His Perfection (Romans 3:23). You are not **Omniscient**, **Omnipresent**, **Omnipotent**, All-Loving, or the Alpha and the Omega—you are not the beginning nor are you the end. To be all you were meant to be, you must empty yourself and be filled with the Holy Spirit of God.

Jesus said, "Blessed are the poor in spirit, for theirs is the kingdom of heaven" (Matthew 5:3; NKJV). Being "poor in spirit" means realizing your need for God in your life. It is becoming desperate for His presence and intervention in all aspects of life. Psalm 34:8 (NLT) says, "Taste and see that the Lord is good, oh, the joys of those who take refuge in Him!" Do you run to Him when you are troubled or do you run to your friends, your wine, your anti-anxiety drug, food, or to the mall? God is Good; He will provide you with everything you need. Of course, He does not give you everything you want, because that is not good for you; but every single need He will provide. As the psalmist says in Psalm 23:1: "The LORD is my shepherd; I have all that I need" (NLT).

Be honest in your evaluation of yourself; you need God! **Jehovah Jireh** (the Lord who Provides) awaits your invitation to fill you with His Spirit. Can you visualize yourself surrendering your control, your fears, and your doubts at the foot of His throne? Will you invite Him to take control? Will you admit your need for Him today and commit to waiting for His guidance while thanking Him for His tender Care over you?

He delights in filling you with His Spirit and bringing good to you.

Your viewpoint and the

actions of others are not the

standards; God's Truth is the

standard.

Sail the River of Life

Ecclesiastes 12:1 (NLT)

Don't let the excitement of youth cause you to forget your Creator. Honor him in your youth before you grow old and say, "Life is not pleasant anymore."

Do you honor your Creator by remembering Him? Do not let today go by without recalling all He has done. You will not get a second chance at living today. Make your peace with God while the day is young! The Lord made this brand new day; rejoice and be glad in it (Psalm 118:24). And let each day, even until your last day, be a new chance to praise and honor your Creator for all He has done.

Understanding you were created by the hand of God gives you purpose and meaning. You were made to walk in alignment with His Ways. Walking with Him saves you from unnecessary suffering and heartache; in His Presence you will find wisdom to guide you. Do you recognize that the fear of the Lord is the beginning of wisdom? Wisdom is like the sail of a ship; with it, you can continually move forward as you travel the river of life; you can even weather the scariest storms.

Will you enjoy your Lord today? Will you ask Him to renew your vigor for Him and for life? Will you ask Him to fill you with the joy and excitement you once knew? Life with the Lord is a breathtaking ride leading to adventures you never imagined possible! Will you remember Him as you sail the river of life?

Flee From Sin

Genesis 34:1–4 (NKJV)
Now Dinah the daughter of Leah, whom she had borne to Jacob, went out to see the daughters of the land. And when Shechem the son of Hamor the Hivite, prince of the country, saw her, he took her and lay with her, and violated her. His soul was strongly attracted to Dinah the daughter of Jacob, and he loved the young woman and spoke kindly to the young woman. So Shechem spoke to his father Hamor, saying, "Get me this young woman as a wife."

1 John 2:15–17 (NKJV)
Do not love the world or the things in the world. If anyone loves the world, the love of the Father is not in him. For all that *is* in the world—the lust of the flesh, the lust of the eyes, and the pride of life—is not of the Father but is of the world. And the world is passing away, and the lust of it; but he who does the will of God abides forever.

Jacob had twelve sons. Most Bible scholars believe Dinah was Jacob's only daughter. It is easy to imagine how spoiled she was in a house full of boys. It is also believed she was fifteen or sixteen when she ventured from her home into forbidden territory—she went "to see the daughters of the land." (The Hebrew word translated here "to see" means to observe their lifestyle, to learn about, to enjoy, to see and to be seen.) Dinah did not seek to hang out with daughters of the King, but with daughters of this world.

Young, spoiled Dinah was somewhere she should not have been; and she certainly should not have ventured out alone. In this ancient culture, such behavior would have been considered very dangerous and inappropriate. Shechem, a prince of the land who was used to getting whatever he wanted, saw Dinah, wanted her, took her, and violated her. The words "He took her" indicate he removed her to an isolated place; not so much by force, but by surprise. Dinah got in too deep; she set herself up by desiring worldly pleasures, and found herself in a place where there was no turning back. Poor Dinah! She was completely disgraced in the eyes of her people, the Israelites. Her lust for the things of the world took her into a place of danger. As a result, she became the victim of Shechem's lust. If only Dinah could have known the wisdom of Paul's words to Timothy, "Flee also youthful lusts; but pursue **righteousness,** faith, love, peace with those who call on the Lord out of a pure heart" (2 Timothy 2:22; NKJV).

Oh, the pain and heartache we suffer when we venture into places we should not be found. A little spark of lust after the world can be fanned into a great, destructive fire. God's Word says to run from anything that stimulates lust because whatever momentary pleasure lust may bring can never be worth the problems sin causes. Run!

Oh, the pain and heartache

we suffer when we venture

into places we should

not be found.

Plant Good Seeds

Psalm 126:5, 6 (NLT)
Those who plant in tears will harvest with shouts of joy. They weep as they go to plant their seed, but they sing as they return with the harvest.

What an incredible encouragement God gives you here! Who are you crying over in your life? Have you tried to share your hope, your joy, or your peace in Jesus with a dear one in your life, to no avail? Keep planting those seeds! God is moving whether your eyes can see Him at work or not. His Words are alive and powerful and they go to work in others' hearts. You plant seeds of Truth and **Grace** every day with your body language, your tone, and your choices.

Some seasons of planting last a lifetime before the harvest is seen. Never give up on another soul! Every person matters; they came from the very hand of God. Cry now, but a day of celebrating is coming! Visualize that day. Will you continue to plant seeds of **Grace** and Truth; asking God for opportunities?

You may weep for your precious one today; but someday you will shout with joy and dance with arms full of praises! God has not given up on your loved one, so you shouldn't either! He desires not one to be lost; no, not one!

Pure Grace

What is pure **Grace**? It is hard for your human mind to grasp. In our human state, we love and give with conditions. God's love is unconditional; it is given regardless of your behavior. He loves you to pieces; you belong to Him. **Grace** means He does not love you more or less based on your performance. There is nothing you can do to make Him love you more. There is no sin you can commit to make Him love you less. He loves you.

You cannot earn what God has already given you. Jesus provided everything for you on the cross. Your walk in **Grace** is not earned; however, it is not without effort. In Matthew 16:24, Jesus told us to follow Him; He was not referring to an effortless walk. Walking in **Grace** requires self-**sacrifice**, the only route to really finding yourself. Walking in **Grace** includes suffering and being uncomfortable because you are a follower of Jesus. Walking in **Grace** does not mean you will not have difficult days or be faced with painful choices.

Luke 13:24 reminds you to make every effort to enter through the narrow gate—Jesus is that Gate; He is the only Way. You can not fit through His gate carrying your self-righteous ways, your self-centeredness, and your pride. You must leave these at the gate, because only a surrendered heart can pass through.

It takes effort to overcome the obstacles to entering His Way. You have to overcome your own flesh, any need for the world's approval, and even **the enemy**'s whispering lies. **Grace** does not exclude effort; it excludes those who would earn God's Love!

You cannot earn what God

has already given you. Jesus

provided everything for you

on the cross.

Humility Brings Blessing

Matthew 5:5 (NLT)
God blesses those who are **humble**, for they will inherit the whole earth.

Why does God promise an incredible blessing if you are **humble**? What does true humility look like? Humility implies an attitude toward God that does not resist Him; but rather, accepts His dealings with you as good. Humility toward difficult people indicates you know your Lord sees all and will deliver you in His perfect timing. Humility also includes the understanding that God allows others' bad behavior to grow you and purify you in Him. The **humble** do not place their trust in their own efforts, but in God's efforts.

True humility demonstrates a teachable spirit. **Humble** people know they don't have all the answers, but they know the One who does! **Humble** people place their confidence in God, because they believe God is watching over them and He will demonstrate His perfect justice. That is why God said the **humble** will inherit the earth. The **humble** are the ones who will reign; they are taken care of by God. Because the truly **humble** trust in their **Omnipotent** God, they do not fear. Fear does not rule over them because they follow the One Who rules the world.

Humbleness is not thinking less of yourself; it is thinking of yourself less and thinking of Him and others more. God blesses the **humble**.

Abundant Life

John 10:10 (NKJV)

The thief does not come except to steal, and to kill, and to destroy. I have come that they may have life, and that they may have it more abundantly.

John 17:3 (NLT)

And this is the way to have eternal life—to know you, the only true God, and Jesus Christ, the one you sent to earth.

Colossians 3:2, 3 (NLT)

Think about the things of heaven, not the things of earth. For you died to this life, and your real life is hidden with Christ in God.

Are you living the abundant life Jesus promised His followers? So many Christians are not. Why? Could it be they are not living the real life God intended them to live?

Jesus said (John 10:10) that the thief (Satan) comes only to steal, kill, and destroy. Satan's tactics always involve lies. His lies can be so subtle they are hard to discern, at times. Some religious leaders teach that Christians should expect health, wealth, and prosperity. The lies of Satan can cause you to believe no trouble should ever come your way. Yet, Jesus said to His followers in Matthew 8:20 (The Message) "Are you ready to rough it? We are not staying in the best inns, you know." Not exactly a picture of wealth and prosperity. Wealth, health, and prosperity are not indicators of the abundant life in Christ.

Paul said that he learned to be quite content, whatever his circumstances (Philippians 4:12, 13). He found the recipe for being happy. Whatever he had, wherever he was, he knew he could make it through anything in the One who made him who he was. Paul understood what Jesus said in John 17:3—real life begins with eternal life and the surety of knowing Jesus.

Are you living the abundant life? Where is your real life hidden . . . in this world or in Christ Jesus?

Wealth, health, and

prosperity are not the

indicators of the abundant

life in Christ.

Growing in Grace and Truth

2 Peter 3:18a (NLT)
Rather, you must grow in the **grace** and knowledge of our Lord and Savior Jesus Christ.

All glory to him, both now and forever! **Amen**.

Are you growing closer to Jesus? Is your relationship growing deeper each day? God gives you **Grace**; He is always standing by, ready to help and engage with you. You, however, must continue to develop and cultivate your relationship with Him. He never forces Himself on you.

The delicious fruit of love, joy, peace, patience, kindness, goodness, faithfulness, gentleness, and self-control (Galatians 5:22, 23) will bud and materialize in your life as your grow in your relationship with Jesus. Growth can be painful at times and can have periods of snail-paced progress. Growing in the promised, abundant life of the **Fruit of the Spirit** can include two steps forward and one step backward. Growth is a continual process of learning, preparing, training, repeating, failing, re-grouping, enduring, rebounding, reclaiming, and succeeding.

Just as a baby learns to walk after many falls, bruises, and bumps, so it will be as you learn to walk in the **Fruit of the Spirit**. Don't let a fall or bruises keep you down. Shortly after learning to walk, a baby is off and running into maturity; and you will grow to strong, stable maturity as you grow in the Lord.

Will you continue to grow in the knowledge of your Savior and become a mature **witness** for Him?

A Clear Conscience

What do you do when your good is returned with evil? How do you react when people slander you and gossip about you because of your walk with Jesus? Peter encourages you to stay close to your Lord and worship Him every day in word and deed. Stay in His Word, sing praise songs to Him; and then when someone asks you about your unusual hope, you can explain it to them.

When you share your Jesus, remember to share with care. Be gentle with others; some take a lot of time and have many questions. Give them **grace** to share whatever obstacles are in their way. Respect where they are coming from. You demonstrate this by really listening to them and understanding their difficulties. Regardless of their response to you and your Jesus, keep your conscience clean by showing patience, respect, and care for them. Their faith is God's responsibility, not yours. Their eternal destination is between them and God. If they speak against you, thank Jesus you belong to Him and answer to Him and not them.

Will you continue to pray for the lost? Will you ask Jesus for His eyes of love and pray those who do not know Him will come to their senses before it is too late?

Betrayal

Psalm 55:12–14 (NLT)

It is not an enemy who taunts me—I could bear that. It is not my
foes who so arrogantly insult me—I could have hidden from them.
Instead, it is you—my equal, my companion and close friend. What
good **fellowship** we once enjoyed as we walked together to the
house of God.

Betrayal by a close friend cuts deep into the heart. In this
Psalm, David is crying to the Lord. He says he could deal
with the hostility of an enemy, but not that of a friend! (Notice
David and his friend once worshiped together in the house of the
Lord!)

Precious and dearly loved child of God, those whom you least
expect may hurt you the most. Christians are humans; they are
always capable of doing good or evil. If evil knocks on your door,
you may experience deep anguish as David did. He said his heart
pounded in his chest and he could not stop shaking (Psalm 55:4,
5). He wished he had wings like a dove so he could fly away and
rest (Psalm 55:6). Can you relate? You are not in heaven yet; you
are still on earth where pain, betrayal, and hurts will occur. If a
friend has brought pain and destruction into your life, perhaps
Abba God is telling you **fellowship** with that person was only for
a season. It is okay to move on; it is good for you to have healthy
boundaries.

Grow from your experiences. David's eyes were opened to his
friend's character. He came to see that his friend broke promises
and spoke smooth words designed to wound. Then David wrote
"I will call on God, and the LORD will rescue me" (Psalm 55:16;
NLT).

Will you call on the Lord? He loves you so much and He longs to demonstrate His Goodness to those who call upon Him, believing He hears them; He moves on their behalf. Will you thank Him when He reveals truth to you even if it is painful to see? He may be protecting you from future heartaches.

Christians are humans; they

are always capable of doing

good or evil.

Talk to Him

John 9:31 (NLT)
We know that God doesn't listen to sinners, but he is ready to hear those who worship him and do his will.

These words were boldly spoken by a poor man to religious Pharisees—the elite. Jesus had just healed the man's blindness and the Pharisees refused to believe Jesus was from God. Jesus did not fit into their set of human standards so they would not accept Him.

Although this poor man had been long blind, he heard God's Truths and listened to God's voice. He worshiped God with his life and longed to honor Him with his choices. He knew God heard his prayers and he believed Jesus healed him. He challenged the Pharisees' heart for God because their motivations focused on exalting themselves and not their Lord. (This is always a red flag with leaders; do they exalt the Lord Jesus or themselves?) God does not respond to prideful, legalistic prayers and motives.

Legalism is a great blinder to **Abba** God's amazing **Grace**. God desires healing and well-being for every soul; yet so many Christians just cannot accept His incredible Love. They focus on insignificant and petty issues, rather than on Jesus Himself.

You can pray to your **Abba** Lord with confidence when your heart is surrendered to Him. Psalm 34:15 says, "The eyes of the LORD watch over those who do right; his ears are open to their cries for help" (NLT). His eye is on you and His ears are open and ready to receive your prayers. Will you talk to Him? He is waiting for you.

Only Seekers Find

Psalm 32:8, 9 (NLT)

The LORD says, "I will guide you along the best pathway for your life. I will advise you and watch over you. Do not be like a senseless horse or mule that needs a bit and bridle to keep it under control."

The horse and mule must be restrained and led with a bit and bridle because they are animals, driven not by reason and understanding, but rather by animalistic desires and passions. You are not an animal without reasoning. You are a child of God knit from His hand and made in His image. Will you allow Him to watch over you and guide you along the path He's created just for you?

In His Word, God gives you the best possible way to live your life. Whenever He says "don't" He is saying, "Stop! I want to protect you." Most pain and difficulty many encounter is from their own faulty choices. God is so Good, Gracious, and Merciful; He has good works for you already planned out and He wants you to fulfill your destiny on earth to His Glory (Ephesians 2:10). His ways are gentle, kind, and trustworthy. He says to ask for wisdom and understanding and He will generously give it to you. Your **Abba** God is not a God of confusion (1 Corinthians 14:33). He has not made it difficult to know Him; He promises that if you seek Him, you will find Him (Proverbs 8:17).

Will you seek **Abba** and His abundant life? Remember, Jesus promised, "For everyone who asks receives, and he who seeks finds" (Matthew 7:8a; NKJV). Are you a seeker of Him?

Will you stop resisting God's leadership and allow Him to guide you? Will you stop being stubborn and difficult? Will you **humble** yourself under His authority (1 Peter 5:6)?

In His Presence

Psalm 89:15 (NLT)

Happy are those who hear the joyful call to worship, for they will walk in the light of your presence, LORD.

Are you happy? Do you feel blessed by God? A negative grumbler or habitual complainer does not have praises for the Lord. Their eyes are not on the Lord at all; that is why they are so unhappy. When you praise God, peace and contentment coats your anxious heart. Praising Him reminds you of Who He is— He is your All-Loving, **Omnipotent**, **Omnipresent**, **Omniscient** God. You are connected to Him at the heart; He has His eye on you and hears your every prayer! Absorb how blessed you are that the Creator of the Universe cares about every hair on your head (Matthew 10:30)! You belong to the One Who promises to care for you, never abandon you, and always tend to your every need. Do you praise Him and thank Him?

A life of worship and praise is a life against nature; it will require that you be intentional in your choices. Paul wrote in Philippians 3:10, 11 that his determined purpose was to know God. Paul set his will to become progressively more deeply and intimately acquainted with the Lord. He wanted to perceive and recognize and understand the wonders of God ever more strongly and ever more clearly. This is a lifestyle of blessing, but one that must be learned.

Don't confuse thanking God with praising Him. When you praise Him, you focus on His character; this helps put your life in perspective and settles your anxious heart. Will you choose an attribute of God from the list included on pages xv through xviii of this book and praise your **Abba** Lord today? In His presence there is healing and new life! Will you enter into His presence with praises to your **King of kings**?

Who Are You?

James 2:22-26 (NLT)
You see, his faith and his actions worked together. His actions made his faith complete. And so it happened just as the Scriptures say: "**Abraham** believed God, and God counted him as righteous because of his faith." He was even called the friend of God. So you see, we are shown to be right with God by what we do, not by faith alone. Rahab the prostitute is another example. She was shown to be right with God by her actions when she hid those messengers and sent them safely away by a different road. Just as the body is dead without breath, so also faith is dead without good works.

Your actions are motivated by your beliefs. If no love, joy, peace, compassion, or generosity is displayed in your life, then these godly actions and reactions do not express what you truly believe. To get a true picture of the beliefs you hold, observe your own choices and interaction with others. What motivates what you do? What are the beliefs that live within your heart?

Have changes happened in your actions and reactions since you accepted Jesus as your Lord and Savior? If you have not experienced changes in your reactions to life or seen your attitudes being transformed, then something is lacking in your relationship with Jesus Christ, your Lord. You may have good ideas about Him and even know many truths about Him. You may even attend church; but without truly surrendering your very mind, heart, and soul to Him, your so-called faith is meaningless. What good is a faith that isn't practiced? Is it apparent to you that faith and works are linked partners; that faith will express itself in works? Belief includes action. What you really believe is made apparent by your actions!

The Message translation of James 2:26 says: "The very moment you separate body and spirit, you end up with a corpse. Separate faith and works and you get the same thing: a corpse." You are not the walking dead! You are a new, vibrantly-alive creature in Christ. Romans 8:16 says "The Spirit Himself testifies with our spirit that we are God's children" (NIV). True Christians cannot deny their Jesus. *You are not who you are because of what you do; you do what you do because of who you are!*

Who are you, a child of God or a child of the world?

To get a true picture of the

beliefs you hold, observe

your own choices and

interaction with others.

Sweet Harmony

James 3:15, 16 (NLT)

For jealousy and selfishness are not God's kind of wisdom. Such things are earthly, unspiritual, and demonic. For wherever there is jealousy and selfish ambition, there you will find disorder and evil of every kind.

Your life is like a field in which you plant seeds. Fruit manifested from seeds of selfishness and jealousy are poisonous; when your life is controlled by your own fleshly desires, confusion, divisiveness, and pain are the result. When you try to look better than others or build yourself up at the expense of others, especially in ministry, you are inviting drama and hurt feelings. You may have some initial success, but eventually things will fall apart.

Do you pray for wisdom when partnering and serving with others? Do you pray for healthy relationships? Do you know the difference between peacemakers and peacekeepers? A peacemaker is gentle, reasonable, and stable. A peacemaker knows how to confront with compassion; always considering the best interest of the other person. A peacekeeper will do anything, even if it's not the wise or godly thing, to avoid conflict. Will you seek to partner with peacemakers instead of peacekeepers? Will you be a Christian who treats others with dignity and honor? Will you ask the Holy Spirit to guide you in Truth and **Grace**?

Will you go before the Lord and ask Him to reveal any jealousy or selfish ambition you might be harboring? Will you **repent** and ask for His **Grace** to enable you to live for His Glory? You have His Spirit living in you; will you plant seeds of compassion and peace with Him, for your own well-being and for the well-being of others?

God Bless America!

Proverbs 28:2 (NLT)
When there is moral rot within a nation, its government topples easily. But wise and knowledgeable leaders bring stability.

Do you pray for your country? You may feel your prayers are like a needle in a haystack to God—so small and insignificant. This is a lie from **the enemy**.

Do you know the story of Elijah from 1 Kings 19? He was a man of God who felt overwhelmed with the moral rot of his nation. When the Lord asked him why he was hiding in a cave; Elijah responded by saying, "I have zealously served the Lord God Almighty. But the people of Israel have broken their **covenant** with you, torn down your altars, and killed every one of your prophets. I am the only one left, and now they are trying to kill me too" (1 Kings 19:10; NLT). The Lord responded by assuring Elijah he was not the only one who still worshiped Him. In fact, there were still 7,000 others who were loyal to God.

You are not alone in your prayers for your country. Will you pray for your country to turn from immorality and back to God and His Love and Truth? Will you pray for our leaders to seek His Wisdom? **Abba** God hears every prayer and every prayer matters to Him. America is worth praying for; God bless America!

Priceless Faith

You will experience **trials**. Everyone does; no one is exempt. **Trials** are an important part of your Christian journey because your faith is tested, purified, and strengthened during **trials**. 1 Peter 2:25 says you were once like a lost sheep with no idea who you were or where you were going. Now you are named and kept for good by the Shepherd of your soul.

Trials test your faith by showing you how well you know your Shepherd. Do you run to Him? Is He your "go to"? Do you trust Him with your problems? Do you cast your cares upon Him? It is good to be tested so you recognize opportunities to trust Him more and know Him better.

Trials also purify your faith. To purify means to cleanse. Just as fire removes the impurities from gold, **trials** help you recognize the impurities of doubt and unbelief you have not yet allowed the Lord to filter from your life. Some **trials** purify your faith by showing you patterns of sin, which need to change.

Finally, **trials** strengthen your faith. **Trials** not only reveal how much you trust and how well you know Jesus; they also serve to strengthen you. When you are privileged to see God moving on your behalf and helping you, your faith in Him is fortified and built up. Every **trial** is meant to strengthen your faith for the next **trial**. According to 1 Peter 4:12-19, you should not be surprised by **trials**, but should continue to commit yourself to God and keep doing what is right through every **trial**. Peter goes on to say that your tried faith is far more precious than mere gold—the most valuable, durable, and purest metal; your faith will carry your soul into eternity. Your faith will result in praise, honor, and glory to **Abba**; very precious indeed!

Trials are an important part

of your Christian journey

because your faith is tested,

purified, and strengthened

during trials.

Incredible Love

Have you received God's incredible love for you? Have you considered what He has written to you? He wrote to you in Lamentations 3:22 that you are not consumed because of His Great Love; His compassions never fail you. He says in 2 Chronicles 16:9 that His eyes range throughout the earth looking for you in order to strengthen you because you are committed to Him. In Isaiah 43:3, 4, He assures you that you are precious and honored in His sight and He loves you. And Isaiah 49:16 says He has engraved you on the palms of His hands! You belong to a God Who adores and loves you to pieces. He is always there for you. It is for freedom that He has set you free (Galatians 5:1)—free to live in the truth that your ever-Loving **Abba** is your Loyal Helper, Healer, and Provider.

Why are you still choosing to wrap the chains of bondage around your heart by entertaining lies about yourself and your God? You wonder why you cannot seem to embrace this abundant life of a Christian—a life that should be joyful, free, and loving. Perhaps everything looks fine on the outside, but something is terribly wrong on the inside. Will you run to your Tender, Caring, and problem-solving **Abba** Lord? He is responsible for you and will help you. Will you ask Him to reveal any lies you have allowed into your mind, heart, and life? Will you ask Him to help you break those chains of bondage around your heart by uncovering and dismantling all the lies with His never-failing Love and Truth? Will you thank Him for the privilege to live His abundant life?

Harvest of Right Living

Hebrews 12:5, 6 (NLT)

And have you forgotten the encouraging words God spoke to you as his children? He said, "My child, don't make light of the LORD's discipline, and don't give up when he corrects you. For the LORD disciplines those he loves, and he punishes each one he accepts as his child."

God loves you; therefore, God will discipline you. To discipline means to train and correct. Your **Abba** God is the Perfect Father. He does not correct in anger; not ever. His correction is motivated by Love, not anger. His training and correction are never to punish you or make you pay for your sins. Jesus already took your punishment and paid the price for your sin on the cross.

If you think you are above God's discipline, consider Hebrews 12:4–11, which tells us that God disciplines His children. You are His child and He desires only the very best for you. Therefore, He will train you in the way you should go. **Abba** God is educating you, not punishing you, so be encouraged because He loves you so much!

He deeply cares how you live. He desires you to live the life for which He created you. Of course, He will prepare you to do just that; and His training results in your maturity. Training is hard work and exhausting, but press on. If you do not give up, there is a peaceful harvest of right living waiting for you!

Healthy Nourishments

Psalm 119:92, 93 (NLT)

If your instructions hadn't sustained me with joy, I would have died in my misery. I will never forget your commandments, for by them you give me life.

God's instructions—His Word—are healthy nourishments for your soul! In these verses the writer of Psalm 119 is thanking God for replacing his depression and misery with joy. God's Word brings such hope and lightens even the darkest places in His people. Will you embrace God's instructions every day? Here is a wonderful habit to begin: each morning when you wake up, thank your **Abba** God for another day. Tell Him you want to know Him better and you need His help today. Finally, ask Him to give you the **grace** to trust Him more and the courage to receive His Love and help. Commit to reading His Word every day so that you may be open and receptive to the life He wants you to have. This is the route to living a more abundant life.

The Hebrew word for "life," used in Psalm 119:93, means to be revived from discouragement and sickness, to be sustained and live a prosperous life, to be revived from death, and to be refreshed. Who wouldn't want this life? Will you learn God's instructions and commit to really knowing Him? Then, will you receive and give to others the joy He generously offers you?

Draw Near to God

1 John 4:4 (NLT)

But you belong to God, my dear children. You have already won a victory over those people, because the Spirit who lives in you is greater than the spirit who lives in the world.

You are of God; you have God's Spirit in you. You are called to rely on God rather than on yourself or the world. God loves the world; He loves His creation. When God was finished creating the earth and all its inhabitants, Genesis tells us He saw all that He made and declared it to be very good (Genesis 1:31).

The "world" to which John refers in 1 John 4:4 is not God's created earth and mankind in general; rather, it is **worldliness**. **Worldliness** is in direct conflict to God's **holiness** and His commands; it is also a threat to Christians because it esteems a set of values, beliefs, and behaviors that have sinful man at the center, instead of esteeming God Almighty. **Worldliness** scoffs at God's value system and calls evil, good and good, evil.

There are forces of spiritual darkness in conflict with God and His children. These dark forces are constantly influencing the world. God's Word exhorts you to purify your heart and not be divided in your loyalty between God and the world (James 4:7, 8). (James 4 also reminds you to resist the **devil** and he will flee from you.)

When you become overwhelmed, will you remember that the Power at work within you is greater than the power at work within the world? Will you draw near to God? He wants to draw near to you!

Don't Quit

Psalm 27:14 (NLT)
Wait patiently for the LORD. Be brave and courageous. Yes, wait patiently for the LORD.

Psalm 27:14 (The Message)
I'm sure now I'll see God's goodness in the exuberant earth. Stay with GOD! Take heart. Don't quit. I'll say it again: Stay with GOD.

It is much easier to keep moving than to be still and wait for the Lord. In Hebrew, the word translated here as "wait" means to hope for and to expect; to anticipate what God is going to do. Do not go weak in the waiting. Stay strong and focus on Jesus, not your circumstances. **Abba** Father's eye is on you; and if you will persevere, you will see the Goodness of God at work. Those who wait upon the Lord gain new strength (Isaiah 40:31) and greater trust in Him. You are becoming a braver, stronger, more alert follower of Jesus when you wait with anticipation, expecting Him to answer.

He loves you more than you can imagine. After all, making you was His idea! Of course He is going to take good care with you all the days of your human life. Then, a day is coming when your time here will come to an end and you will cross over into Jesus' arms for all eternity. Everything will be clear then and there will be no more questions, doubts, or heartaches. You will be home and all will be well with you forever and ever.

Will you determine to wait with anticipation and keep on keeping on in Jesus' name?

Silence the Crowing Roosters

You worship the God Who is the **Ancient of Days** (Daniel 7:9)—a Forgiving, Just, and Loving **Abba**. He is ever so patient with His children, longing for you to seek Him. He is a relational God who created you to know Him and "do life" with Him. He waits patiently for you to yield to His Truth and **Grace**. He is the same God whose patience is demonstrated in His timeless love letter (the Bible) written for you.

God called Moses to lead the Israelites (His **chosen people**) out of the land of slavery to the **Promised Land** flowing with blessings. On the way to this **Promised Land**, while God Almighty was explaining to Moses how to follow Him and live in freedom, His children were choosing bondage by building a golden calf to worship. (See Exodus 24 and 32.) They were denying **Abba** as their Lord and choosing a false god.

For more than 1,000 years, God demonstrated inconceivable patience with His **chosen people** by sending prophets, teachers, and righteous leaders to them. Over and over again, they ignored or rebelled against the Truth. God demonstrates this same patience with you—His chosen child.

Will you choose to ignore or rebel; or will you honor your **covenant** relationship with your **Abba** God? Will you turn from anything in your life that dishonors Him? Are there roosters crowing in your life—voices that accentuate doubt or denial? Will you embrace who you are in Christ and stop denying Him so you can silence the crowing roosters?

He is a relational God who

created you to know Him

and "do life" with Him.

One Truth; One Way

God's written Word to us, in the form of the Old Testament and New Testament, is our Truth. Testament means evidence, proof, confirmation, and **witness**. God's Testaments to us are written, tangible proofs of His Truths; they are His testimony. You, too, are to be a testimony—a testimony of God's Love, Truth, and Life. Living a holy life that pleases God will produce this testimony.

Jesus prayed to **Abba** Father, imploring Him to make you holy by His Truth (John 17:17–19). Holy means different from the world and dedicated to God. Is your life distinguishable from those who do not live yielded to God's ways? Are you a **witness** to the Truth or are you a confusing compromiser—claiming to be a Christian, yet not committed to the Truth? If you claim to be a Christian, you are claiming to follow Christ—the Way, the Truth, and the Life (John 14:6). You are to prove this claim through choices that reflect His Glorious rays of light instead of the darkness of **worldliness**.

There is only one Truth; but there are two powers at work. You have an **adversary** who accuses you day and night of wrong doing (Revelation 12:10). Will you refuse to give him ammunition to use against you? When you behave in a way that is not holy, when you do not live according to God's Truths, you can immediately go before the throne of **Grace** and **Mercy** and claim the blood of Jesus (Hebrews 4:16). His blood washes you as clean as freshly-fallen snow. The **adversary**'s attacks and accusations will be completely defeated by the blood of Jesus.

The victory that enables you to live holy and different is yours. Will you claim the **salvation** and power that is yours to live a life of Truth and **Grace**?

The adversary's attacks

and accusations will be

completely defeated by the

blood of Jesus.

He Chose You!

1 Peter 1:2, 6-8 (NLT)

God the Father knew you and chose you long ago, and his Spirit has made you holy. As a result, you have obeyed him and have been cleansed by the blood of Jesus Christ. May God give you more and more **grace** and peace . . . So be truly glad. There is wonderful joy ahead, even though you have to endure many **trials** for a little while. These **trials** will show that your faith is genuine. It is being tested as fire tests and purifies gold—though your faith is far more precious than mere gold. So when your faith remains strong through many **trials**, it will bring you much praise and glory and honor on the day when Jesus Christ is revealed to the whole world. You love him even though you have never seen him. Though you do not see him now, you trust him; and you rejoice with a glorious, inexpressible joy.

Your **Abba** Father knows you and chose you. Imagine! The All-Powerful, All-Knowing, **King of kings** and Lord of lords has His eye on you! David was overwhelmed by this and wrote, "What are mere mortals that you should think about them, human beings that you should care for them?" (Psalm 8:4; NLT). Although your Loving, Caring **Abba** would never tempt you to sin (James 1:13), He does allow **trials**, measured by Him, in order to prove your faith as trustworthy.

God promises to never let you be tempted beyond what you can bear (1 Corinthians 10:13); therefore, when you trust Him with every trouble, you are purifying your faith; you are proving Him to be real. When you trust Him by saying, "Jesus, I trust you" and "**Abba**, I know You are working good from this," you are ascending to a place of genuine faith where there is evidence of things unseen (Hebrews 11:1). The result of trusting in your Lord will be a stronger love for Jesus. This love expresses itself with the delicious fruit of joy because you know that He holds your hand through everything that comes your way and you can always trust Him to help you.

Will you trust Him? Will you rejoice? He chose you and He adores you!

The result of trusting in your

Lord will be a stronger love

for Jesus.

Intentional Obedience

Abba Father desires to open your eyes to things unseen. Will you ask Him for His thoughts to be your thoughts? You need God's Holy Spirit to enlighten your understanding to His wonderful Truths.

The real you was created to live in harmony with God. You belong to Him and your real home awaits you in heaven. As a **sojourner** in this world, you must be intentional with your life. The world is like a powerful magnet pulling you toward a path of lies. Your Christian path is narrow (Matthew 7:14) and your feet will wander if you are not walking according to the Truth.

There is only one Truth; it is found in the timeless letters of the Old and New Testaments. Please do not ignore these life instructions from the very mind of God. If your prayers are not being answered, is it possible you are ignoring God's Word to you? Is it possible you might be reading it, but not living in intentional obedience to it? Will you ask **Abba** to open your eyes to His divine instructions?

Give and Receive Mercy

You were lost and now you are found. You were empty; now
you have the Holy Spirit within you. You were aimlessly
wandering through life without real purpose; now you are called
a son or daughter of the King. You are called His chosen one (1
Thessalonians 1:4), His appointed one (John 15:16), His beloved
(Colossians 3:12), the apple of His eye (Psalm 17:8), and His precious one (Isaiah 43:4). You have been called to a high calling; you
are an ambassador for Christ (2 Corinthians 5:20). You are God's
instrument; He desires to speak though you to encourage others
with His words of eternal life. You are called to represent Him to
lost souls.

You are God's vessel; He desires you to reach out your arms to
hug and help others in Jesus' Name. You have been shown much
Mercy. Do you acknowledge the **Mercy Abba** Father has given
you? Matthew 5:7 says, "Blessed are the merciful, for they shall
obtain **mercy**" (NKJV). Are you merciful? Are you compassionate
and kind? Do you give unconditionally—with no strings attached

and expecting nothing in return? **Abba** Father lavishes His **Mercy** on you. Do you thank Him for His **Mercy** and then do as He says and extend that **mercy** to others? (See Matthew 5:7; Luke 6:36.)

You are someone very special with a divine calling. You are royalty (Revelation 1:6). Are you acting like a child of the King? Ask **Abba** Father to stir up an eagerness in you to live for Him by showing **mercy** to others. Thank Him for His great **Mercy** and the joy of receiving and sharing it.

You have been called to

a high calling; you are an

ambassador for Christ.

Immeasurably More

Psalm 37:4 (NLT)
Take delight in the LORD, and he will give you your heart's desires.

Proverbs 28:13 (NLT)
People who conceal their sins will not prosper, but if they **confess** and turn from them, they will receive **mercy**.

1 Peter 2:11, 24 (NLT)
Dear friends, I warn you as "temporary residents and foreigners" to keep away from worldly desires that wage war against your very souls . . . He personally carried our sins in his body on the cross so that we can be dead to sin and live for what is right. By his wounds you are healed.

Is there a war waging in your soul? Are you indulging your appetite for pleasure or wealth at the expense of your soul? God's Word says worldly desires wage war within us. For you to really find life, you must loosen your greedy, preoccupied grip on material and worthless things and turn your attention to spiritual matters.

What occupies your mind? If you are preoccupied with anything or anyone more than **Abba** Father, you are practicing **idol**atry. This is sin. Remember, there is no sin you can commit that will keep God from loving you. You are His child; His Love is unconditional and forever. However, when you live in patterns of sin, it interrupts your intimate connection with Him. You forfeit so many blessings!

Will you live for what is right and for what is forever? Will you live for God? If you will commit to keeping company with Him every day, He will give you immeasurably more than anything or anyone else ever could!

Be of One Mind

1 Peter 3:8–12 (NLT)

Finally, all of you should be of one mind. Sympathize with each other. Love each other as brothers and sisters. Be tenderhearted, and keep a **humble** attitude. Don't repay evil for evil. Don't retaliate with insults when people insult you. Instead, pay them back with a blessing. That is what God has called you to do, and he will bless you for it. For the Scriptures say, "If you want to enjoy life and see many happy days, keep your tongue from speaking evil and your lips from telling lies. Turn away from evil and do good. Search for peace, and work to maintain it. The eyes of the Lord watch over those who do right, and his ears are open to their prayers. But the Lord turns his face against those who do evil."

In verse 8 of this passage, Peter says all of us should be of one mind. Of what mind does he speak; your mind? No. God is speaking through Peter to encourage Christians to be of the mind of Christ (1 Corinthians 2:16).

If we should all have the same mind, why are there so many conflicts within the church? Many have been hurt by another believer or may even have caused pain for another believer. Why? Because Christians don't always have the mind of Christ; for us to think like Jesus, it is imperative that we know what He teaches. Christians must know the Word of God.

This life is a test and every day you are being tested. Will you represent Christ today? You will receive your test results one day in the future when you stand before the **Judgment Seat of Christ**. On that day, we must all give an account for the things we said and did on earth. You will be blessed and rewarded for your obedience to God and suffer loss for the times you dishonored your **Abba** Lord. 1 Corinthians 3:12–15 says that even good deeds done with the wrong motives will burn as wood, hay, and stubble.

You are called to love others with the mind of Jesus. Peter tells you how to do this; he says to sympathize with others, be tender-hearted toward others (especially the difficult believers in your life), and do not repay evil for evil. Do not try to defend yourself or get even by gossiping or slandering your brother or sister. Instead, will you bless them by showing **mercy**? Will you bless them by praying for them?

The eyes of the Lord are watching over you, hoping you will have His mind. When you do, you bless **Abba** Father; and you will be blessed in turn with the Peace of the Lord for doing what is right.

You are called to love others

with the mind of Jesus.

Love One Another

Psalm 119:73 (NLT)

You made me; you created me. Now give me the sense to follow your commands.

1 John 2:6-9 (NLT)

Those who say they live in God should live their lives as Jesus did. Dear friends, I am not writing a new commandment for you; rather it is an old one you have had from the very beginning. This old commandment—to love one another—is the same message you heard before. Yet it is also new. Jesus lived the truth of this commandment, and you also are living it. For the darkness is disappearing, and the true light is already shining. If anyone claims, "I am living in the light," but hates a Christian brother or sister, that person is still living in darkness.

Are you a person of good, common sense? Proverbs 2:7 promises that God grants a treasure of common sense to the honest. The honest person is one who does what is right before the Lord.

God tells you in His Word that it is right for you to love your brothers and sisters. He created you to be in relationships with others. These relationships reflect your **fellowship** with and maturity in Christ. The evidence of your growing relationship with Jesus is manifested in how you treat your brothers and sisters. You will not save your soul by simply knowing about Jesus; you save your soul by knowing Him personally. When you know Him, you experience His amazing **Grace** and Love and you cannot help but extend it to others. Will you do the hard work required to rid your heart of any hardness toward a brother or sister? This may require more than prayers; this ridding may require **fasting**, as well. Do whatever it takes to gain freedom from the bondage of unforgiveness and bitterness.

Will you choose to live in God's warm light of **Grace**? Will you walk away from the cold, dark, empty, and unfruitful ways of the past? You are a new creation in Christ (2 Corinthians 5:17), created to live in Truth and **Grace**. Are you living in darkness or in the light of Christ? "If anyone claims, "I am living in the light," but hates a Christian brother or sister, that person is still living in darkness" (1 John 2:9; NLT).

The evidence of your

growing relationship with

Jesus is manifested in how

you treat your brothers

and sisters.

What Do You Crave?

1 John 2:15–17 (NLT)

Do not love this world nor the things it offers you, for when you love the world, you do not have the love of the Father in you. For the world offers only a craving for physical pleasure, a craving for everything we see, and pride in our achievements and possessions. These are not from the Father, but are from this world. And this world is fading away, along with everything that people crave. But anyone who does what pleases God will live forever.

What do you crave? Do you crave comfort, a new car, granite counter tops, diamonds, the perfect weight, a big title in front of your name, a platform, perfect kids, or exotic vacations? There is a difference between craving things of this world and appreciating blessings. Proverbs 14:23 says hard work produces a profit. We can enjoy the blessings that profit may bring without craving worldly pleasures and possessions. To crave means to long for something with an overpowering desire. Many things of this world are not sinful in and of themselves; for the Christian however, it is sinful to desire and focus on temporary things above knowing **Abba** Father and living for Him.

What keeps you up at night? Does your craving for wealth or pleasure or fame keep you awake; or does your desire to honor your heavenly Father have your focus? Do you crave Him? Do you ask Him to give you a desire to spend more time in His Word and a desire to seek Him in the details of your life? In the passage above, John warns you to not love this world. He is not referring to God's beautiful creation or to human beings. John is encouraging you to not love the world's ways—its paths to alleged material success, its standards, and its value system. The world will forfeit God's values and authority for the sake of advancement. This advancement may

NOURISHMENTS 🌾 267

promise to make you "better off"; but its promise is empty and it can never make you "better."

Do you crave pleasing your **Abba** Father? Will you ask Him to stir up this craving every day so you may experience a full life that is better than you could ever have imagined?

We can enjoy the blessings

that profit may bring

without craving worldly

pleasures and possessions.

Deep Cries Out to Deep

Daniel 10:17-19 (NLT)

"How can someone like me, your servant, talk to you, my lord? My strength is gone, and I can hardly breathe." Then the one who looked like a man touched me again, and I felt my strength returning. "Don't be afraid," he said, "for you are very precious to God. Peace! Be encouraged! Be strong!" As he spoke these words to me, I suddenly felt stronger and said to him, "Please speak to me, my lord, for you have strengthened me."

Are you feeling weak and weary? Has your strength been sapped? Do not fear, precious loved one. You have been marked for all eternity as a child of God. He watches over you day and night, waiting for your invitation to help. Will you open His Word and feed your famished soul with nourishing encouragements? Will you sit with Him and ask your Loving, Caring, Good Shepherd (John 10:14) to touch you with His **Grace** and Strength? You will not suffer want when you spend time beside the deep, still waters of Life. When you are still and quiet with your **Abba**, deep cries out to deep—the deepest places of your soul cry out to connect with the very essence of your **Abba**; in this **communion**, your soul is restored. When you walk with Him, you walk in green pastures; even if you walk through the valley of troubles, He is with you every step of the way, holding your hand and strengthening your soul. (See Psalm 23.)

Do not fear evil because He is with you to strengthen you for the journey. Will you thank Him continually for His Care and provisions? Will you thank Him today for His **Grace** and Truth; and will you determine to dwell in the house of the Lord today and forever? Will you say to **Abba** Father, "Please speak to me, my Lord, for You have strengthened me"?

Fellowship with God

Do you remain in **fellowship** and connection with your **Abba** Father? After believing in Jesus as your Savior and Lord over your life, have you continued to sin? 1 John 1:8 tells us that if we claim we have no sin, we are only fooling ourselves and not living in the Truth. Of course you have sinned! You are not Jesus; and therefore, you are not perfect.

John wants to be clear that, if you continue in patterns of sin, you are living in spiritual darkness. You prove by continued patterns of sin that you really don't know Jesus. If you are abiding in sin, you are intentionally choosing to live a life consisting of sinful choice after sinful choice. And that is not living in **fellowship** with God. When sin is a lifestyle, you abide in sin, not in Christ (John 15:4–7).

There is a difference between committing a sin and abiding in sin. When you are living in **fellowship** with God, your heart will be convicted when you commit a sin. You can then **repent** and restore the **fellowship** that sin attempted to interrupt. When you do sin, when you rebel against God or do anything that brings Him dishonor, simply **confess** to Him and **repent**, and you will be clean again. To be clean means you are again in relationship or **fellowship** with God. Positionally, you were forgiven of all sins—past, present and future—when you received Jesus as your Lord and Savior. No sin can change your "position" as His child. However, your God is a relational God and made you to be in **fellowship** with Him. When you sin and do not **confess**, you have stopped His intimate **fellowship**. (It is the same in a marriage. When a spouse offends another spouse, they don't get divorced, but they also are not inclined to snuggle up together and enjoy each other's company.) There cannot be true reconciliation without **repent**ance. Will you **confess** all your known sins to **Abba**? In His **Grace**, He also forgives all unknown offenses. He is faithful and just to forgive your sins and remove them from you as far as the east is from the west. He is always ready to re-engage with you. Will you remain in **fellowship** with Him?

Will you ask Jesus to help you? Will you ask **Abba** Father, through His Holy Spirit in you, to reveal to you the reality of how deep His Love for you is? His deep and amazing Love is there for you even if you are struggling with a particular sin; let Him strengthen and nourish you, dear one. Will you start by choosing to know Him more every day? Will you commit to look up His names and study His character as presented on page xv through xviii of this book?

When sin is a lifestyle, you

abide in sin, not in Christ.

Look to the Lord

Where do you look for help? Does your help come from the Lord? Do you look to the Creator of the heavens and earth for help? He is **Jehovah Jireh**, the Lord who Provides. Your **Abba** Lord loves you and adores you; you matter to Him. His eye is on you. Will you step away from fear of your circumstances and step toward trusting in Him? When you are afraid or worried will you say, "Thank You, **Abba** Father, for Your promise to be my protective shade who watches over me as I come and go"? Will you write His promise to be your help on the fiber of your being?

In this life, you will slip and stumble; but you will not fall if you look to your Lord and Savior for help. He never says "no" to a cry for help. You have the Spirit of the Holy God within you. God's Spirit within you will protect and guide you all the days of your life, even unto death. God's Spirit is your eternal **Comforter** (John 14:16; KJV). Will you look to Him? Will your help come from the Lord?

Be Still and Know the Lord

Psalm 23 (NIV)

The LORD is my shepherd, I lack nothing. He makes me lie down in green pastures, he leads me beside quiet waters, he refreshes my soul. He guides me along the right paths for his name's sake. Even though I walk through the darkest valley, I will fear no evil, for you are with me; your rod and your staff, they comfort me. You prepare a table before me in the presence of my enemies. You **anoint** my head with oil; my cup overflows. Surely your goodness and love will follow me all the days of my life, and I will dwell in the house of the LORD forever.

Isaiah 32:16–20a (NLT)

Justice will rule in the wilderness and **righteousness** in the fertile field. And this **righteousness** will bring peace. Yes, it will bring quietness and confidence forever. My people will live in safety, quietly at home. They will be at rest. Even if the forest should be destroyed and the city torn down, the LORD will greatly bless his people.

You do not belong to this world. You are God's prized possession. You are one of His people. Those who do not belong to Him do not rest in peace or confident hope. True peace and hope are unique qualities only experienced by God's children. When you focus on your **Abba** Father who is full of **Grace** and Goodness, His Love will quiet you. You shall not want. The mountains may fall into the sea and the earth may shake and tremble, but you have been marked in Him with a seal, the promised Holy Spirit (Ephesians 1:13). When you are still and quiet, you can know Him even more. Perhaps you have heard the saying, "if the **devil** cannot make you sin, he will keep you busy." There is truth in that saying. Be still and know the Lord.

Will you ask **Abba** Father to **anoint** you with His Peace that surpasses all understanding (Philippians 4:7)? Will you make this request possible by allowing Him to lead you in righteous living? If you are living to honor Him, under His authority and for His Glory, your cup will overflow with thanksgiving, even in the presence of many enemies and difficulties. Will you choose His Righteous Ways? Will you tell Him you trust Him with every detail of your life and allow your life to be filled with His promised blessings of peace, quietness, and confident hope? Will you commit to living in the house of the Lord forever; surely Goodness and Love will follow you all the days of your life.

True peace and hope

are unique qualities only

experienced by

God's children.

Suffering for Right

As a Christian, how do you react when evil is returned for good you have done? You must understand, this is to be expected in a **fallen world** that does not subject itself to God's standards and values. Darkness hates light and will sometimes return evil for good done in the Light of Christ. **Abba** Father promises you a special reward if you suffer for doing what is right. If your life is a reflection of Jesus to others, **Abba** Father is greatly pleased with you and will reward you.

In order for you to do what is right, you must worship Christ as Lord of your life. When you worship Him, you will be dedicated to learning of Him by spending time with Him in His Word. You behave differently from those who don't believe. You must separate yourself from compromising circumstances that are sinful in God's eyes. You demonstrate you are different by being like Jesus—a compassionate, kind, and generous person who loves others. Do you give of your time, talent, and treasures? When you show **mercy**, the Lord shows you even more **Mercy**! Lamentations 3:22, 23 tells you the faithful Love of the Lord never ends; His mercies never cease. Great is His Faithfulness!

He is Faithful to you; will you be faithful to Him?

Suffering Will End

Psalm 103:2–5 (NIV)

Praise the LORD, my soul, and forget not all his benefits—who forgives all your sins and heals all your diseases, who redeems your life from the pit and crowns you with love and compassion, who satisfies your desires with good things so that your youth is renewed like the eagle's.

Psalm 119:92 (NLT)

If your instructions hadn't sustained me with joy, I would have died in my misery.

1 Peter 4:12, 13 (NLT)

Dear friends, don't be surprised at the fiery **trial**s you are going through, as if something strange were happening to you. Instead, be very glad—for these **trial**s make you partners with Christ in his suffering, so that you will have the wonderful joy of seeing his glory when it is revealed to all the world.

1 Peter 5:10 (NLT)

In his kindness God called you to share in his eternal glory by means of Christ Jesus. So after you have suffered a little while, he will restore, support, and strengthen you, and he will place you on a firm foundation.

God is more concerned with your character than your comfort. You have all of eternity to be comfortable. While on earth, you will have fiery **trial**s and smoldering troubles. There will be relational stresses and strains within your natural family and your eternal family. This is a time to build your life on the foundation of God's promises and instructions.

When King David was so miserable, hurt, and depressed that he wanted to die, he turned to **Abba** Father for instructions and was greatly encouraged. He wrote Psalm 103 to the Lord. God gave David His perspective, and that made all the difference. He will also give you His perspective, which brings hope and joy. You can know that no matter what happens, everything will end well for you, as a child of God.

What is the worst thing that can happen in your life? There is nothing in this world that can separate you from Father **Abba**'s Love and Care for you, neither life nor death (Romans 8:38). Will you determine, regardless of what you are experiencing, that you are being called to **glorify** God through your circumstance? Will you thank Him because, after you have suffered a little while, He will restore, support, and strengthen you? **Amen!** Let it be so.

This is a time to build

your life on the foundation

of God's promises and

instructions.

Walking Along God's Path

> **2 Peter 1:5–8 (NLT)**
> In view of all this, make every effort to respond to God's promises. Supplement your faith with a generous provision of moral excellence, and moral excellence with knowledge, and knowledge with self-control, and self-control with patient endurance, and patient endurance with godliness, and godliness with brotherly affection, and brotherly affection with love for everyone. The more you grow like this, the more productive and useful you will be in your knowledge of our Lord Jesus Christ.

As a Christian, you are either pressing toward Jesus or retreating away from Him. There is no neutral ground with Him. You have obtained a precious faith accompanied by divine Power that allows you to participate in God's divine nature and ways. Peter exhorts you to give your all in your walk with Jesus. Step-by-step, Peter explains this difficult but incredibly rewarding way for you: he encourages you to make every effort to live a morally excellent life of godly character and to develop a deeper understanding of your Savior. He encourages you to be discerning and to demonstrate self-control with your words and actions. You demonstrate growth by graciously showing patience and love to others. Do you reflect a reverent sense of wonder for your Jesus and a tender heart for your brothers and sisters in Christ? Oh, how **Abba** Father will use you to advance His kingdom as you grow in these qualities!

In Matthew 7:14, Jesus said: "Narrow is the gate and difficult is the way which leads to life, and there are few who find it" (NKJV). Are you walking on the path of life or the path of destruction? Will you choose today to be one of the few who truly commits to doing life **Abba's** way? Will you walk the path paved with productivity for the kingdom of God?

Wake up!

Luke 9:28-35 (NLT)

About eight days later Jesus took Peter, John, and James up on a mountain to pray. And as he was praying, the appearance of his face was transformed, and his clothes became dazzling white. Suddenly, two men, Moses and Elijah, appeared and began talking with Jesus. They were glorious to see. And they were speaking about his exodus from this world, which was about to be fulfilled in Jerusalem.

Peter and the others had fallen asleep. When they woke up, they saw Jesus' glory and the two men standing with him. As Moses and Elijah were starting to leave, Peter, not even knowing what he was saying, blurted out, "Master, it's wonderful for us to be here! Let's make three shelters as memorials—one for you, one for Moses, and one for Elijah." But even as he was saying this, a cloud overshadowed them, and terror gripped them as the cloud covered them.

Then a voice from the cloud said, "This is my Son, my Chosen One. Listen to him."

Are you listening to Jesus? He has something to say to you. Are you sleep-walking through your day, unaware of His Ever-present Spirit? Have you tasted the Glory of the Lord? He desires to share His dazzling Magnificence with you; slip your hand into His and sit with Him and His Word. Ask Him for a new revelation today; He loves to speak to His own. He loves to give you a preview of coming attractions; a preview of His Glory. You will enjoy glimpses of the Glory of the **King of kings** on earth; but there is a day coming very soon when you will live every moment basking in His warm, loving, and dazzling Glory!

Your days are numbered; will you make the most of them? Ask the Holy Spirit to open your eyes to the Glory of God all around you. Will you seek Him with all your heart and renew your life with His nourishing words? Will you stop questioning Him and start thanking Him? Will you stop doubting Him and start praising Him?

Will you keep your eyes on the goal and not sleep-walk through today, missing glorious glimpses of your **King of kings** and Lord of lords?

Your days are numbered;

will you make the

most of them?

Be an Agent of Change

Are you sickened by the increase of the shameful immorality sweeping across our land? The children of our land are indoctrinated in public schools with information about how to have sex rather than being told the blessings that accompany waiting until marriage. Openly immoral speakers are invited into our children's schools, college campuses, and even churches, promoting practices of sexual deviance that go explicitly against God's commands. As if this weren't enough, our media promotes immorality day and night.

God credited Lot as a righteous man because his soul was tormented by the immorality he saw in his community. However, is it enough to be troubled in your heart, yet fail to act on your **conviction**s? We are called to look different than the ungodly; to use our voice of Truth and **Grace** in hopes of bringing about change. Lot allowed his family to "do life" with proud and arrogant people who despised God's authority (read Lot's story in Genesis 18 and 19). Yes, God, because of His **Grace**, **saved** Lot and his daughters, but Lot escaped only with his life. He lost his wife, his home, and everything else he had worked to achieve. Was the life he chose to live fruitful? Lot, no doubt, was a man of sorrows in his aging years; although he did recognize good from evil, he did nothing about the evil surrounding him.

Where is God calling you to speak up with Truth wrapped in Love? God gave you a voice to use; if you do not use it, you may very well lose it. Do not lose the opportunity to be an agent of change; the resulting loss can be too great.

Where is God calling you

to speak up with Truth

wrapped in Love?

He is Near

Living in this world is hard at times. Jesus said in John 16:33 that we will encounter sorrows, **trial**s, and troubles in this world. This is not heaven; earth is your temporary home. Will you thank the Good Lord for being your **Jehovah Shammah**, the Lord Who is There? He is right here with you in this troubled world.

Jesus knew you would have stresses and pressure; it is part of your journey. Every sorrow and **trial** places you at a crossroads. You can choose the wide, popular road of worry, anxiety, and leaning on your own understanding. Or, as a child of **Abba** Father, you can choose the road less traveled and cast your cares upon Him. To "cast upon" means to place upon; can you visualize placing your troubles at the throne of **Grace** and **Mercy** and leaving them there, knowing your Loving **Abba** is moving on your behalf? Will you tell Him you choose to trust Him rather than worry?

Will you rise in the quiet of the morning and meditate on **Abba**'s Love for you and His promises to you? When anxiety begins to stir in your heart, will you say the Lord's Prayer (Matthew 6:9–13) or Psalm 23? Do you know these passages? If not, do not wait another day to memorize these timeless words of wisdom, guidance, comfort, and support.

Abba Father is near and He can always be trusted. Will you give Him time to show you how He will do immeasurably more than you could have ever imagined (Ephesians 3:20)?

God Favors the Humble

> **Philippians 2:5-11 (NLT)**
>
> You must have the same attitude that Christ Jesus had. Though he was God, he did not think of equality with God as something to cling to. Instead, he gave up his divine privileges; he took the **humble** position of a slave and was born as a human being. When he appeared in human form, he **humble**d himself in obedience to God and died a criminal's death on a cross. Therefore, God elevated him to the place of highest honor and gave him the name above all other names, that at the name of Jesus every knee should bow, in heaven and on earth and under the earth, and every tongue **confess** that Jesus Christ is Lord, to the glory of God the Father.

God's favor is upon the **humble**. He promises to save the **humble** (Psalm 18:27), to guide and teach the **humble** (Psalm 25:9), to sustain the **humble** (Psalm 147:6), and to crown the **humble** with victory (Psalm 149:4). Are you **humble**? Do you have a teachable spirit; or do you think you already know everything? Are you okay with being second for the sake of others? Do you assert your will and your way or do you submit to **Abba** Father's will? Do you try to control situations or do you ask Him for guidance and wait for His leading? Do you live most of the day without communicating with God or do you consistently call upon the Power at work within you?

Jesus is the **King of kings**. He is in complete control of heaven and earth; yet He **humble**d Himself to walk in flesh and blood on the dirty streets of earth. Why would He lower Himself to die a painful, criminal's death? He **humble**d Himself for two reasons: 1) He chose to obey **Abba** Father because He trusted Him; 2) He chose to **sacrifice** Himself because His eye was on you. He wanted to save you, to provide you with true life both now and for all eternity. He wants to be with you forever. This is **Grace** in action—the perfect picture of God's unmerited favor. He did it all and He gives you all; you just say, "Yes, I receive Your gift of life." James 4:10 implores you to **humble** yourself before the Lord and promises He will lift you up. The Message translation says it this way: "so let God work His will in you. Yell a loud *no* to the **devil** and watch him scamper. Say a quiet *yes* to God and he'll be there in no time. Quit dabbling in sin. Purify your inner life. Quit playing the field. Hit bottom and cry your eyes out. The fun and games are over. Get serious, really serious. Get down on your knees before the Master; it's the only way you'll get on your feet."

Will you **humble** yourself and choose the same attitude of Christ?

Jesus is the King of kings.

He is in complete control of

heaven and earth.

Open Your Heart

> **Acts 16:13-15 (NLT)**
> On the Sabbath . . . we sat down to speak with some women...One of them was Lydia . . . who worshiped God. As she listened to us, the Lord opened her heart, and she accepted what Paul was saying. She was baptized along with other members of her household, and she asked us to be her guests. "If you agree that I am a true believer in the Lord," she said, "come and stay at my home." And she urged us until we agreed.

Paul was in Philippi—an ancient city in Macedonia (present-day Greece). He went there to plant a church. Because there was not a synagogue to attend, he went to the riverbank prayer meeting. There, he shared the **Good News** of Jesus Christ with a woman named Lydia and "the Lord opened her heart, and she accepted what Paul was saying."

The Lord opened Lydia's heart. The Lord is the heart's Maker and He alone has the key that opens its door. What evidence will appear when you allow the Lord's key to open your heart? There will be change. Lydia immediately obeyed the Lord and was baptized. She desired connection with her Lord and demonstrated this desire with obedience to Jesus' command in Matthew 28:19 to be baptized in the name of the Father and of the Son and of the Holy Spirit. Lydia then further demonstrated her acceptance of Jesus by caring for her brothers in Christ. She demonstrated love and kindness and hospitality by insisting they stay in her home.

Do you demonstrate an open heart for Jesus? Do others see you obeying Him and loving your fellow believers? Where is God asking you to demonstrate your open heart as evidence of your faith in Him?

Choose Encouraging Words

Psalm 119:79 (NLT)
Let me be united with all who fear you, with those who know your laws.

Ephesians 4:29 (NLT)
Don't use foul or abusive language. Let everything you say be good and helpful, so that your words will be an encouragement to those who hear them.

Do you have a friend who encourages you? To encourage another means to speak courage into them. Courage does not mean lack of fear; rather, it means you move forward though the fear. We all need encouragers who know the Lord and are familiar with His ways to inspire us and embolden us. If you do not have an encourager in your life, ask **Abba** Father to send you one. He loves to give such gifts to His children.

Protect yourself by limiting the time you spend with those who use discouraging words that cut like a sword into your soul. And be careful how you use your own words; your words can be a gift that brings forth hope and life; or your words can be a weapon that brings forth destruction and death. Do not kill another's dreams or purposes with harsh, harmful words. Will you commit to saying only what helps another? Will you ask the Holy Spirit within you to give you His Words when opening your mouth? Watch the way you talk; your Lord Jesus is standing beside you listening.

Be united whenever possible with those who respect and honor your Lord with their words; and pray that everything you say will be helpful to others. Are you an encouragement to those who hear you?

Loyalty

Hosea 5:7 (NKJV)
They have dealt treacherously with the LORD, for they have begotten pagan children. Now a New Moon shall devour them and their heritage.

Have you considered the deep Love your Savior has for you? He absolutely adores you. He sits at the right hand of the Father interceding for you (Romans 8:34). He prays for you to remain strong and faithful! He is Ever-Present (Matthew 28:20), watching over every detail of your life like a Shepherd tending to His lamb (John 10:1–18). In what ways have you received His **Grace** in your life? You are a son or daughter of the King on your way to a heavenly home He has prepared for you.

Have you dealt honorably with your Lord? Have you kept your promise to be faithful? Have you intentionally sought Him in **communion**? Do you pray with fervency and faith, knowing He is listening to every whisper and shout to Him? Do you passionately ask for opportunities to honor Him by letting your light shine on others (Matthew 5:16)? When is the last time you spoke His Truth to someone with respect and gentleness? Have you been disloyal to your Lord? Do you rationalize sinful choices? Do you give the greatest portion of your time and attention to temporary matters or worldly pursuits?

Oh, child of God, let today be the day you honor your Lord! Jesus never forgets you. He stands before the mighty throne of **Abba** with your name written on His hand pleading for you (Isaiah 49:16). Do not betray His honor.

Will you commit your loyalties to your biggest Supporter? Will you commit to Jesus? Today is the day to honor Him!

Saturated

Acts 2:1–4 (NLT)
On the day of Pentecost all the believers were meeting together in one place. Suddenly, there was a sound from heaven like the roaring of a mighty windstorm, and it filled the house where they were sitting. Then, what looked like flames or tongues of fire appeared and settled on each of them. And everyone present was filled with the Holy Spirit and began speaking in other languages, as the Holy Spirit gave them this ability.

Abba Father always keeps His promises. He promised to send the Holy Spirit and, on the day of Pentecost, that promise was fulfilled. Jerusalem was full of worshipers from many different countries, gathered to observe the Feast of Pentecost—a time of remembrance commemorating the giving of **God's Law** to Moses on Mount Sinai. All the believers present were filled with the Holy Spirit. The Greek word for "filled" means: to fulfill, to satiate, to be full to the brim, to wholly take possession of, and to complete. The same word is used to describe the sponge *filled* with sour wine offered to Jesus as He was dying on the cross (John 19:28–30); the sponge was saturated with the sour wine. The believers on that Day of Pentecost were saturated—filled to the brim—with the Holy Spirit. They received and welcomed Jesus as Lord and Savior, their all in all. They did not leave room for any other gods in their lives.

How about you? Are you saturated with Jesus? Do you soak up His words and Love for you? **False gods** will never fulfill or complete you. You are a temple of the Holy Spirit (1 Corinthians 6:19); invite Him into every nook and cranny; allow Him full possession of your mind, heart, and spirit.

Will you allow the Holy Spirit full access? Will you allow Him to fill you to such fullness there is no room for any **false gods**?

Put On the New Self

Ephesians 4:22–24 (NKJV)

Put off, concerning your former conduct, the old man which grows corrupt according to the deceitful lusts, and be renewed in the spirit of your mind . . . put on the new man which was created according to God, in true **righteousness** and **holiness**.

Colossians 3:10, 11 (NKJV)

Put on the new man who is renewed in knowledge according to the image of Him who created him, where there is neither Greek nor Jew, circumcised nor uncircumcised, barbarian, Scythian, slave nor free, but Christ is all and in all.

In both these passages, Paul says to "put on the new" self. This phrase is the same one used for changing clothes. Every day, you have a choice—you can put on soiled, stinky clothes, or you can choose fresh, clean ones. The **devil** loves it when you refuse to put on the new self the Lord provides and choose to walk about your days in your stinky, dirty, old clothes. But you can choose to operate with the Power at work within you and be renewed by knowing your God and being in an intimate relationship with Him.

You were made in the image of God; you were created after the likeness of God Almighty (Genesis 1:27)! As you grow in the **Grace** and knowledge of Jesus Christ, the real you emerges— the you that was knit together in the image of God. The real you that God created and patiently waits for you to discover is kind, patient, forgiving, tender-hearted, compassionate, and **humble**. As a believer, you are part of a family that favors no race, class, culture, or nationality. Your family favors Jesus.

Do you know who you really are? Have you put on the new self?

Be Clothed in White

Revelation 3:4, 5 (NKJV)

"You have a few names even in Sardis who have not defiled their garments; and they shall walk with Me in white, for they are worthy. He who overcomes shall be clothed in white garments, and I will not blot out his name from the Book of Life; but I will **confess** his name before my Father and before his angels."

White is worn on festive occasions; it is the color that signifies innocence and purity of the soul. **Abba** Father spoke through John in Revelation 3:1, 2 rebuking Sardis for being a dead church; it was notoriously evil and needed to wake up. Yet, there was a remnant who chose good over evil and to clothe themselves in the white garments of Jesus' teaching.

In Ecclesiastes, 9:7, 8a, King Solomon wrote: "Go, eat your food with gladness, and drink your wine with a joyful heart, for God has already approved what you do. Always be clothed in white" (NIV). Solomon understood that seeking God with a pure heart will enable you to see Him with new eyes, understand His Love and Grace, and bring a greater desire to know and obey His Truths. Oh, the joy you gain when God's favor is upon you!

Could it be that so many Christians are depressed, lonely, and unfulfilled because their clothes are stained with sinful choices that compromise their walk with God? Have you lost the joy of your **salvation**? Your name *is* written in the Book of Life; can you visualize your name recorded there and the future God has waiting for you? Will you step into **fellowship** with Jesus, turn from all garments of compromise, and clothe your soul in white? Will you walk hand-in-hand with Jesus, both today and forever?

The victory is yours; all who are victorious will be clothed in white!

The Incense of Prayer

> ### Revelation 5:8 (NLT)
> And when he took the scroll, the four living beings and the twenty-four elders fell down before the Lamb. Each one had a harp, and they held gold bowls filled with incense, which are the prayers of God's people.
>
> ### Revelation 8:4 (NKJV)
> And the smoke of the incense, with the prayers of the saints, ascended before God from the angel's hand.

God's Holy Spirit within you is encouraging you to cry out to Him. You live in perilous times; are you calling out to **Abba** Father? Will you cast your cares upon Him today? Will you share your desires and dreams with Him? Your prayers ascend to the altar of **Abba** Father; there they are mixed with incense and the intercession of Jesus Himself (Romans 8:34) as they ascend before your heavenly Father.

We see in these passages from Revelation how important our prayers are; they are held in golden bowls and are a sweet-smelling incense to God. In Psalm 141:2, the psalmist asked that his prayer be set before God as incense, the lifting up of his hands as the evening **sacrifice**. Are you willing to **sacrifice** your time and commit to praying to **Abba** God? What will you lift before Him today?

It takes fire to ignite incense. Do you have a fire in your heart to connect with your Lord and Savior? If not, do not despair. He responds to even the smallest embers of a prayer. Will you ask Him to fan your embers into burning flames of desire?

You are very important to **Abba** Father; He is with you right now. Will you lift up your hands to Him and pour out your heart to the One Who hears and moves on your behalf?

New Life

There is a time to actively serve Jesus and a time to be still and sit with Jesus. Lazarus was dead and Jesus raised him to life. Lazarus desired to be close to Jesus; to sit with Him. He longed to be near his Savior. You, too, have been raised from the pit of death. You have been given new life in Christ. Do you present yourself as one who has been brought from death to life?

Go to God; do whatever it takes to connect with **Abba** Father. Will you sing praise songs to Him today? Will you focus on His character? Are you reading a Bible with good study notes or a daily format? Do you have friends who speak God's Truth and live in **Grace**? If not, ask **Abba** for such friends.

Are you serving **Abba** in ministry? Wherever God has placed you at this time, there is a ministry opportunity for you right there. Will you ask Him for opportunities to share the Hope within you with gentleness and respect? Will you declare this day that you will sit with Jesus, walk with Him, and live everyday with Him?

He waits at the table for you; don't allow your chair to go unoccupied. Be occupied with Him. You are an instrument to do what is right for the Glory of God; this is why you were given new life!

Meaningful Life

John 10:9, 10 (NKJV)

"I am the door. If anyone enters by Me, he will be **saved**, and will go in and out and find pasture. The thief does not come except to steal, and to kill, and to destroy. I have come that they may have life, and that they may have it more abundantly."

What is the rich, satisfying and abundant life God promises? Jesus gives us four glimpses of a meaningful life in this passage.

Firstly, you can rest assured of your eternal **salvation**. Those who accept Jesus are **saved**. So you can be sure, no matter what happens to you on earth, your eternal destiny is set. What is the worst thing that can happen to you? You are never alone; even if your temporary body dies, your soul crosses over into Jesus' arms.

Secondly, you are free every day to "go in" and connect with Jesus. He invites you to nourish your soul with His Word, to strengthen your life with His promises, and to find the peace and joy of holding His hand through it all.

Thirdly, the blessings that accompany you as you "go out" compare to nothing this world can offer. When you reach out to someone with Truth and **Grace** in the Power of Jesus name, you are confirming to yourself who you really are—a son or daughter of the King. As you serve others more with your time, talents, and treasures, your eyes are open wider to God's amazing **Grace** in your life. Don't miss opportunities to reach out to others!

Finally, it is in the "going in" when you connect with Jesus and in the "going out" when you connect with others. Are you going in and going out through Jesus? Are you walking in the green pastures of Truth, Love, and **Grace**?

Do not let **the enemy** close the door to your abundant life.

Bear Good Fruit

Psalm 1:1-3 (NLT)

Oh, the joys of those who do not follow the advice of the wicked, or stand around with sinners, or join in with mockers. But they delight in the law of the LORD, meditating on it day and night. They are like trees planted along the riverbank, bearing fruit each season. Their leaves never wither, and they prosper in all they do.

The One Who knit you together desires blessings for you. Your God has a prosperous path carved just for you. Finding this path begins with sitting with the Lord, meditating on His Word, and then obeying it. The way to happiness and blessings starts by opening God's Word and chewing on it day and night.

What did the psalmist who wrote Psalm 1 mean when he wrote about standing around with sinners or joining in with mockers? He was referring to seeking advice and guidance from those who have no interest in your **Abba** Lord and joining the company of those who scorn and disrespect His Ways. You will be blessed when you seek God's guidance and godly counsel rather than seeking advice from the ungodly or walking compromising paths with the openly sinful person.

Do you consider yourself a prosperous, fruit-bearing person? A tree cannot produce fruit unless it is firmly rooted and nourished. God's Word written on your heart and stewing in your mind keeps you rooted and well equipped for every good work (2 Timothy 3:16, 17). His Word teaches you how to live prosperously, it convicts you of sinful choices so you can **confess** and turn from death to life (Hebrews 4:12) and it comforts you and gives you hope in your troubles and hardships (Psalm 23:4; Psalm 119: 49, 50). His Word trains you in right living. If you commit to standing for Him and living in His Word, your feet will always be on a firm foundation, even if the earth is moving and shaking under you. You will not wither and live an unproductive life when your eyes are on Jesus.

Will you cast every doubt, care, and question upon Him and live your life as a tree planted by the riverbank, bearing eternal fruit?

God's Word written on your

heart and stewing in your

mind keeps you rooted and

well equipped for every

good work.

Tapestry of Life

1 Timothy 4:8, 10–13, 16 (NLT)

Physical training is good, but training for godliness is much better, promising benefits in this life and in the life to come . . . This is why we work hard and continue to struggle, for our hope is in the living God, who is the Savior of all people and particularly of all believers. Teach these things and insist that everyone learn them. Don't let anyone think less of you because you are young. Be an example to all believers in what you say, in the way you live, in your love, your faith, and your purity. Until I get there, focus on reading the Scriptures to the church, encouraging the believers, and teaching them . . . Keep a close watch on how you live and on your teaching. Stay true to what is right for the sake of your own **salvation** and the **salvation** of those who hear you.

God is forming a beautiful tapestry from your life on earth. You see only threads of this tapestry and may feel as though the struggles of life are not producing anything of significance in you. **Abba** Father uses everything in your life to grow you closer to Him and to encourage others to have hope as they **witness** you leaning on Him. These golden threads of training come with promised benefits of God's blessings. God's eye is on you even while you perform the same old task each day. It is in the simple, daily tasks where you can shine the most. It is in your daily commitments to honor Him with your gentleness, gratefulness, and hope for your future where the fragrant aroma of Christ reaches another's senses.

Every day is a gift that moves you closer to your eternal destination. Paul encouraged Timothy to give his complete attention to how he lived; to throw himself into his tasks so that everyone would see his progress.

Your tapestry is being fashioned every day. For the sake of your own destiny and for the **salvation** of those who hear you and see you, will you continue training for godliness? The promised benefits will not disappoint and the finished tapestry will be oh, so glorious!

Every day is a gift that

moves you closer to your

eternal destination.

Shine Out

Isaiah 58:9, 10 (NLT)

Then when you call, the LORD will answer. "Yes, I am here," he will quickly reply. "Remove the heavy yoke of oppression. Stop pointing your finger and spreading vicious rumors! Feed the hungry, and help those in trouble. Then your light will shine out from the darkness, and the darkness around you will be as bright as noon."

God is Good! Yes, He is Good all the time! His Word to you today is to shore up any areas of weakness in your life. He longs to reply quickly when you call to Him; yet, you hinder His response with your ungodly choices. Will you make the choice today to stop gossiping and slandering your brothers and sisters? You hurt yourself and cause lacerations in your soul when you tear others down. Your role as a follower of Christ is to build your eternal family up and encourage them. Your job is to feed the physically and spiritually hungry whom God brings to you.

Of course, your desire to help others in trouble flows from your connection to Christ. He reaches out to you continually with a cup of His **Living Water** (John 4). Will you take it, ingest it, and live on it?

Will you stop pointing your finger at others and start drinking the **Living Water** of Truth and **Grace**? Do this and your light will shine out from the darkness and the Lord will guide you continually (Isaiah 58:11). Then you will call and **Abba** Father will answer.

Never Give Up

Isaiah 30:18 (NLT)

So the LORD must wait for you to come to him so he can show you his love and compassion. For the LORD is a faithful God. Blessed are those who wait for his help.

When Samuel anointed David as King of Israel, David was between twelve and sixteen years of age. 2 Samuel 5:3, 4 tells us David was thirty years old when he finally took the throne. For more than a decade, David fled from Saul's torments; he lived in caves and prayed for God's deliverance. But David knew God is Faithful, so he trusted and waited for God to fulfill His promise to make him King of Israel.

Have you been waiting for God to move on your behalf? Have you been praying the same prayer over and over? Does it seem as if God is not answering you? Do you wonder why God delays in answering your prayers? Rest assured; He has heard your prayers; your requests are ever before Him. **Abba** God deals with you in absolute Love, **Mercy**, **Grace**, and Justice. He has His reasons for keeping you waiting and they are always for your good. Could it be God is waiting so your prayers become more fervent and focused? Could it be He is waiting so you know, beyond any doubt, He heard your requests and His awaited answer will demonstrate more powerfully His Love, Justice, and Compassion for you? He may be waiting in hopes that you seek to know Him more intimately so your heart is fully committed to Him. There may be some bitter root of sin in you that needs to be dug out and removed. Perhaps you are confusing His Truth with false ideas or perhaps you trust more in your own solutions than in His.

Will you go to **Abba**, lay it all at His throne, tell Him you trust Him, and then wait with anticipation for His answers? Your **Abba**

God is a Faithful Father; blessed are those who wait for His help.

Don't go weak today and don't give up on Him; He never gives up on you.

Abba God deals with you in

absolute Love, Mercy, Grace,

and Justice.

Ears that Hear

Isaiah 30:20, 21 (NLT)

Though the Lord gave you adversity for food and suffering for drink, he will still be with you to teach you. You will see your teacher with your own eyes. Your own ears will hear him. Right behind you a voice will say, "This is the way you should go," whether to the right or to the left.

Why is it that we must sometimes learn the hard way before learning the easy way?

God's Words are full of instructions and promises. When you seek to obey Him, you often walk past many valleys of hardship and pain instead of through them. When you do get off track, God, in His incredible **Mercy**, will not allow Hope, Peace, and Joy to accompany you. Rather than choosing His nourishing, satisfying, **Bread of Life**, you sometimes choose the bread of adversity—the hard, sorrowful path. God will allow suffering when you are not walking with Him in order to teach you His ways are better for you.

In Isaiah 55:9, God says, "For just as the heavens are higher than the earth, so my ways are higher than your ways and my thoughts higher than your thoughts" (NLT). Will you stay on His path and thank Him for showing you the better way to live? Will you make it your goal every day to gain godly understanding and accept His instructions with a thankful heart? This will enable you to hear Him more clearly. You will hear the voice of the Holy Spirit telling you which way to go, whether to the right or to the left.

Grace without Limit

Ezra 7:21–23 (NKJV)

And I, even I, Artaxerxes the king, issue a decree to all the treasurers who are in the region beyond the River, that whatever Ezra the priest, the scribe of the Law of the God of heaven, may require of you, let it be done diligently, up to one hundred talents of silver, one hundred kors of wheat, one hundred baths of wine, one hundred baths of oil, and salt without prescribed limit. Whatever is commanded by the God of heaven, let it diligently be done for the house of the God of heaven. For why should there be wrath against the realm of the king and his sons?

In this passage of Ezra, we see the Lord using a **heathen** king for His Glory. It is the Lord who bestows favor and honor upon those whose walk is intentional; and Ezra was known throughout Persia as a man who committed himself to studying the revelations of God and obeying His instructions. King Artaxerxes, an ungodly, **heathen** king, was so moved by Ezra's devotion to the One True Living God, he not only allowed those who wanted to return to Jerusalem to leave **Babylon**, but he also opened his treasure chest and sent them home with silver and gold! (Read Ezra 7 for more of the story.)

King Artaxerxes proclaimed: "whatever is commanded by the God of heaven, let it diligently be done for the house of the God of heaven." This pagan king offered salt without prescribed limit. Charles Spurgeon says, "Salt was used in every offering made by fire unto the Lord, and from its preserving and purifying properties it was the grateful emblem of divine **grace** in the soul."[1] Just as

---

1. Charles Spurgeon, Morning and Evening Devotional, Morning December 16; Public Domain

Ezra's earthly king offered him salt without limit, your heavenly and eternal **King of kings** offers you **Grace** upon **Grace** without limit.

God does limit His judgments and wrath with you, but there is no limit to His **Grace**! If you need **grace**, go before the Mighty throne of God and request His preserving **Grace** of faith to help you trust Him more; and request His purifying **Grace** to help you desire to obey Him more. He will honor your request without limit.

Your heavenly and eternal

King of kings offers you

Grace upon Grace

without limit.

Let Him Quiet You

Zephaniah 3:17 (NIV)

The LORD your God is with you, the Mighty Warrior who saves. He will take great delight in you; in his love he will no longer rebuke you, but will rejoice over you with singing.

The Lord is **Jehovah**; this is the proper name of the One true God. Imagine! The One true God is with you! Matthew 1:23 says, "The virgin will conceive and give birth to a son, and they will call him Immanuel (which means "God with us")" (NIV). God is not only with you, He is a Mighty Warrior always ready to deliver you from troubles (Psalm 70:5), liberate you from bondage (Isaiah 42:7), defend you against **the enemy** (Isaiah 12:2), avenge you from fools (Psalm 94:1), save you from mistakes (Psalm 37:23, 24), and preserve you until you are in heaven in His presence forever (1 Thessalonians 5:23).

He longs to delight in you because He is the perfect **Abba** Father. He is full of **Grace** and **Mercy** and always ready to connect with you. As your Creator and **Omniscient**, Ever-Present **Abba**, only He knows your heart well enough to quiet it. Will you ask Him to **anoint** you with His Peace and give Him your anxieties? He is **Jehovah**; He can handle whatever you give Him. You are the object of His Love. Will you acknowledge His Love for you and tell Him you receive it?

You have victory in Jesus Christ. When you choose to connect with Him, you ignite the process of His transforming **Grace**, which creates a deep, abiding quietness within you as you begin to recognize His Rule and Trust in His Name. The natural consequence of this trust is God's ultimate delight in rejoicing over you with **Grace** and **Mercy**.

Be at peace; the Lord your God is with you.

Are you Ready?

1 Thessalonians 4:16-18 (NIV)

For the Lord himself will come down from heaven, with a loud command, with the voice of the archangel and with the trumpet call of God, and the **dead in Christ** will rise first. After that, we who are still alive and are left will be caught up together with them in the clouds to meet the Lord in the air. And so we will be with the Lord forever. Therefore encourage one another with these words.

O happy day; a shout from Jesus Himself will ring throughout the earth! The trumpet will blast and those with eyes to see and ears to hear will join Him in the clouds to be with Him forever. He is coming to get you. Are you ready? He delays because He desires that not one be lost; no, not one.

Are you doing your part to share Jesus with others? Will you ask for more opportunities to share Him? In 1 Thessalonians 4:1–3, the Message translation says you should strive to please God "not in a dogged religious plod, but in a living, spirited dance." It is a dance of worship that speaks to all the Glory of your God. You know the guidelines laid out for you from the Master, Jesus. God wants you to live a pure life filled with the joy of your **salvation** (Isaiah 61:10).

When Jesus returns from heaven, the **dead in Christ** get to go first (1 Thessalonians 4:16). Then, those still living will join in that happy meeting! Oh, what a glorious reunion it will be! You will be with your forever family and you will finally see Jesus. You will really see Him! The day is coming when your faith will be rewarded with sight! O happy day! Are you ready?

The Land of Meribah

Psalm 81:6, 7 (NLT)

"Now I will take the load from your shoulders; I will free your hands from their heavy tasks. You cried to me in trouble, and I **saved** you; I answered out of the thunder cloud and tested your faith when there was no water at Meribah."

The biggest battle you will ever face is the battle to trust **Abba**. Your flesh will constantly be at war with your spirit. Will you cry to Him for His protection, provision, and guidance; or will you fret, worry, stress, and move forward in your own understanding?

At some point, you will find yourself in the land of Meribah—the land of strife and hardship (see Exodus 17:1–7). Will you linger; will you fall apart; or will you cry out to Jesus? Will you reach for His hand of relief and rescue? Your shoulders are not big enough to carry the weight of the world and God does not intend you to be burdened beyond what you can bear (1 Corinthians 10:13). Will you invite Him to take the load from your shoulders and free you from your heavy tasks?

God will test your faith in Meribah. Will you pass the test? Will you cry out to Jesus and tell Him you are going to trust Him? Will you tell **Abba** Father you are going to thank Him constantly for allowing you to be His child? He is the most Amazing Father. He will give you everything you need, including Strength and Peace for the journey. Anything and everything is possible with Him. Now, tell Him you believe this and relax in His divine control.

Divine Control

Psalm 34:8-10 (NLT)

Taste and see that the LORD is good. Oh, the joys of those who take refuge in him! Fear the LORD, you his godly people, for those who fear him will have all they need. Even strong young lions sometimes go hungry, but those who trust in the LORD will lack no good thing.

Romans 8:6 (NLT)

So letting your sinful nature control your mind leads to death. But letting the Spirit control your mind leads to life and peace.

Do you have a decision to make? How do you really know what to do? How can you be sure of God's will? Will you seek Him in prayer and in His Word? Will you ask Him to give you a burning desire for His will? Will you ask Him to give you a check in your spirit that causes unrest if you are not in His will, or incredible peace with your choice if it is His will? Will you ask Him to open and close doors and give you the wisdom to recognize which is which?

You are blessed when you respect the Lord's will and way for you. When you live life your way, you may achieve a certain amount of success—a fancy title, and even material blessings; but in your soul there will be an unshakable gnawing and emptiness. The mind of the flesh—the mind centered on doing what it thinks above what God says—will lead your body and soul to fatigue and frustration. It is exhausting to run against the wind. Why do it? Will you set your mind on whatever is of the Lord and ask for strength to fulfill His will?

Revere and honor the Lord and be prepared to be astonished with how Good He is to you!

The Lord is Your Shepherd

> **Isaiah 58:11 (NLT)**
> The LORD will guide you continually, giving you water when you are dry and restoring your strength. You will be like a well-watered garden, like an ever-flowing spring.
>
> **Psalm 23:1-3 (NIV)**
> The LORD is my shepherd, I lack nothing. He makes me lie down in green pastures, he leads me beside quiet waters, he refreshes my soul. He guides me along the right paths for his name's sake.

Your Forever Father is completely Loyal, Faithful, and Trustworthy. Your temporary family is going to frustrate and disappoint you at times; but your **Abba** Father will never leave your side nor forsake you. You are His namesake, part of His family. Go to Him, reflect on His names, sing praise songs, and receive His restoration for your weary soul. He is the Architect of your soul; He knows best how to refresh, revive, and restore you. He is willing and faithful to give; will you tell Him you are willing to receive and embrace Him?

Oh, the good plans He has for you! He delights in guiding you in His Ways of goodness, purity, and prosperity. Circumstances and the actions or influences of others may cause you to stumble, but your **Abba** is always a safe refuge waiting to restore you. Will you let Him? If you walk hand in hand with Him, you will not miss the right path He has prepared in advance for you. He sees yesterday, today, and tomorrow with absolute wisdom and clarity. Your God loves sharing with His children. He shared His son Jesus; will He not share His perfect guidance when you ask?

Jehovah is waiting for your invitation to lead you. Place your hand in His and follow Him along the paths of right living.

Safe Beneath God's Wings

1 Corinthians 15:33 (NIV)
Do not be misled: "Bad company corrupts good character."

2 Peter 3:17, 18 (NLT)
I am warning you ahead of time, dear friends. Be on guard so that you will not be carried away by the errors of these wicked people and lose your own secure footing. Rather, you must grow in the grace and knowledge of our Lord and Savior Jesus Christ.
  All glory to him, both now and forever! Amen.

You are safe and sound when you are connected to Jesus. Being connected to Him will manifest itself in your life with increased overtures of **grace**; a tender, caring, kindness toward others will flourish from your words and intentions. John tells us that the Word was made flesh and lived with us filled with Grace and Truth. Jesus did not come to earth so you could just know about Him; He wants to "do life" with you through the ebb and flow of your days. He desires you to experience Him in the moments of your life by talking to Him, praising Him, seeking His Wise guidance, and thanking Him for His presence and provisions. The more you connect with Him, the greater your **grace** toward others.

Do you pay attention to your daily walk? It only takes one very wrong turn to get you off course. **The enemy** loves nothing more than for you to lose your safe position in Jesus. Of course you will never lose your **salvation**, but you can walk out from under the safety of His wings (Psalm 91:4). Be on guard so that you are not led astray. Do not be misled by those who call evil, good and good, evil.

Will you intentionally seek to understand God's Truth and ask for opportunities to demonstrate **grace**? This path will keep you steady, safe, and continually growing in strength.

Grace, Truth, and Legalism

> ### Psalm 119:136 (ESV)
> My eyes shed streams of tears, because people do not keep your law.
>
> ### John 1:17 (NIV)
> For the law was given through Moses; **grace** and truth came through Jesus Christ.
>
> ### Colossians 2:20-23 (NIV)
> Since you died with Christ to the elemental spiritual forces of this world, why, as though you still belonged to the world, do you submit to its rules: "Do not handle! Do not taste! Do not touch!"? These rules, which have to do with things that are all destined to perish with use, are based on merely human commands and teachings. Such regulations indeed have an appearance of wisdom, with their self-imposed worship, their false humility and their harsh treatment of the body, but they lack any value in restraining sensual indulgence.

L egalists feel they are superior because they avoid certain activities such as drinking or smoking; but no avoidance of any activity can cause your heart to love or trust Jesus. The legalist focuses on outward performances; but those who truly seek the Lord grow in the knowledge of Him and connect often with Him simply by talking to Him, praising Him, and **fellowship**ping with those who are yielded to Him.

As you grow in **Grace** and Truth, the desire of your heart will be to honor your Loving **Abba** Father and **glorify** your Savior, Jesus. Your focus, as you grow spiritually, will be more on your behavior and less on other's behavior. The mature believer is a man or woman of **grace**; but the spiritually immature do not and cannot extend love and **grace** because they have not chosen to use what has been given to them. Colossians 2:23 says that they give the illusion of being pious and **humble**, but they are really just showing off to make themselves look important.

You are called by God to grow in **Grace** and Truth and to avoid legalistic tendencies. Galatians 3:24 says the Law was our guardian until Christ came, in order that we may be **justified** by faith. Of course, the Law is and was good; but you must always remember its purpose is meant to lead you to Jesus. Keep the Law as an obedient child of God; but focus on Jesus. He is the only Way to God and the only One who can enable you to live in ways that please Him.

You are called by God to

grow in Grace and Truth

and to avoid legalistic

tendencies.

Who is Your Master?

Everyone has a master. Who is your master?

Sin is a harsh master. Do not walk through your days as though you are walking the "dead man's walk" under a dark cloud of a death sentence. Jesus has laid a path of freedom, life, and renewal for your daily walk. Are you walking in freedom?

Jesus is a Loving and Life-giving Master. You have the Power of His Spirit at work within you because He knocked on your heart's door and you opened the door and invited Him in as Lord and Savior of your life (Revelation 3:20). You no longer live under the tyranny of sin and death.

Sometimes it takes intentional, bondage-breaking prayers to walk in freedom. Sometimes, **Abba** Father will ask you to fast and pray in order to get you to the end of yourself so you can begin fresh with Him. If you seek to walk in Jesus' freedom, **Abba** will show you exactly how to do so; just ask Him.

You were not created to be miserable and calloused. You were not created to limp through this life. The victory has been won for you. God has divine work waiting for you to do.

Will you let today be the day you begin asking your Adonai, which means Lord and Master, to show you His Greatness and Mighty hand in your life? Deuteronomy 3:24 (NKJV) says, "O Lord GOD You have begun to show Your servant Your greatness and Your mighty hand, for what god is there in heaven or on earth who can do anything like Your works and Your mighty deeds?"

God has a divine work

waiting for you to do.

Step it Up

Is it time to make some changes and grow up? Do you reflect Christ to others and bring honor to your Christian title? You started out as a babe in Christ; with your limited knowledge of Him, you, of course, spoke, thought, and reasoned as a child. Have you put away former ways, the ways in which you used to speak and act? Today is the day to pack up the bottles and to move from your baby seat to a chair at the feasting table of the Lord. You are washed clean by the blood of Jesus; you have a new life. Will you commit to being a mature **witness** of Christ no matter how crazy a family member, friend, or co-worker is making you? Will you reflect His Glory no matter how oppressive your circumstances?

Your brothers and sisters in the Lord are sitting at His table with you; ask them for their support and prayers. Most of all, ask your **Advocate**, Jesus, to talk to the Father for you. Will you ask Him to increase your trust and to forgive you for any unbelief?

Jesus is inviting you to "go higher" with Him. What is your response?

Unveil your Heart

The access through the **curtain** to God Almighty was opened
by Jesus. Will you enter with a **humble** heart and go before
your **Abba** Father, acknowledging His **Mercy** for you? The Holy
Spirit of God within you is crying out to the innermost part of
you—deep cries out to deep (Psalm 42:7). He wants your whole
heart; He desires to commune with you.

Many Christians choose the easy path of outward observances
and rituals; these feed the flesh and create good feelings; but feelings are temporary and change with circumstances. What happens
to those good feelings when troubles knock on your door or death
waits at the threshold?

Any practice of religion not accompanied by a **humble**, sincere
heart is in vain. The deep recesses of your soul cry out for more
than human traditions. Your soul craves intimate connection to its
Maker—**Abba** Father. This connection requires being honest and

real, setting all pretensions aside, and admitting your deep need for **repent**ance, provision, guidance, and the Love of your Savior.

Will you un**veil** your heart, open it wide, and invite **Abba** Father into every nook and cranny? Will you surrender all to Him, do what is right, love **mercy**, and walk hand in hand with the Lover of your soul?

Any practice of religion not

accompanied by a humble,

sincere heart is in vain.

Continue to Trust Him

Romans 4:2, 11 (NLT)

If his good deeds had made him acceptable to God, he would have had something to boast about. But that was not God's way . . . Circumcision was a sign that **Abraham** already had faith and that God had already accepted him and declared him to be righteous—even before he was circumcised. So **Abraham** is the spiritual father of those who have faith but have not been circumcised. They are counted as righteous because of their faith.

Colossians 1:10 (NLT)

Then the way you live will always honor and please the Lord, and your lives will produce every kind of good fruit. All the while, you will grow as you learn to know God better and better.

Colossians 2:6, 7 (NLT)

And now, just as you accepted Christ Jesus as your Lord, you must continue to follow him. Let your roots grow down into him, and let your lives be built on him. Then your faith will grow strong in the truth you were taught, and you will overflow with thankfulness.

Does your pulse beat for Jesus? Is your life rooted in Him? If you have determined to know Him, your trust in Him is growing stronger with every situation in your life. Do you recognize the ebb and flow developing between you and your Savior? Have you noticed how your connection to Him has proven to you how incredibly Trustworthy He is? Is His Trustworthiness prompting you to be less and less tempted to place your trust elsewhere? Are you overflowing with thankfulness? Paul says in Colossians that as we, God's children, choose to build our lives on His truths, we will begin to develop a grateful attitude. Will you determine to acknowledge His blessings with thanksgiving?

The manifestation of growing thankfulness is a greater desire to obey God and **glorify** Him with your life. Like your spiritual ancestor, **Abraham**, you trust **Abba** Father; as a sign of your faith in Him, you seek to obey Him. God considers you righteous; not because of what you do, but because of what motivates you to do what's right—your trust and faith in Him.

Will you keep following Him and build your life on **the Rock of Ages**? God Almighty is counting you as righteous because you trust Him.

The manifestation of

growing thankfulness is a

greater desire to obey God

and glorify Him with

your life.

A Peaceful Harvest

Psalm 77:7-9, 11, 14 (NLT)

Has the Lord rejected me forever? Will he never again be kind to me? Is his unfailing love gone forever? Have his promises permanently failed? Has God forgotten to be gracious? Has he slammed the door on his compassion? . . . But then I recall all you have done, O LORD; I remember your wonderful deeds of long ago . . . You are the God of great wonders! You demonstrate your awesome power among the nations.

Hebrews 12:6-11 (NLT)

"For the LORD disciplines those he loves, and he punishes each one he accepts as his child." As you endure this divine discipline, remember that God is treating you as his own children. Who ever heard of a child who is never disciplined by its father? If God doesn't discipline you as he does all of his children, it means that you are illegitimate and are not really his children at all. Since we respected our earthly fathers who disciplined us, shouldn't we submit even more to the discipline of the Father of our spirits, and live forever? For our earthly fathers disciplined us for a few years, doing the best they knew how. But God's discipline is always good for us, so that we might share in his **holiness**. No discipline is enjoyable while it is happening—it's painful! But afterward there will be a peaceful harvest of right living for those who are trained in this way.

Are you going through a hardship? Will the Lord ever leave you or forsake you? No! Will He reject a cry of help? No!

Is it possible **Abba** Father may be disciplining you through hardship and **trial**; may He be trying to work out something good in your life? Will you let Him? If you have sought the Lord and feel your hardship may be His divine discipline, what should you do?

Your **Abba** Father only disciplines those He loves (Hebrews 12:6). Thank Him for choosing you to be in His family and tell Him you trust Him as a God of Perfect Justice and Fairness. Then, submit to His discipline by thanking Him that He is more concerned about your spiritual growth than your comfort. Finally, tell Him you look forward to His promise of a peaceful harvest of right living because you agree to be trained in His Holy ways.

A new day is on the horizon when you seek **Abba** Father even in the midst of pain. His Love is unfailing and you will soon rejoice in His Compassion, **Mercy**, and **Grace**.

Do you acknowledge all He has already done for you and look forward to all He will continue to do for you, both in this life and the next?

A new day is on the horizon

when you seek Abba Father

even in the midst of pain.

Pray for Your Country

2 Kings 21:1–6 (The Message)

Manasseh was twelve years old when he became king. He ruled for fifty-five years in Jerusalem. His mother's name was Hephzibah. In God's judgment he was a bad king—an evil king. He reintroduced all the moral rot and spiritual corruption that had been scoured from the country when God dispossessed the pagan nations in favor of the children of Israel. He rebuilt all the sex-and-religion shrines that his father Hezekiah had torn down, and he built altars and phallic images for the sex god Baal and sex goddess Asherah, exactly what Ahaz king of Israel had done. He worshiped the cosmic powers, taking orders from the constellations. He even built these pagan altars in The Temple of God, the very Jerusalem Temple dedicated exclusively by God's decree ("in Jerusalem I place my Name") to God's Name. And he built shrines to the cosmic powers and placed them in both courtyards of The Temple of God. He burned his own son in a sacrificial offering. He practiced black magic and fortunetelling. He held séances and consulted spirits from the underworld. Much evil—in God's judgment, a career in evil. And God was angry.

2 Kings 22:1, 2, 8–13, 16–20 (NLT)

Josiah was eight years old when he became king, and he reigned in Jerusalem thirty-one years . . . He did what was pleasing in the LORD's sight and followed the example of his ancestor David. He did not turn away from doing what was right . . . Hilkiah the **high priest** said to Shaphan the court secretary, "I have found the Book of the Law in the Lord's Temple!" Then Hilkiah gave the scroll to Shaphan, and he read it. Shaphan went to the king and reported, "Your officials have turned over the money collected at the Temple of the LORD to the workers and supervisors at the Temple." Shaphan also told the king, "Hilkiah the priest has given me a scroll." So

Shaphan read it to the king. When the king heard what was written in the Book of the Law, he tore his clothes in despair. Then he gave these orders . . . "Go to the Temple and speak to the LORD for me and for the people and for all Judah. Inquire about the words written in this scroll that has been found. For the LORD's great anger is burning against us because our ancestors have not obeyed the words in this scroll. We have not been doing everything it says we must do." . . . 'This is what the LORD says: I am going to bring disaster on this city and its people. All the words written in the scroll that the king of Judah has read will come true. For my people have abandoned me and offered **sacrifice**s to pagan gods, and I am very angry with them for everything they have done. My anger will burn against this place, and it will not be quenched.' "But go to the king of Judah who sent you to seek the LORD and tell him: 'This is what the LORD, the God of Israel, says concerning the message you have just heard: You were sorry and **humble**d yourself before the LORD when you heard what I said against this city and its people— that this land would be cursed and become desolate. You tore your clothing in despair and wept before me in **repent**ance. And I have indeed heard you, says the LORD. So I will not send the promised disaster until after you have died and been buried in peace. You will not see the disaster I am going to bring on this city. . .'"

Will you **humble** yourself before the Lord for the sake of your great country? Will you pray for your country's leaders to be sorry for the moral rot that has infected your homeland?

Manasseh was a leader who steered God's people toward wickedness. He encouraged them to consult mediums for advice, to worship **false gods**, and to practice sexual immortality. He angered God with his spiritual corruption and moral rot.

Manasseh's son, Josiah, was different. He chose to read God's truths and to obey them. He **humble**d himself before the Lord and was sorry for the evil that had permeated the land and the people's hearts. He demonstrated the seriousness of his **repent**ance by pouring resources into restoring God's temple—His place of worship. He pledged before the people to obey the Lord with all his heart and soul and He got rid of the mediums and psychics, the household gods, and the **idol**s. We are told no other king was ever like Josiah who turned to the Lord with all his heart and soul and strength, obeying all the laws of Moses.

The Lord was angry with the people for abandoning Him and living in spiritual decay under Manasseh's rule; but God held back His hand of punishment. He heard Josiah's heartfelt **repent**ance and He did not send the promised disaster.

Will you cry out to **Abba** Father for **Mercy** on behalf of your great land and your leaders?

Will you humble yourself

before the Lord for the sake

of your great country?

Teach us to Number our Days

Do you love the Lord with all your heart, mind, and soul? You have God's Holy Spirit within you, empowering you to desire a deeper relationship with Him. His Holy Spirit pours out His Love in your heart (Romans 5:5) and encourages you in the enduring Hope you have because of Jesus Christ (1 Thessalonians 1:3) Will you ask Him to help you? He Loves you and has chosen you to be part of His eternal family. He promises in His Word to guide you through this life (John 16: 13, 14) and awaits your arrival into the next. This life will fade away as quickly as a beautiful flower—alive and vibrant one day and wilted and lifeless the next. You are like a vapor that appears for a set time (Psalm 39:5); God has already recorded a set number of days for you. Are you making your days count for all of eternity?

In 1 Thessalonians 1, Paul tells us what to do with our precious limited time here. He says to labor in love for others by never ceasing to set an example of trust in Jesus and joy in Him, no matter your circumstances. Paul encourages us to be examples to all believers by serving the One True God and by looking forward to the coming of Jesus, whom God raised from the dead.

You cannot imagine what God has prepared for you because of the love you demonstrate for Him and others. Will you make your days count?

You have God's Holy Spirit

within you, empowering

you to desire a deeper

relationship with Him.

Love Covers Sin

1 Peter 4:7, 8 (NLT)

The end of the world is coming soon. Therefore, be earnest and disciplined in your prayers. Most important of all, continue to show deep love for each other, for love covers a multitude of sins.

In these last days, you are called to live for God. This is where you find real life, truth, grace, peace, hope, and joy. Talk to Him in the morning, throughout your day, before you close your eyes at night, and when you awake during the night. He is always near and always listening. But how else do you live for God?

God made you to be in relationship with your brothers and sisters in Christ. This is why He encourages you in His Word to cover others' sins with love. Where love is demonstrated, small offenses are overlooked and large ones are addressed in prayer and in person, with the goal of reconciliation. God designed family; it was His idea. Your Abba Father is well pleased with you when you love your family.

Your archenemy, the devil, is thrilled when you withhold love. He delights in destroying relationships through divisiveness and conflict because relationships are important to your Abba God.

Will you determine today to honor your Lord by showing deep love for others and letting your love cover a multitude of sins? 1 Peter 4:13 says trials make you partners with Christ in His suffering, so you will have the wonderful joy of seeing His Glory when it is revealed to the entire world. Oh, what joy awaits you whose love covers short-comings!

The end of this world is coming soon; will you continue to show deep love for others?

Table Manners

Proverbs 18:21 (NLT)
The tongue can bring death or life; those who love to talk will reap the consequences.

Ezekiel 37:4 (NLT)
Then he said to me, "Speak a prophetic message to these bones and say, '**Dry bones**, listen to the word of the LORD!'"

James 1:26 (NLT)
If you claim to be religious but don't control your tongue, you are fooling yourself, and your religion is worthless.

1 Peter 3:10 (NLT)
For the Scriptures say, "If you want to enjoy life and see many happy days, keep your tongue from speaking evil and your lips from telling lies."

Be careful with your words. Your God hears everything you say. Your poisonous words can kill dreams, hopes, imagination, and joy in others. Oh, please be very careful!

On the other hand, your words can revive hope, renew a forgotten dream, and flow fresh, **living water** into a parched, dry soul. Your words can speak courage where fear abounds and your words can bring fresh life to **dry bones**—those whose faith lies withered and dry.

God is serious about you using your words to help heal and encourage; He said in James that your religion is worthless if you do not control your tongue. Will you consider the seriousness of His words? Will you guard your words with great intentionality? Will you commit to not sharing words that could hurt another? If you have some special knowledge that could damage someone's reputation, don't share it with anyone, except to intercede for them in your prayers.

Abba Father is the only true Judge and He knows best how to deal with your brothers and sisters. A.W. Tozer said, "After you are seated at the Father's table, He expects to teach you table manners. And He won't let you eat unless you obey the etiquette of the table. And what is that? The etiquette of the table is that you don't tell stories about the brother who is sitting at the table with you."

1. A.W. Tozer, *Five Vows for Spiritual Power.* Public Domain.

Your words can revive hope,

renew a forgotten dream,

and flow fresh, living water

into a parched, dry soul.

Founded in Godliness

Just as Israel was birthed into the ways of the Lord, so was America. God's Word and ways laid a foundation for this great country.

In Exodus 33:13, Moses pleaded with **Abba** Father that he might know Him better and continue to enjoy His favor. Will you do the same? Moses had tasted and seen the Lord's Goodness and was hungry for more of Him. He experienced amazing **Grace**— God's unmerited favor and unfailing kindness toward him. He accepted God's **Forgiveness** and **Mercy** and, as a result, desired more and more intimacy with His Maker. Moses remembered the people he was leading were God's special nation. Israel was a nation that would show a lost world the way to **salvation**, and a nation that would bring light and goodness to a dark and cruel world. Moses sought the Lord's presence and Glory, and how did the Lord respond? According to Exodus 33:17, the Lord replied that He would indeed do what Moses asked because He looked favorably on him; **Abba** God knew him by name.

Will you ask God to ignite the flicker burning inside you to know Him and love Him into an all-consuming fire? Will you implore the Lord to remember America was founded as "One Nation under God" and to lead us back to living as a nation under God? Will you seek the Lord with everything in you; will you seek His presence and His Glory? He is looking favorably on you and He knows your name, will you ask Him to increase your knowledge of and intimacy with Him?

You belong to Him; you are His prized possession and He longs for you to enjoy His favor.

Ask God to ignite the flicker

burning inside you to know

Him and love Him into an

all-consuming fire.

Glossary

Abba

This word expresses a very close, intimate relationship, much like a parent/child bond. The English word that most closely compares to the biblical meaning is "Daddy."

Found in Mark 14:36; Galatians 4:6.

Abraham

The story of Abraham is found in the Book of Genesis. He was the founding father of the Israelites—God's chosen people. His name means "Father of a Multitude."

Found in Genesis, chapters 12 through 25.

Acts of the Flesh

When the term "the flesh" is used in Scripture, it nearly always refers to the rebellious, disobedient part of us that operates in opposition to God's desires for His children. "Acts of the flesh" are, therefore, the actions such attitudes produce.

Found in Galatians 5:19–21.

Adversary

An adversary is an enemy or one who acts in opposition. For Christians, the "adversary" is Satan. He hates whatever God loves and seeks to destroy those who belong to the Lord.

Found in 1 Peter 5:8.

Advocate

An advocate is one who speaks on behalf of another in pleading a cause in much the same way as a modern-day lawyer does. This is a translation of the Greek word meaning "intercessor" or "consoler." Jesus intercedes on our behalf from His throne in heaven, where He is seated at the right hand of the Father (Mark 16:19).

Found in 1 John 2:1.

Alpha and Omega

Jesus called Himself the Alpha and Omega in the Book of Revelation. Alpha and Omega, respectively, are the first and last letters of the Greek alphabet. In referring to Himself in this way, Jesus proclaimed He was present when all things began and will be present at the end. He is eternal—He always existed and will always exist. Because He is God, He is the beginning and end of all things. Through Him, we are saved; and by Him we will be taken into heaven on the last day. Only God Himself can make the claim, "I am the Alpha and the Omega."

Found in Revelation 1:8, 21:6, 22:13.

Amen

The word translated as "amen" in Scripture is an affirmation of truth. It is an interjection (or exclamation) of solemn, strong agreement. When one speaks the word "amen" it is as if to say, "Yes! That is true. Before God, I agree!"

Found in Psalm 41:13, 72:19, 89:52; Matthew 6:13; Revelation 22:20, 21.

Ancient of Days

This is the name given to our eternal God in the Book of Daniel. It conveys the image of One who is above and beyond time. The context of its use expresses an honor, dignity, and wisdom that is transcendent—far beyond that of any other being.

Found in Daniel 7:9–14.

Angels of God

Angels are heavenly beings—a distinct creation of God.

Contrary to the belief of some, Scripture makes it clear that angels are not and never have been human beings. The Greek word translated as "angel" means a messenger or one who is sent as an envoy. Angels were created by God to serve Him. However, a mutiny in heaven resulted in one third of the angel host choosing to serve Satan. The Angels of God have remained loyal to their Creator and continue to serve Him; the mutinous angels (fallen angels) operate in vehement opposition to the plans and purposes of God.

Found in Genesis 28:12; Matthew 22:30; Luke 12:8, 9; John 1:51; Hebrews 1:6.

Anoint(ed)

To be anointed is to be set apart for divine use. In Old Testament days, oil was poured upon the head of one who was to be dedicated to the Lord's service—a symbolic act of devotion. Those so anointed were empowered by God for powerful service to Him. Vessels and implements used in the Lord's service were also anointed—dedicated to the purposes of God.

Found in Exodus 28:41, 29:7, 40:15; 1 Samuel 10:1, 16:12, 13; Psalm 23:5, 45:7.

Armies of Heaven

The Armies of Heaven are God's holy angels who fight against the fallen angels on behalf of the children of God. The heavenly angels are loyal soldiers to their Commander, God Almighty. They are warriors operating under divine orders to affect the lives of men and the course of the world according to the purposes of God.

Found in 2 Kings 6:16, 17; Revelation 19:14.

Atonement

In the Old Testament, atonement was the method God ordained through which sinful man could be reconciled to Holy God. By the sacrifice of certain animals in a prescribed fashion, the sin of man could be "covered" for a period of time; the barrier between God and man created by sin was temporarily removed. In the New Testament, Jesus became the Sacrificial Lamb. When we trust in Him, His shed blood covers our sin for all time. Through Him, sinful man can be forever reconciled to Holy God.

Found in Exodus 29:36; Leviticus 4:20, 19:22; Psalm 79:9.

Babylon

In the days of Jehoiakim, King of Judah, God's people had ceased to follow God's Law and had begun to worship idols. God had warned the people of Judah repeatedly of the consequences of their rebellious ways. As a result of the continued sin of the people of God, the evil King Nebuchadnezzar of Babylon set siege against Jerusalem, the seat of power in Judah, and Jerusalem fell into his hands. Thousands of God's people were taken captive into Babylon, an idolatrous, wicked land; and their captivity lasted for decades. The Babylonians so disregarded God Almighty that they robbed God's temple of its priceless, consecrated treasures. From that time, Babylon became synonymous with sinfulness and idolatry.

Found in 2 Kings 20:17, 18, 25:13; Isaiah 13:19, 14:22, 21:9; Jeremiah 51:6–12; Revelation 14:8, 18:2, 21.

Balm

In general, the word "balm" means an ointment that has soothing, recuperative effect. Biblically, the word is associated with the "Balm of Gilead," an ointment so scarce it was twice as costly as silver in Old Testament days. This balm was cherished, not only for its value, but also for its ability to heal wounds.

Found in Jeremiah 8:22, 46:11, 51:8.

Belial

This is a biblical name for Satan or one of his fallen angels (demons). The word literally means "worthless" or "lawless." Belial, as used in Scripture, is the personification of all sinfulness and wickedness combined.

Found in Deuteronomy 13:13; Judges 20:13; 1 Samuel 2:12; 1 Kings 21:10, 13; 2 Corinthians 6:15.

Bema Seat

This term is not found in Scripture. However, "Bema" is the Greek word translated as the Judgment Seat of Christ where those who are born again by believing in Jesus will have their works and motives judged; they will be rewarded for their service to their King.

Found in 2 Corinthians 5:10.

Bread of Life

Twice, in the Gospel of John, Jesus referred to Himself as the "Bread of Life." Throughout Scripture, bread is spoken of as the staple—the basic necessity—to sustain life. It is representative of the nourishment needed to keep our bodies healthy and alive. Therefore, the symbolism conveyed by Jesus' assertion that He is the "Bread" conveys the truth that only by receiving Him can we know the spiritual health and eternal life God desires for us.

Found in John 6:35, 48.

Chaff

Generally, chaff is the outer layer of husk that surrounds grain as it grows. To harvest, the grain must be threshed (beaten) to remove the husk and expose the grain. The chaff is the dry, dead particles that are left; these are light and easily blown away by the wind. Biblically, chaff means worthless matter or something with no substance or purpose that will easily be swept away. In Scripture, godless people, ungodly doctrine, and hypocrites are referred to as chaff—worthless, empty, and insignificant.

Found in Psalm 1:4; Jeremiah 23:28; Matthew 3:12.

Chosen People

From the very beginning, God focused His love and attention on the Israelites, the nation He began through Abraham. To them He revealed His nature and His Law. He chose them to be the recipients of His redemptive love through the sacrificial ordinances He instituted. Israel continually strayed from God—ignoring His Law and worshiping false gods. However, through Israel, God brought forth a Savior, Jesus, the Son of God. Now, those who believe in Jesus and accept His sacrifice on their behalf are "adopted" into God's family—they become a part of the Chosen People of God.

Found in Deuteronomy 7:6; 1 Kings 11:36; 1 Chronicles 16:13; Psalm 33:12, 132:13; Isaiah 44:1; Matthew 20:16; 1 Peter 2:9.

Comforter

Jesus referred to the Holy Spirit as "Comforter." In the original language, this word was *parakletos*, meaning one called alongside to help. It also conveys the meaning of consoler or intercessor. The Holy Spirit was sent by Jesus to aid believers in their walk of faith. He consoles us in our distress, and comforts us by reminding us of all the promises of God.

Found in John 14:16, 26, 15:26, 16:7.

Communion

This word has a dual meaning in the kingdom of God. To be in communion with another is to share deepest, most intimate thoughts and feelings. It is to participate together in a deeply emotional and/or spiritual exchange. It is possible Paul had this definition in mind when he referred to the Lord's Supper as the "communion" of the body and blood of Christ.

Found in 1 Corinthians 10:16.

Confess

To confess means to admit guilt. It is necessary for anyone who wishes to be in right relationship with Holy God to recognize and be forthcoming with God regarding his or her sinful state. It is not necessary to confess because God is not aware of sin within our hearts; we confess because we must come to God with an open heart, in true and honest transparency. The heart that would attempt to hide sin from the Lord is a heart that is not willing to stand humbly before God; pride is a sin that will attempt to hide other sins.

Found in Mark 1:5; 1 John 1:9.

Consecrate

When a thing is consecrated, it is separated from worldly matters and dedicated to God. Things, as well as people, may be consecrated. A vessel used solely for the purpose of worshiping Abba God—whether the vessel is an implement, container, device, or person—is consecrated to the service of the King.

Found in Exodus 28:41; Joshua 6:19; Hebrews 10:20.

Conviction

Conviction speaks to the awareness of and sorrow for sin. It differs from guilt in that conviction will draw a repentant one to God's throne of grace; guilt may well drive one from their God. Conviction is an act of the Holy Spirit within a believer; guilt is most often a ploy of Satan, the enemy of the children of God.

Found in John 8:9, 16:8; James 2:9; Jude 1:15.

Covenant

In general terms, a covenant is a legally binding agreement. Biblically, a covenant is a much more powerful bond. It is, in nature, much like a last will and testament in that it is an endowment bestowed by one party of greater means upon another party of lesser means—the one who possesses much bequeaths to the one who possesses less. Just as loyalty and devotion is often the motivation for choosing an heir, so it is with the Lord. He has covenanted with us to bring to pass all His promises; all He asks in return is loyalty and devotion—a heart filled with faith and love for our Abba God.

Found in Genesis 9:9, 17:7; Nehemiah 1:5; Psalm 89:34, 111:9; Jeremiah 31:31–33; Matthew 26:28; Romans 11:27; Hebrews 9:15.

Curtain (Veil)

After the Israelites were freed from their slavery in Egypt, they wandered in the wilderness for 40 years. During that time, they worshiped God in a tent-like structure called the Tabernacle. Later, when they settled their own land, they built a grand and majestic Temple in which to worship God. In both structures, the area at the back (furthest from the entrance) was the area where God's Presence resided. It was separated from the rest of the worship structure by a massively thick, woven curtain, also known as a veil. This curtain had no opening and no one could go past it except the high priest (see definition below), and he only once per year. At the moment Jesus died on the cross, the curtain in the Temple was split from top to bottom. This signified that, because of Jesus' sacrifice, all are now able to enter into the very Presence of God.

Found in Exodus 26:33; Leviticus 16:2; Numbers 18:7; Matthew 27:51; 2 Corinthians 3:14.

Dead in Christ

Those who accept Jesus as Savior and Lord become a part of His body on earth; they are His hands, His feet, and His voice to the world. The Bible tells us we are positionally located "in" Christ. Therefore, when one who belongs to the Lord dies, that person is "dead in Christ," meaning at the point of death, that person was "in Christ."

Found in Romans 12:5; 2 Corinthians 5:17; Galatians 3:28; Ephesians 2:13; 1 Thessalonians 4:16.

Devil

The devil's name is Satan. He began as a superb creation of God named Lucifer, which means "carrier of light." Pride caused Lucifer to consider himself equal to God. He wanted to rule as God rules and convinced a third of all God's angels to follow him instead of God. As a result, God cast Lucifer and the rebellious angels from heaven. Now known as Satan or the "devil," he is eaten up with jealousy, anger, and hatred—he hates everything God loves, especially mankind. So he is on a mission to destroy mankind and cause us to follow him instead of God. Those who choose to follow Satan will suffer the same fate awaiting him—an eternity separated from God and all that is good and holy—an eternity in hell.

Found in Isaiah 14:12–15; Ezekiel 28:12–19; John 10:10; Revelation 20:15.

Dominion of Darkness

The word "dominion" means to have the power to rule or control. And the term "darkness" refers to the unenlightened state of those who have not seen, known, and experienced the "light" of God's Truth. Therefore, this term is used in the Bible to describe those who do not know Christ as their Savior. They remain slaves to sin—totally under the dominion, or control, of Satan. Only the blood of Christ can free us from the devil's evil power.

Found in Colossians 1:12, 13. See also John 3:16–20; Romans 6:16–22; 1 Corinthians 4:3, 4.

Dry Bones

The Book of Ezekiel contains an account of a vision given to Ezekiel. In the vision, Ezekiel was instructed to speak the Word of the Lord to a pile of dry, human bones. When he did, the bones began to be reconnected, grow muscle, sinew, and flesh—they came back to life. The symbolism spoke of the nation of Israel's return to the Lord and the reestablishment of its own land. However, the symbolism also speaks loudly of the need for all people to receive the Word of the Lord in order to find true life—to be saved from their dead, dry state and become renewed and enlivened by the water of life available through the Word of God.

Found in Ezekiel 37:1–14.

El Roi

Hagar was the slave of Sarah, Abraham's wife. Sarah was barren. Because she could not give Abraham a son, Sarah gave Hagar to Abraham so he could father a child by her. A son, Ishmael, would be born from the union. Once Hagar had become pregnant, she began treating Sarah with contempt. Sarah repaid her with harsh treatment. So Hagar escaped and ran away into the desert. But God met her there and told her to return to Sarah. He promised Hagar she would have a son and, through him, she would be the mother of many descendants. Hagar praised God for His faithfulness and called Him El Roi, which means "The God Who Sees Me." Hagar is the only one who called God by this very descriptive name. (For further information, see the Names of God article on pages xv–xviii.)

Found in Genesis 16:1–16.

Fallen Realm

The angels who followed Satan in rebellion against God (see Glossary entry "devil") accepted Satan as their lord and master. They were cast from heaven and fell away from God's grace. They are now a part of Satan's kingdom—his fallen realm. Before we accept Jesus as our Lord and Master, we are also a part of Satan's fallen realm—we are slaves of sin and under the dominion of darkness (see Glossary entry "dominion of darkness").

Found in Isaiah 14:12; Colossians 1:12, 13.

Fallen World

This world is under the curse of sin. Adam and Eve enjoyed perfect communion with God (see Glossary entry "communion"). However, they allowed Satan to deceive them into sin—they disobeyed God (see Genesis 3:1–19). They and all their descendants suffered the same fate—they became disconnected from God and alienated from His righteousness. They became slaves of a new master—Satan. Before we accept Jesus as our Savior and Lord, we are slaves to sin and sinful citizens of the fallen, sin-filled world.

Found in John 3:16–20, 7:7; Romans 5:12, 13, 12:2; James 4:4; 1 John 2:15–17.

False gods

False gods consist of anything that is worshiped in the place of God Almighty. These are also known as "idols" (see Glossary entry "idols"). A false god need not be a counterfeit deity. We may worship money, fame, status, or even another human being. Anything we value above our relationship with God is a false god—it takes the highest priority in our lives and we are subservient to its demands.

Found in Deuteronomy 32:17; Psalm 4:2; Jeremiah 16:19; Jonah 2:8; Ephesians 5:5; Colossians 3:5; 1 John 5:21.

Fasting

Fasting, in the biblical sense, is a time of abstaining from food, drink, or certain activity for a period of time in order to offer more focused attention upon the Lord. Fasting requires the spirit of man to override the flesh of man—it is forcing oneself to ignore the demands of the flesh (hunger, thirst, desire) and place greater importance upon the spiritual aspects of life. Fasting is a strengthening agent of prayer; by having a more singular focus, it is possible to enter into a time of intense fellowship with God, which forges a much closer bond. Fasting also serves to increase the ability to "hear" God's voice; when the voices of your physical desires are ignored, the voice of God is much easier to hear. Fasting is also a dynamic that allows for much more powerful intercession on behalf of others. At times, believers may fast in repentance; though not required for God's forgiveness, it is a sign of absolute sincerity and the desire to deny all the sinful works of the flesh (see Glossary entry "Fleshly Lusts" below).

Found in 1 Samuel 7:6; 2 Samuel 12:16–23; Ezra 8:21–23; Esther 4:16; Joel 2:12; Matthew 6:16–18; Acts 14:23.

Fellowship

In worldly terms, fellowship is to gather together with those who have similar interests or goals. Biblical fellowship includes this aspect, yet goes far beyond. Fellowship in the kingdom of God is to be indelibly linked to other believers; it is to have lives so intertwined as to share sorrow and joy at the deepest levels. It is a unity of spirit that has its foundations in the Lord Himself. The Apostle Paul likened the community of believers to a body (1 Corinthians 12:12–27); he wanted to convey the degree to which we are connected to one another. More importantly, believers collectively form the body of Christ on earth (Romans 12:5)—we are His hands, His feet, and His voice, to one another and to an unbelieving world.

Found in 1 John 1:1–8.

Fleshly Lusts

The Apostle Peter used this term to describe temptations to operate according to our sinful natures (1 Peter 2:11, 12). Even once we have accepted Jesus as our Lord and Savior, Satan still tempts us to fall into old patterns of sin. He tempts our flesh, for he cannot touch our spirit; our spirit belongs to God. Yet, we can and do continue to make sinful choices when we fall for Satan's tempting lies. Far too often, Christians fail to follow God's perfect will and choose to operate according to the desires ignited by our flesh—that part of us that is still of the world and will not be renewed until we leave this world behind and receive a new spiritual body from our Abba God.

Found in 1 John 2:15–17; Romans 7:13–25; Galatians 5:19–25.

Forgiveness

Forgiveness is not a term limited to things of the kingdom. The world practices a form of forgiveness; but it is only a pale shadow of the forgiveness offered by our Abba Father. In the world, forgiveness is often conditional and always limited. Human beings are not capable of totally forgetting a wrong; forgiveness cannot be total when the wrong is remembered. However, when our holy God forgives those who come to Him with repentant hearts, He chooses to forget the sin ever happened. Once we have repented and received the forgiveness of God, it is as if we had never sinned. But God has given us one stipulation to His forgiveness—we must forgive others if we wish God to forgive us. How can a heart that refuses to love enough to forgive receive the unconditional love of God as manifested in His total and undeserved pardon and removal of our sins?

Found in Psalm 103:12; Isaiah 43:25; Mark 11:25; Luke 6:37; 1 John 1:9.

Fruit of the Spirit

An apple tree brings forth apples because the seed planted caused the plant to grow according to its kind; just so should those who have been given the Spirit of God bring forth fruit that is according to the nature of the Spirit of God. The Holy Spirit is alive within the hearts of believers; His very nature is contained within us. Therefore, as we grow attuned to the Spirit's voice when He prompts us to act with godly actions and reactions, the "fruit" that is produced in our lives should become more and more representative of God's nature.

Found in Galatians 5:22–25; Ephesians 5:8–10.

Glorify

To glorify God means to reveal through our actions and attitudes His Holy nature, limitless love, and majesty. It means to bring recognition to His magnificent splendor. Glorify is a verb; it requires action. When we praise our God, when we lift His name high by extolling His virtues, when we give Him the honor due His Name, we reveal to the world the character and attributes of our Abba Father.

Found in Psalm 69:30; Luke 2:20; 1 Peter 2:12.

The Bible also tells us that those who belong to the Lord will be glorified. This does not mean we will be honored and revered, praised and extolled. It means God will transform us from these earthly vessels into perfected spiritual beings. When we have left this world and entered into the kingdom of God, we will become like Jesus. We will be given a new body; our spirit will be completely in tune with the Spirit of God; we will be perfected and take on the very nature of Christ. Scripture tells us we will share in the glory of our Lord.

Found in Romans 8:17, 28–30; 1 Peter 5:1.

God's Law

The first five books of the Old Testament are sometimes called the books of the law. In them we read the account of Moses receiving directly from God the laws that were to govern the Israelite nation. These laws contained very specific directions from God for all aspects of life: dietary, legal, spiritual, relational, and medical, just to name a few. The entire code of behavior prescribed by God is known as the Law of God. Since we no longer live under the law of the Old Testament, but under the grace of the New Testament, God's Law now most often refers to the Ten Commandments.

Found in Matthew 22:34–40.

Good News

Good News refers to the truth of God's redemptive love. The first to refer to it as "good news" was Ezra in the Book of First Chronicles. Isaiah spoke of the message of salvation as "good news." The gospels, Matthew, Mark, and Luke also use this term to speak of the message of salvation available through Christ. As a matter of fact, the word "gospel" means "Good News."

Found in 1 Chronicles 16:23; Isaiah 52:7; Matthew 4:23; Mark 1:14; Luke 3:18; Luke 8:1.

Gospel

The word gospel as used in Scripture literally means "good news" or "glad tidings." The first four books of the New Testament are called "gospels"; they are the good news about Jesus' life, death, and resurrection. They contain the "glad tidings" of the salvation available to us through His death on our behalf. In the world, "gospel" conveys the meaning of something absolutely, undoubtedly true. Such is the good news of our Lord. His truth is sure and His salvation is available to all who will call upon His name. This is the gospel of our Lord.

Found in Matthew 24:14; Mark 16:15; Acts 15:7; Romans 1:16; Philippians 1:27; Revelation 14:6.

Grace

Very simply, grace is the undeserved support, assistance, and partiality shown to us by Abba God. We do not deserve His favor and we cannot earn it. His grace is a gift to us. It is God's grace that compelled Him to send His Son, Jesus, into the world to die for the sins of mankind. It is God's unmerited favor that sustains us and redeems us.

Found in John 1:16, 17; Romans 3:22–24, 5:15–17; Ephesians 2:4–8.

Great Commission

The Great Commission is the name given to the directive of Christ: "Therefore go and make disciples of all nations, baptizing them in the name of the Father and of the Son and of the Holy Spirit, and teaching them to obey everything I have commanded you" (NIV).

Found in Matthew 28:16–20.

Great White Throne of Judgment

The Great White Throne of Judgment will occur when this world comes to an end. God will judge the lives of all mankind. Two books will be opened at that time—one will be the Book of Life in which the names of all who belong to the Lord are written. Any whose names are not found written in that book will be condemned for not believing in the Name of the Son of God.

Found in Revelation 20:11–15.

Heathen

A heathen is one who does not accept the truth of God or believe Him to be the only true God.

Found in Matthew 6:7, 18:17.

Heavenly Citizenship

The moment you believe on Jesus as your Lord and Savior, you establish your heavenly citizenship—you become a full citizen of God's eternal kingdom. Though you may be years from actually abiding in His Presence on those heavenly shores, when you accept Jesus as your King, you are accepted as one of His own.

Found in Philippians 3:20, 21.

High Priest

In Old Testament times, the servant of God who would act as High Priest was chosen by the people of Israel. The High Priest offered sacrifices on behalf of the people, other priests, and himself. Only the High Priest was allowed to enter into the Holy of Holies, the veiled off portion of the Temple or Tabernacle (see Glossary entry "Curtain") where the Ark of the Covenant rested and the Presence of God dwelt. Once per year, on the Day of Atonement (a holy day set aside for the atonement of sins), he would sacrifice a bullock and seven lambs and collect some of the blood. Only on this day was the High Priest allowed to enter the Holy of Holies. He would enter and sprinkle the blood on the Ark of the Covenant (also known as the Mercy Seat). Through this sacrifice and ritual, the sins of the people were cleansed for the period of one year.

Jesus is the High Priest of God. Through the sacrifice of His own life and His spilt blood, the sins of all people are cleansed for all time; we only need accept His sacrifice on our behalf and we are made clean and sinless in the eyes of God.

Found in Hebrews 5:1, 7:1–28.

Holiness

Holiness is a state of being absolutely spiritually pure and clean, without fault or spiritual blemish. Because sinful man can never achieve this state on his own, God Himself, the only true Holy One, imparts the ability, through the Holy Spirit, to manifest in our own lives a shadow of His true and singular holiness—we can show forth the Fruit of the Spirit: love, joy, peace, patience, kindness, goodness, faithfulness, gentleness, and self-control. For holiness to be appropriated into our lives, we must be wholly committed and set apart for the Lord's service. We must be attuned to God's heart with worship for the only true God filling our own hearts.

Found in Romans 6:22; Hebrews 12:10–14.

House of Levi

The Israelite nation was divided into twelve tribes; each tribe was made up of the descendants of one of Jacob's sons. (Jacob's name was changed to Israel by God.) His sons were: Reuben, Simeon, Levi, Judah, Dan, Naphali, Gad, Asher, Issachar, Zebulun, Joseph, and Benjamin. The tribe (or house) of Levi was appointed by God as the caretakers and ministers of the Tabernacle in the wilderness (after the Israelites were freed from slavery in Egypt) and the Temple in their own land.

Found in Genesis 35:23–26; Numbers 1:50–53, 3:5, 6, 9, 12; Deuteronomy 21:5; 1 Chronicles 23:32; Jeremiah 33:22.

Humanism

Humanism is a world view that considers man of prime importance and dismisses the concept of a deity or supernatural power. This mindset has become ever more pervasive in the last few decades. This is not a biblical term; however, Scripture speaks of the humanistic beliefs that will overtake man in the last days.

Found in 2 Timothy 3:1–7.

Humble

Humbleness is an attitude of unselfish concern for others and the absence of conceit, arrogance, and pride. Jesus described Himself as "gentle and lowly in heart" (Matthew 11:29; NKJV); this makes it clear that humility is not the actual state of being less than or lower than another (for there is no being of more importance or significance than the Lord), but to be humble is to make the choice to place others' welfare above your own.

Found in Matthew 18:4; Philippians 2:5–8; James 4:10; 1 Peter 5:5, 6.

I AM

When God told Moses to go to Pharaoh and demand that he free all Hebrew (Israelite) slaves, Moses asked God what he should tell the Hebrews if they asked who had sent him to free them. I Am Who I Am is the name God gave Himself in answer to Moses' question. In the original language of Scripture, the name God gave Himself is related to the verb "to be" and conveys the absolute existence of God.

Found in Exodus 3:13–15.

Idol

When spoken of in Scripture, an idol is most often an image or statue of a false god (see Glossary entry "false god") or some imaginary deity conceived by the mind of man. However, in general terms, an idol is anything that is worshiped in the place of God Almighty. It may be anything to which you give your time, energy, loyalty, and affection. Anything that usurps top priority in your life above your Abba God is an idol in your life.

Found in Leviticus 26:1; Ezekiel 14:1–7; Colossians 3:5–7.

Idolatry

Idolatry is the worship of anything other than Abba God. See Glossary entries "false gods" and "Idol."

Found in 1 Corinthians 10:14.

Immutable

To be immutable is to be totally without change or alteration of any kind. God is perfection embodied; that which is perfect cannot change or it would cease to be perfect. Our Holy God is devoid of any change in His character, attributes, and promises. He is the same, yesterday, today, and forever.

Found in Hebrews 13:8.

Inheritance

An inheritance is the estate (assets, property, wealth) received by a specified individual following the death of the owner. When Christ died, He left to all who would believe in Him the greatest inheritance—the riches of His kingdom.

Found in Ephesians 1:11–18; Hebrews 9:15; 1 Peter 1:3, 4.

Jehovah

The Hebrew name of God was YHWH; this is called the Tetragrammaton. It appears in ancient Bible texts without vowels. Its exact pronunciation is debated: Jehovah, Yehovah, Jahweh, Yaweh. God chose this name as the one by which He was to be called by His chosen people. The Jewish people considered this name too holy to be spoken. It means Self-Existent or Eternal One.

Found in Genesis 2:4; Exodus 3:14–17.

Jehovah Jireh

This name of God means "The Lord Who Sees and Will Provide" or simply "The Lord Who Provides." For further information see Names of God article on pages xv–xviii.

Found in Genesis 22:12–14.

Jehovah Raah

This name of God means "The Lord My Shepherd." For further information see Names of God article on pages xv–xviii.

Found in Psalm 23; Isaiah 40:11; John 10:11, 27, 28; Matthew 18:12, 13; Revelation 7:17.

Jehovah Shalom

This name of God means "The God of Peace" or "The Lord of Peace." For further information see Names of God article on pages xv–xviii.

Found in Judges 6:24.

Jehovah Shammah

This name of God means "The Lord Who is There." For further information see Names of God article on pages xv–xviii.

Found in Ezekiel 48:35

Judgment Seat of Christ

The Judgment Seat of Christ (also known by the Greek name the Bema Seat) is not a place where judgment will be passed regarding one's salvation. However, all believers will stand before Christ and He will judge the things done or not done in His Name. Some will hear "Well done" and some will be found wanting. What sorrow it would bring to stand before the Lord and be found wanting.

Found in Romans 14:10; 2 Corinthians 5:10.

Judgment Day

Judgment Day is the day when all people will stand before Almighty God. Those who have accepted Christ as their Lord and Savior will be welcomed into eternal blessing in the Presence of God. Those who have not will be exiled from His holy Presence for eternity. The unsaved will find their fate to be the same as the fallen angels (see Glossary entry above) and their master, Satan (see Glossary entry "devil").

Found in Matthew 25:41; Acts 17:30, 31; Romans 2:5; 1 Corinthians 6:9, 10.

Justified

The biblical meaning of this word is to be completely guiltless in the eyes of God through the blood of Christ. When you accepted Jesus' sacrifice on your behalf, your sins were washed away—you were cleansed of your guilt before God. Through Christ, you can make the claim "it is just as if I'd never sinned." This play on words conveys the meaning of justified in a very clear, memorable way.

Found in Romans 3:21–24, 5:9; 1 Corinthians 6:11; Galatians 2:16; Titus 3:4–7.

King of kings

When Jesus was arrested and stood before Pilate, Pilate asked Him, "Are you the King of the Jews?" Jesus answered, "My kingdom is not of this world." Jesus is the King of heaven; being one with God the Father (John 10:30), He is the Ruler of all creation. He is above all and is, literally, King over all kings.

Found in John 18:33–36; 1 Timothy 6:15; Revelation 19:16.

Lake of Fire

When this world has ended and time is no more, Satan (see Glossary entry "devil") and his demons (see Glossary entry "fallen angels") will face God's wrath for the evil they have inflicted on mankind. Their punishment will be an eternity outside of God's Presence in a place of continual torment; this is described in Scripture as a "lake of fire." Those who reject Jesus Christ as their Lord and Savior will also be cast from God's Presence to spend eternity in hopeless torment in a place devoid of all that is good and holy.

Found in Matthew 25:41; Revelation 20:10.

Legalism

Legalism is to rely upon actions and good works to gain favor with God rather than to depend solely on grace (see Glossary entry above). Legalism is the strict adherence to a code of conduct (the Law), or a faithful commitment to ritual and ceremony; but these can never bridge the gap between sinful man and Holy God. According to Ephesians 2:8, "by grace you have been saved through faith" (NKJV). Only God can bridge the chasm of sin that separates us from Him; the Bridge is Jesus, the Son of God. Once a person has received Christ, they may attempt to gain God's blessings through works. This is also legalism. We cannot earn God's favor; it is a gift of God purchased for us by the blood of Christ.

Found in Romans 8:1–4; Ephesians 2:8–10.

Living Water

Water is a necessity of life. Without it, we die. Undoubtedly, we cannot drink once and be satisfied forever. However, Jesus offers "Living Water"—a fountain of spiritual, life-giving water that flows from Him into the lives of believers, and from them into the lives of those they touch with their lives. Unlike the physical waters that must be consumed frequently, Jesus' Living Water is a continuous supply; and it does not lead only to physical life, but to eternal, spiritual life to those who drink from His fountain. The Living Water Jesus gives is a manifestation of the Holy Spirit in the lives of believers; He satisfies the soul thirsty for God and pours His life-sustaining waters as a stream through the lives of those who belong to the Lord.

Found in John 4:10–14.

Magnify

To magnify a thing is to enlarge it to the point where it can be easily seen and recognized. Such it is when we magnify the Lord—we tell of His goodness and mercy to others, magnifying His nature so others can see and know the wonders of our God.

Found in Psalm 34:3; Acts 10:46.

Mercy

Mercy is the compassionate, forgiving attitude of one who has the power to harm, yet chooses to act with empathy and benevolence. In the justice system, when someone wishes to beg leniency from a judge, it is said he or she may "throw themselves on the mercy of the court." God is a merciful God. Though sinful man deserves to suffer the eternal consequences of sin (spiritual death), God has shown limitless compassion and forgiveness by sending

His Son to pay our penalties and provide a way for us to appear sinless before Abba God.

Found in Psalm 23:6, 36:5, 86:5, 103:8; Isaiah 55:7; Luke 1:50, 6:36; Ephesians 2:4-7; Hebrews 8:10–12.

Messiah

Messiah means "Anointed One" in Hebrew (original language of the Old Testament). This was the term used when the One God would send to save the world was prophesied. The Greek word for Messiah, used in the New Testament, is *Christos*. Thus, when Jesus is called "Jesus Christ," He is proclaimed as the One sent from God to save the world from sin—Jesus the Messiah.

Found in Daniel 9:25; John 1:41, 4:25.

New Covenant

The word "covenant" means a contract, pact, or a last will and testament. It is a binding agreement between two parties. The Old Covenant of God (see Glossary entry below) was between God and Israel—God's decree and pact to save His people—sealed by the blood of animal sacrifice. The New Covenant is the testament of Christ—the salvation of the world promised through Jesus' death and resurrection—sealed by His blood.

Found in Jeremiah 31:31–33; Matthew 26:28; Romans 11:26, 27; Hebrews 9:15.

Old Covenant

The Old Covenant was a binding agreement God made with the people of Israel (His chosen people). The people agreed to follow the Law of God and regularly seal their promise through the blood sacrifice of prescribed animals.

Found in Genesis 17:7; Exodus 19:5–8; Psalm 50:5.

Omniscient

To be omniscient is to know all things; to be perfect in knowledge and wisdom. Only God Himself is omniscient. Though this word is not found in Scripture, many passages describe Abba as an all-knowing, all-wise God.

Found in Job 37:16; Psalm 147:5; 1 John 3:19, 20.

Omnipotent

Omnipotent means possessing unlimited power, to be almighty. There is no power greater than the power of God. He created all things, and through Him all things continue to exist (Colossians 1:16–17).

Found in Revelation 4:11, 19:6.

Omnipresent

To be omnipresent is to be in all places at all times. To be omnipresent, it is necessary to exist outside of space and time—the aspect of creation that limits mere mortals to a moment-by-moment existence and the limitation of experiencing only the here and now. Abba God is not mortal; He is above and beyond all things.

Found in Jeremiah 23:24; Psalm 139:7–12.

Prince of this World

The "prince of this world" is Satan. He is also referred to as "the god of this age" (2 Corinthians 4:4; NKJV), "prince of the power of the air" (Ephesians 2:2; NKJV), and "ruler of this world" (John 12:31; NKJV). This means Satan has major control over the world of men: ideas, perspectives, opinions, goals, and objectives. Satan is not all powerful and God is the Sovereign of this world. However, in His wisdom, God has allowed Satan limited power in the world to affect the lives of men. But we must remember, Satan does not possess power over believers for we belong to Christ. Those who have not accepted Jesus as Savior and Lord are still a part of Satan's fallen realm (see Glossary entry "fallen realm"). They are, therefore, under the rule of Satan.

Found in John 12:31, 14:30, 16:11.

Promised Land

In the Book of Genesis, the Lord promised a special land to Abraham and all his descendants. It was to be a land "flowing with milk and honey" (Deuteronomy 26:15). Long after Abraham had left this life behind, God fulfilled His promise and the Israelites finally were given possession of this land, the land of Canaan. Although Scripture never uses the term "promised land," the Israelite people held on to the promise God gave Abraham to provide a special land for His people. The Israelites waited for centuries for God's promise to be fulfilled. Today, this term has come to mean the heavenly home God has prepared for us.

Found in Genesis 15:18; Exodus 3:17; Joshua 5:6; Ezekiel 20:6.

Redemption (Redeemed)

The literal meaning of "redemption" is to be set free from bondage by the payment of a ransom. It is to be delivered from captivity or to be set free. In the Old Testament, a master would ransom a slave from captivity—procuring his redemption. In the New Testament, "redemption" is available to all through Christ's sacrifice. A ransom has been provided to all who are captives of the "prince of this world" (see Glossary entry above). The payment is Christ's blood and, by it, we can be set free—redeemed by the blood of Jesus, the Son of God.

Found in Luke 1:68; Galatians 3:13; Revelation 5:9.

Remission

Remission is the cancellation of a debt. When Christ paid the penalty for our sins by dying on the cross, our account—the debt we owed for our sinful existence—was paid in full.

Found in Matthew 26:28; Acts 2:38, 10:43; Hebrews 9:22.

Repent

The Greek word translated in Scripture as "repent" is *metanoeo*. This Greek term is formed of two words: *meta*, meaning "after," and *noeo*, meaning "to think." These combined words define repentance as a change of mind. It conveys the idea of a complete change of perception and displeasure with one's past choices. True repentance results in a drastic change in course, action, and attitude. It means to change your mind, turn, and go another way.

Found in Ezekiel 18:30; Acts 3:19; Revelation 2:5.

Righteousness

The biblical definition of "righteousness" is to be in right standing before God. By the cleansing work of the blood of Jesus, God declares a believer acquitted—found innocent and sinless. Only by the impartation of God can sinful man become righteous—freed from all sin and darkness and able to stand before their holy God.

Found in Romans 3:21–26; Romans 5:17–19.

Sacrifice

In the Old Testament, the word "sacrifice" meant the offering of a life in the course of worship. (See Glossary entry "Atonement.") It is a sign of giving all in reverence. In the Book of Leviticus, God says "the life of the flesh is in the blood . . . it is the blood that makes atonement for the soul." As Christians, we no longer offer animal sacrifices to God because Jesus was the final and complete sacrifice—He paid the penalty of sin for all men for all time. However, we are still called to sacrifice as a sign of our reverence for God. A sacrifice can be anything surrendered to the Lord in worship—time, money, talent, anything of value that can be given over to the Lord for His service and His glory.

Found in Mark 12:33; Romans 12:1; Ephesians 5:2.

Salt and Light

Salt and light are two elements that permeate and transform. Jesus told His disciples that they were to be salt and light in the world—we are to permeate and transform the world around us by living and proclaiming the gospel of Christ. Jesus did not tell us we have the option of being salt and light; He made the proclamation that we *are* salt and light. As salt, we should permeate society with the "flavor" of our Lord and His kingdom; we should be agents used by God to transform society by adding a preserving element to stop moral decay. As light, believers should permeate their world by shining brightly with the love of the Lord and, thereby, overcome the darkness that has overtaken the world.

Found in Matthew 5:13–16.

Salvation

In the original Greek, the word translated as "salvation" is *soteria*. At its root is the word *soter*, which means a deliverer or one who saves. With that in mind, the meaning of salvation is to depend upon our Deliverer, our Savior, for liberation, rescue, safety, forgiveness, and healing. The salvation of our Lord is complete; it encompasses all that we are. Salvation is a process that begins at the moment of new birth—the moment we recognize our own sinfulness, repent and ask forgiveness, and accept Jesus as our Savior and Lord—and continues throughout our lives. As the Lord changes us, we are being perfected as sons and daughters of our King—we are in the process of "being saved."

Found in Psalm 25:5; Psalm 74:12; 1 Corinthians 1:18; 2 Corinthians 2:15, 3:18.

Saved

Most often, when believers use the word "saved," they are speaking of the moment of new birth—the moment when a person recognizes his or her own sinful state, repents and asks forgiveness, and accepts Jesus as his or her Lord and Savior. The word translated in the New Testament as "saved" is the Greek word *sozo*, which means to save, keep safe, make whole, or to heal. When we are "saved" by the blood of Jesus, we no longer need fear facing the penalty for our sin (spiritual death) because Jesus has paid the price. He saved us from the punishment for our sin and put a new heart within us (Ezekiel 36:26) with which we can live a new, abundant life in Him.

Found in Psalm 80:19; Isaiah 45:22; Joel 2:32; Mark 16:16; Acts 4:12; Romans 10:9–11, 13; Ephesians 2:8.

Servants of Satan

Those who do not serve the Lord are slaves of darkness. There are only two choices as to whom we will serve—we either serve God or we are slaves of darkness—servants of Satan. Failure to make a conscious choice does not override the fact that all people serve one or the other. Is it not infinitely better to choose to serve God than to be a slave of darkness by default?

Found in Romans 6:16–22; 2 Peter 2:19.

Shalom

Though most often translated as "peace," shalom has a much deeper meaning than our modern-day understanding of peace. The full meaning conveys the idea of wholeness, completeness, health, prosperity, tranquility, and fullness. It is the opposite of strife and chaos. Shalom describes the state of perfect unity with our Creator wherein we can experience the harmonious state of mind and soul each of us craves at the depth of our being.

Found in Genesis 43:23; Nahum 1:15; John 20:19; 2 Peter 1:2. (Note: In the New Testament, the Greek word *eirene* is used, which corresponds to the Old Testament *shalom*.)

Sodom

Sodom was a large city located near the Dead Sea in the days of Abraham. It was a center of trade and commerce and an extremely sinful, immoral, wicked place. Because of unrepentant sin, God passed judgment upon Sodom and its neighboring city, Gomorrah—He rained down "fire and brimstone" and the cities, along with all the inhabitants, were completely destroyed. Sodom and Gomorrah have become synonymous with unrepentant, sinful behavior.

Found in Genesis 13:13, 19:1–28.

Sojourner

As used in Scripture, this word means a stranger who travels through a foreign land. As Christians, this world is not our home;

we wait for the day when God will take us into His kingdom, our true home. Until that day, we travel through this world as foreigners and aliens who are just passing through.

Found in 1 Peter 2:11 (NKJV).

Son of Man

When Jesus walked this earth, He was 100% God and 100% man—He was born through the Spirit of God to a human woman. Through Adam, the first man, sin entered the world. In order to set man free from the wages (or penalty) of sin—death—it was necessary that a man without sin die a substitutionary death. So Jesus chose to be born as a human baby—He became the second Adam. Jesus became a Son of man as well as the Son of God.

Found in Mark 2:9–11; Luke 9:43–45, 12:8, 18:31; John 6:53, 8:28; Acts 7:56.

Sovereign

To be sovereign is to possess ultimate, supreme authority and power. The only One who possesses true sovereignty is God Almighty. All things are under our Father's absolute rule and authority. Nothing happens without His direction or permission. He is our Sovereign, our King of kings and Lord of lords.

Found in NIV translation in Deuteronomy 3:24; 2 Samuel 7:22; Psalm 71:16, Ezekiel 20:5; Acts 4:24; Revelation 6:10.

Stand in the Gap

In biblical days, cities were surrounded by walls designed to protect the inhabitants from enemy attack. If the wall was damaged, the resulting gap in protection required someone to stand guard—to stand in the gap so enemies could not enter in. What is true in the physical is also true spiritually. We have an enemy who searches for "gaps" in the "walls" of protection we need around our lives. These walls are formed of prayer, the Word of God, and in close communion (see Glossary entry above) to our Abba God. When a gap in our protective wall appears, we need the prayers of others to overcome the threats of the enemy. "Standing in the gap" is a metaphor for intercessory prayer—praying diligently for the needs of others.

Found in Ezekiel 22:30.

The Enemy

The enemy of God's people is Satan. He desires to destroy those who belong to God. See Glossary entry "devil."

Found in John 8:44, 10:10; Mark 4:15.

The Rock

Moses was the first to refer to God as "the Rock." In Deuteronomy 32:4, he said, "[God] is the Rock, His work is perfect." God is the absolute sure foundation; He is solid, strong, and immutable (see Glossary entry above).

Found in 2 Samuel 22:47, 23:3; Psalm 18:2; 89:26, 95:1; Luke 6:46–48.

Trial

A trial is synonymous with troubles, strife, and difficulties in life. No one is immune to trouble. A trial for the people of God may be a test or proving ground. But not for the purpose of proving ourselves to God: He already knows all about us. Trials in the life of a child of God allow the child to know just how strong (or weak) his or her faith has grown. If faith is weak, trials give the child a chance to grow in trust of Abba. If faith is strong, the child knows he or she only need wait upon God for the life-storm to pass, knowing that, in the Lord, the sun will always shine again.

Found in Psalm 66:8–12; Romans 8:31–39.

Unresolved Sin

If any sinful act or attitude of heart is not confessed, repented of, and forgiven, it remains as a barrier between the unrepentant, unforgiven sinner and God. The blood of Jesus washes us free from sin; but to receive the benefit of His sacrifice, we must appropriate its power by repenting of our sin (see Glossary entry "repent").

Found in 1 John 1:9.

Witness

As a noun, a witness is one who can attest to the facts. As a verb, to witness is to speak the known truth—to testify to facts as they are known. We are Christ's witnesses, for we know the truth of His life, death, and resurrection. And we are called to tell others of the truth that has been revealed to us by the Holy Spirit.

Found in Matthew 24:14; John 15:27; Acts 1:8, 4:33, 5:32.

Worldliness

Worldliness, as it pertains to Christians, is to think, act, and respond according to the accepted norms of society even when those norms are contrary to the teachings of Christ. As Christians, we are to be in the world. For, if we are to be salt and light (see Glossary entry above), we cannot hold ourselves apart from those who do not know the Lord. However, being involved does not mean we partake of the ungodly elements of this world—we do not allow worldly attitudes and ungodly actions to overtake our lives.

Found in John 17:14, 15; Romans 12:2.

Yeshua

Yeshua is the Hebrew name for Jesus. It means "Yahweh (the LORD) is salvation." The English spelling of this Hebrew name is actually "Joshua." In Greek, it translates to Iesous; the English translation of Iesous is Jesus. It is important realize that our Savior's very name reveals His love for us—He came to bring us God's salvation (see Glossary entry "salvation") by paying the price for our sin and restoring us to right standing and relationship with God.

Found in Matthew 1:21; Luke 1:31.